From Dublin to Bull Run

to Baghdad and Beyond

The Story of the Fighting 69th

James P. Tierney

Dedication

This book is dedicated to the Soldiers of the 69th Regiment—past, present, and future—whose courage, sacrifice, and unwavering commitment have shaped our history and continue to inspire generations.

Acknowledgments

The New York State Military Museum and Veterans Research Center and Courtney Burns must be recognized for their excellent work transcribing the Adjutant General's Reports.

Stephen Harris' book "Duffy's War" provided in depth study of the Regiment's contributions to World War I.

Sean Michael Flynn's book "The Fighting 69th: From Ground Zero to Baghdad" provided a insight into the Regiment's recent history.

Sergeant Brian Danis'(69th Infantry Regiment) research into the Regiment's early history and links to Ireland was extremely helpful in understanding the culture of the regiment in its first 60 years.

About the Author

James P. Tierney was born in New York City, the son of two Irish Immigrants, James Patrick Tierney, Sr. and Mary Patricia Ryan. His father and two uncles were members of the 69th Regiment, New York Guard.

Mr. Tierney received a bachelor's degree from the University of the State of New York. He has a Master of Arts (MA) in Management and Supervision from Central Michigan University and a Master of Business Administration (MBA) with Distinction in Marketing from Long Island University.

Mr. Tierney enlisted in the 69th Infantry Battalion, New York Army National Guard, in 1966 and served in the National Guard until 1981, when he entered active duty in the Army. He served in the Army Operations Center in the Pentagon during Operation Just Cause (Panama) and Operation Desert Storm (Iraq).

He retired from Active Service in September 1996 with the rank of Colonel. Colonel Tierney is an Army Command and General Staff College, Air War College, and the Army War College graduate.

Colonel Tierney served for ten years as a Historian of the 69th Infantry Regiment and appeared in a History Channel TV presentation entitled "On the Frontlines" in 2005. He wrote and published the Complete History of the Fighting 69th - Sixty-Ninth Infantry Regiment from 1849 until 2016.

He was appointed the Honorary Colonel of the 69th Regiment in March 2013 and serves in that position today. Mr. Tierney is a Knight Commander of the Equestrian Order of the Holy Sepulchre, an Honorary Lifetime Member of the Knights of Columbus (Fourth Degree), a Knight Commander of the Sovereign Military Order of the Temple of Jerusalem, a Distinguished Member of the Sixty-Ninth Infantry, and a member of several veteran organizations.

He serves on the Advisory Board of the New York St. Patrick's Day Parade and is the Secretary of the 69th Infantry Officers Club, Inc. He is also a Trustee of the Sixty-Ninth Infantry Regiment Historical Trust and serves as an Honorary Board Member of the Thomas F Meagher Foundation in Dublin, which promotes pride in and respect for the Irish Flag and its meaning for peace.

Since his parents were born in Ireland, Mr. Tierney is recognized as an Irish citizen. Due to his uncle's participation in the Easter Rebellion in 1916, he is a member of the 1916 Relatives Association in Dublin. Mr. Tierney has been married to his wife, Clare, for over 50 years. They have four children, nine grandchildren, and one great-grandchild.

He lives in Virginia but travels to New York City frequently due to his duties in the 69th Infantry Regiment.

Chapter One
69th Infantry Regiment

In the Army National Guard, the regiment was the primary tactical unit from 1636 until 1959. Each regiment had its roots in a particular community or geographic area within a State. The regiment was not only the repository for history and tradition, but it also served as the basic personnel and administration organization. Before 1959, National Guard soldiers often spent their entire military careers in a particular regiment. However, in 1959, regiments were replaced by battle groups, which were later replaced by battalions as the primary tactical organization of the Guard. In 1993, the National Guard re-established the Regimental System as a framework for battalions to continue their identity and affiliations to their parent regiments without restricting changes in force structure. The regiment is the proponent for and the repository of the lineage, honors, traditions, history, and heraldry of the regiment. Everyone in the U.S. Army must belong to a regiment and an honorary regimental staff is appointed for each regiment. In the National Guard, the regimental staff consists of an Honorary Colonel, Regimental Adjutant, Honorary Regimental Sergeant Major, and Regimental Historian.

As the symbolic head of the Regiment, the Honorary Colonel of the Regiment (HCOR) or Regimental Colonel is the custodian of Regimental heritage and traditions. The HCOR links all elements of the regimental family, including regimental veterans' organizations, to promote espirit de corps throughout the regiment. The Regimental Colonel may serve as the president of the Regimental Association. As ceremonial head of the Regiment, the HCOR represents the Regiment at military and civic functions. The Regimental Colonel chairs Regimental committees but is not in the chain of command. The Regimental Colonel can assist Battalion Commander with history, customs, espirit de corps, and public affairs matters affecting the Regiment. The HCOR directs the activities of the Regimental Adjutant, Honorary Regimental Sergeant Major, and Historian. Regimental Staff serve without pay but may be reimbursed for official travel when authorized by the State.

It is not uncommon for a Regiment to have multiple units in its lineage which co-exist. Between 1849 and 1858, there were three Regiments in the lineage of the 69th (the First Irish Regiment, (9th), the Second Irish Regiment (69th), and the Fourth Irish Regiment (75th). Again, during the Civil War, there were three Regiments in the Sixty-Ninth's lineage which co-existed and those three regiments: Sixty-Ninth Regiment New York State Militia (NYSM) or Sixty-Ninth

Regiment, New York National Guard (NYNG), the Sixty-Ninth Infantry Regiment, New York State Volunteers (NYSV), and the Sixty-Ninth Artillery Regiment (Serving as Infantry) New York State Volunteers (NYSV)(later to be designated the 182d Infantry Regiment NYSV) are all part of the today's Sixty-Ninth Infantry Regiment's proud lineage and history.

During World War I and World War II, there were two Regiments in the lineage of today's 69th, (the 165th Infantry Regiment (a Federal Regiment) and the 69th Regiment, New York Guard (a State Guard Regiment formed to replace the National Guard Regiment when it was Federalized and activated for the war). During Federalizations after World War II (i.e., Iraqi Freedom, War on Terror, and Horn of Africa, etc.), a New York Guard Regiment was not formed to replace the unit since a cadre of personnel from the unit were not deployed and continued to serve as National Guard soldiers.

The Sixty-Ninth Infantry Regiment has many names in its lineage (i.e., 69th Infantry Regiment, New York State Militia, 69th Infantry Regiment, New York National Guard, 69th Infantry Regiment, New York State Volunteers, 69th Artillery Regiment (serving as Infantry), 182d Infantry Regiment, New York State Volunteers, 69th Infantry Battalion, 165th Infantry Regiment, 69th Air Defense

Artillery, and 1st Battalion, 69th Infantry) but in Army lineage, names are not what matters. Lineage follows people, and all those units are in the lineage and are part of the history of the 69th Infantry Regiment ("The Fighting 69th).

The Regimental March is the "Garryowen". The Regimental Mascot is the Irish Wolfhound. The Regimental Motto is "Gentle when Stroked, Fierce when Provoked" (motto of the Irish Wolfhound). The Regimental Nickname is the "Fighting 69th". The Unit Day is March 17th. "RIAM NAR DRUID O SBAIRN LANN" was written on a scroll below a harp on the First Irish Colors carried by the Irish Brigade. It translates to "Who Never Retreated from the Clash of Spears" (taken from an ancient tale about Ossian, the son of Fionn Mac Cumhail) (anglicized to Finn McCool). (Fenians took their name from Finn and his followers, Fianna).

The information used in this book comes from numerous sources. Most of the information was gleaned from the New York State Adjutant General's Reports and the information in the Regimental archives. "The Complete History of the Fighting 69th, Sixty-Ninth Infantry Regiment 1849 – 2016" has all the references used (until 2016) listed in footnotes. There are over 600 footnotes in the book which cite where the information was obtained. The book was published in a limited quantity and was offered on the Regiment's website.

It can be found in the Pentagon and New York State Military Museum libraries. The New York State Military Museum has published the Adjutant General's Reports, which are available on their website. Several books and manuscripts are essential to understanding the history of the Regiment. Numerous books were written about the 69th and the Irish Brigade during the Civil War. Stephen Harris's book, "Duffy's War," is an excellent source of information on World War I. Sean Flynn's Book, The Fighting 69th, is the best source of information about the Regiment's role in Operation Iraqi Freedom.

The Regiment has a glorious history and many traditions. It is that history and those traditions that link the soldiers who came before, to the soldiers now serving to the soldiers who will serve in the future. "The Fighting 69th".

Chapter Two
Conception and Formation

The formation of the 69th Infantry Regiment can be traced directly to the Young Irelander Revolt in 1848 and events in Ireland in the 1840s. For Catholics, the conditions in Ireland in the 1840s were intolerable. Catholics could not vote, hold office, assemble in groups, own weapons, or speak their own language (Gaelic or Irish). Furthermore, a potato famine (the main food stable at the time) plagued the country for over four years, leaving people starving in the street. Ireland's population in the 1840s decreased by over 33%. However, during that time, Protestant landlords in Ireland exported wheat.

Giuseppe Mazzini had formed the Young Italy (Giovine Italia) Party. Young Italy was a revolutionary movement that called for creating a united Italian republic. It was the stimulus for other "Young" movements throughout Europe. Based on Mazzini's efforts in Italy, William Smith O'Brien formed Young Ireland with the goal of creating a free Irish Republic.

Many of the leaders of Young Ireland came from wealthy and powerful families. William Smith O'Brien was born in Dromoland Castle in County Clare, Ireland. He was the second son of Baron Sir Edward O'Brien and Charlotte Smith from County Limerick. William took his mother's maiden name as an additional surname when he inherited her estate in Limerick. The O'Brien's were descendants of Brian Boru, an eleventh-century High King of Ireland. William Smith O'Brien attended Trinity College, Cambridge, and studied law at King's Inns in Dublin. In April 1828, Smith O'Brien was elected as a Tory Party Member of Parliament (MP) in the House of Commons. Although Protestant, he supported Catholic rights. In 1835, he switched his affiliation to the Whig Party and served as an MP for County Limerick. He served in the House of Commons until 1849. Although Smith O'Brien had been a member of Daniel O'Connell's Repeal Association, he left that association to join the Irish Confederation which believed in independence for Ireland. Smith O'Brien would be very important to the formation of the Regiment.

Thomas Francis Meagher also came from a wealthy, politically active family. Thomas Francis was born on 3 August 1823. His father, Thomas Meagher, was a wealthy merchant who entered politics. He was elected Mayor of Waterford twice and was elected to the House of Commons. He served there until 1857. As a young man, Thomas Meagher lived in Waterford but left and migrated to Newfoundland. Thomas' wife and Thomas Francis' mother,

Alicia Quan, died when TF was three. Thomas Francis Meagher attended school at Clongowes Wood College in County Kildare, where he developed his skills as an orator. After Thomas Francis studied at Stonyhurst College in Lancashire, England.

In 1844, Meagher traveled to Dublin with the intention of studying for the bar. He became involved in the Repeal Association, which worked to repeal the Act of Union between Britain and Ireland. Meagher was influenced by writers of "The Nation," a newspaper that denounced British liberalism in Ireland. Meagher and the other "Young Irelanders" (the name Daniel O'Connell used to describe the Irish Republicans referring to the Young Italian movement.) denounced any movement toward English political parties so long as Repeal was denied.

O'Connell's followers introduced resolutions to declare that under no circumstances was a nation justified in asserting its liberties by force of arms. Meagher responded with his famous "Sword Speech" when the Peace resolutions were proposed. Abhor the sword? Stigmatize the sword? Be it for the defense or be it for the assertion of a nation's liberty, I look upon the sword as a sacred weapon. The speech was interrupted by John O'Connell, MP, son of the "Liberator," to prevent Meagher from continuing. The Young Irelanders left Conciliation Hall forever. In January

1847, Meagher, together with John Mitchel, William Smith O'Brien, and Thomas Devin Reilly, formed a new repeal body, the Irish Confederation. In 1848, Meagher and O'Brien went to France to study revolutionary events there and returned to Ireland with the new Flag of Ireland, a tricolor of green, white, and orange given to them by French women sympathetic to the Irish cause.

Meagher flew this flag on 7 March 1848 from 33 The Mall, Waterford. Ten Days later, Meagher presented the Tricolour in Dublin. He said during the presentation, "The white in the center signifies a lasting peace between the orange and the green, and I trust that beneath its folds, the hands of the Irish Protestant and Irish Catholic may be clasped in generous and heroic brotherhood." On the day Thomas Francis Meagher presented the Tricolour in Dublin, William Smith O'Brien, leader of the Young Irelanders, called for raising an Irish Brigade in New York City and training that brigade in the New York State Militia (National Guard). Within weeks, independent Irish companies were formed in Manhattan which evolved into three Irish Regiments. Those three regiments are part of the lineage of today's 69th Infantry Regiment.

Michael Doheny

Unlike O'Brien and Meagher, Michael Doheny did not come from a wealthy and powerful family. He was, however, a well-established lawyer in Cashel, Tipperary. Michael Doheny was born in Tipperary on May 22, 1805. His father was a farmer who could not send his son to school. Michael learned to read and write in the evenings beside his father's fireside under the direction of a poor scholar who sometimes visited his father's farm. Michael Doheny was probably the most important person in forming the 69th Regiment.

Another Young Irelander who escaped from Ireland and came to New York was James J. Houston. Houston would play an important role in the history of the Regiment, although his role is cloaked in secrecy. He was a Captain in the First Irish Regiment (9th Infantry Regiment, NYSM), which was commanded by Benjaman C. Ferris. Colonel Ferris was appointed Colonel of the Regiment when it was formed in 1849. Although Colonel Ferris was in command, the regiment was really controlled by a secret organization within its ranks, the SF (Silent Friends or Sein Fein), headed by Captain James Houston. In 1854, Houston and Corcoran would quarrel over the organization and management of the secret societies within the three regiments. Corcoran brought charges against Houston, accusing him of mishandling funds. These disputes between the leadership would be a major reason for consolidating the three regiments into one in 1858. Houston would transfer to the Second Regiment of the New York Militia and Commanded Company "E" at the Battle of Bull Run. The Second Regiment's name was changed to the 82d Infantry, and James Houston commanded the regiment at the Battle of Gettysburg. He was killed during that battle in 1863.

Michael Corcoran was not a member of the Young Irelanders. However, he was a member of another revolutionary group in Ireland that called for the freedom of Ireland, the Ribbon Men. Like Houston, much of his activities in Ireland and the United States were secretive. He was one of the founders of the Fenian Brotherhood, along with Doheny and other Young Irelanders. He was the ranking member of the Fenians in the United States when the Civil War broke out. The Fenians were the precursor to the Clan na Gael, another Irish Republican organization. Secret Irish Republican organizations (e.g., Irish Republican Brotherhood, Phoenix Brigade, Irish Volunteers, IRA, etc.) would have links to the 69th Regiment for the first fifty years of its existence. Since these organizations did not leave records, the depth of their involvement in managing the Regiment is unknown. What is known is the 69th Regiment can be directly traced to events in Ireland in 1848 and the Irish Republican movement in the U.S. and Ireland during that year.

James Cavanaugh

Another important figure during and after the Civil War who was not a member of Young Ireland (but was most probably a Fenian) was James Kavanaugh (Cavanaugh). He was born in Tipperary in 1831 and emigrated to New York in 1847, probably due to the potato famine. He enlisted in the 69th in 1852 and eventually became the longest-serving Commander in the Regiment's history.

The year 1848 witnessed rebellions all over Europe. 1848 has been called the "Spring of Nations". There were revolutions in France, the German States, the Kingdom of

Denmark, Poland, Hungary, Switzerland, Romania, Brazil, the Austrian Empire, and Ireland. In 1848, the Potato Famine was in its fourth year. Although many organizations and individuals sought to provide relief to Ireland during that time (e.g., the Jewish Community in New York, the Sultan of the Ottoman Empire, the Choctaw Indians, and the Committee of Colored Citizens in Philadelphia, etc.), England's efforts to assist were totally inadequate. Due to the famine and intolerable conditions, the younger generation in Ireland grew weary of attempts to use negotiation to gain self-rule and rights for the Irish. Young Irish Leaders formed the Young Ireland Movement.

The leaders of Young Ireland wore green frock coats (Club 82 Jackets) with "1782" embossed on the buttons (commemorating Gratton's Parliament and the Irish Volunteers of 1782). The Club 82 Jacket would inspire the early uniforms of the 69th Regiment. Young Irelanders believed the only way to obtain freedom for Ireland was through the use of force and not negotiation. An attempted rebellion in 1848 failed miserably and would have a dramatic impact on the history of the 69th Regiment. After the failed rebellion, the center of Irish Republicanism moved from Dublin, Ireland, to New York City. The leaders of Young Ireland who were not captured, especially Michael

Doheny, left Ireland and came to New York and were crucial in forming the Regiment.

In Manhattan, the newly formed Irish Companies became known as the Irish Brigade of Young Ireland (which was not part of the State Militia). There were several "monster meetings" in 1848 where the Irish Brigade of Young Ireland marched with Meagher's Tricolour. At one of these monster meetings in Williamsburg, Brooklyn, on July 4, 1848, an Irish Declaration of Independence was proclaimed and adopted.

The Irish Brigade of Young Ireland consisted of the following companies:

Company 1, Captain M.T. O'Conner, and Lt. James Bergen

Company 2, Captain Dwyer

Irish Fusiliers / Irish Patriot Fusiliers, Captain Maurice Walsh

John Mitchel Guard, Captain James Markey

Guyon Cadets Captain Michael Phalen

The above units were armed with pikes, muskets, bayonets, and fusils (light flint-lock muskets). The brigade attempted to procure rapid-fire fusils, colt revolvers, and light artillery but failed. It may have had a troop of lancers. At the end of July 1848, members of the Irish Brigade of

Young Ireland traveled from New York to Ireland to serve as "force multipliers" (cadre would train individuals recruited in various towns throughout Ireland) for the Young Ireland Rebellion of 1848. The face of warfare changes most often due to changes in technology. (e.g., rifled weapons in the Civil War, fragmentation shells leading to the use of steel helmets in World War I, etc.). Sometimes, strategy or tactics change how war is fought. Although the concept of force multipliers failed in the 1848 Rebellion, Wild Bill Donovan adopted the concept in World War II for the Office of Strategic Services. It is unknown whether William J. Donovan (Wild Bill), who commanded the Regiment during World War I, knew the early history of the Regiment and specifically the concept of force multipliers. He did, however, use that concept for the primary strategy of the Office of Strategic Services (OSS), which he organized and commanded during World War II. The Special Forces of the U.S. Army (Green Berets) modeled their strategy after the OSS when they were organized in 1952.

When, in August 1848, the Young Ireland Rebellion failed, 500 Pounds were offered for the capture of William Smith O'Brien and 300 Pounds for Thomas Francis Meagher, John B. Dillon, and Michael Doheny. O'Brien and Meagher were captured and sentenced to be hung, drawn, and quartered. The

William Smith O'Brien

sentence was commuted, and the captured leaders were transported to a Penal Colony in Australia (Van Diemen's Land / Tasmania).

After the failed revolt, the remnants of Irish revolutionary (republican) leaders left Ireland and joined Irish American revolutionaries in New York City. The central doctrine of these Irish republicans was the freedom of Ireland could only be achieved by the force of arms. In November 1848, members of the Irish Brigade of Young Ireland (who traveled to Ireland to take part in the failed uprising) returned to New York City. The Irish Brigade of Young Ireland would later become the nucleus of the First Irish Regiment.

In February 1849, Michael Doheny arrived in New York City. He played a major role in organizing three Irish

Regiments in Manhattan (in 1854, these three regiments were known as the Irish Brigade of the New York Militia). These three Irish Regiments are in the lineage of the 69th Infantry Regiment of today.

Lineage of the 69th Infantry Regiment units from 1849-1858:

First Irish Regiment, 9th

Second Irish Regiment, 69th

Fourth Irish Regiment, 75th

In the summer of 1849 and continuing until the fall, Irish leaders in New York City began negotiations with the State to form an Irish regiment consisting of the existing and future independent Irish companies. The Irish Brigade of Young Ireland was reorganized with other independent militia companies into the "First Irish Regiment." The First Irish Regiment is the earliest Regiment in the Sixty-Ninth Regiment's lineage. The First Irish Regiment was formed on 21 December 1849 and mustered into the New York State Militia on 29 May 1850 as the Ninth Regiment.

Within the Ninth Regiment, Captain James Houston commanded a secret organization known as the "SF," which was comprised of Irish revolutionaries. The "SF" ("Silent Friends" was called the "Sinn Fein" by J.C.P. Stokes, the Historian of the Ninth Regiment).

1851 marked the first year the 69th marched in the St Patrick's Day Parade. The Regiment wore their green frock coats (fashioned after the Club 82 Jacket worn by the Young Irelanders). The formation of armed Irish Regiments caused uneasiness among American "Nativists." The Know Nothing Party was rising in power, and in the 1850s, Nativists were successful in forming a new regiment in Manhattan to counterbalance the Sixty-Ninth. The Seventy-first Infantry Regiment, NYSM (with the motto of the "American Guard") was formed to keep watch on the 69th Regiment because New York did not like Irish marching around with green uniforms and rifles. These two regiments would later become sister regiments serving in the same brigade.

On May 27, 1852, Meagher walked into the law office of Dillon and O'Gorman (Richard O'Gorman) on William Street and announced he was Thomas Francis Meagher, who had recently escaped from Australia. Thomas Francis Meagher had been sentenced to death for his part in the Revolution of 1848 but was pardoned by Queen Victoria in 1849 and exiled for life to Australia. He escaped by withdrawing his parole and sailing away in a ship paid for with money from the United States. Meagher would take a very active role in the Irish Republican movement in New York City.

On the west coast of Ireland, in County Sligo, Michael Corcoran resigned his position as a tax collector in the Royal Irish Constabulary. While working for the Crown, Corcoran was also a member of a local guerilla group known as the Ribbon Men. At night, the group would burn the landlord's crops and barns and kill their livestock. Corcoran was 6 foot 2 inches, and when he came under suspicion of sedition, he left Ireland and emigrated to America. Arriving in New York, he joined the 69th, joining the company formed by Captain John Judge, which was known as the "Irish Rifles." He secured a position working for John Heeney, who owned the Hibernian Hall. On Heeney's retirement, Corcoran succeeded him as the owner. Corcoran also held a position in the Customs Service (which was no doubt a political favor).

On November 3, 1851, the Regiment was assigned to the Fourth Brigade of the First Division. Major Charles S. Roe, formerly of the Washington Grays, was elected Colonel. On June 24, 1854, Michael Corcoran was promoted to Captain with a Date of Rank of May 29, 1852.

1855 was a very turbulent year in New York City. Racial, religious, and political fervor reached the highest pitch in the history of Manhattan. In January 1855, Bill Poole (Bill the Butcher), a member of the "Bowery Boys" and champion of the Native-American faction, was shot in a barroom brawl at

Stanwix Hall. The Know-Nothings made political capital out of the shooting since two of the men arrested for the shooting had Irish names. The Know-Nothings stirred up anti-Catholic sentiments. There were several riots in the city, and the militia (including the 69th) had to be called out to restore order.

Discussions about canceling the St. Patrick's Day Parade were held, and although the Parade was allowed, military units were prohibited from participating. Militia Regiments were held at the regimental parade grounds to await orders. The weather was poor, and hail began to fall as soon as the parade marchers formed. As the parade moved downtown, group after group dropped out, leaving only the longshoremen to finish at City Hall. The only spectators were the police, and often they sought shelter. When the regiments were finally dismissed, the Sixty-Ninth marched with fixed bayonets. The other regiments did not attempt to march.

In February 1856, the Crimean War between England and Russia ended, and hopes to take advantage of "England's difficulties" were dashed. The Irish in New York were disillusioned because the Irish Regiments did nothing to take advantage of the war. Instead, the leadership of the Irish Regiments fought amongst themselves. From then on, recruiting for the Irish Regiments suffered greatly. On

March 14, 1858, the three Irish Regiments were consolidated into one regiment and designated the 69th Infantry Regiment.

On September 7, 1858, New York Governor John A. King issued a proclamation calling for 250 officers and men of the First Division to proceed to the Quarantine Station on Staten Island. They were to defend the property of the State from a lawless mob. On October 18th, the Seventy-first Regiment was relieved by a detachment from the Sixty-Ninth. On November 1, the 69th Regiment departed Staten Island. They were relieved by the 55th Regiment.

In 1858, the 69th Regiment consisted of the following:

- Colonel, James Ragget Ryan, Date of Commission: April 18, 1855, Date of Rank: March 23, 1855, Residence: New York City.

- Lieutenant Colonel, Edward L. Butler, Date of Commission: May 14, 1856, Date of Rank: March 3, 1856, Residence: New York City.

- Major, Robert Nugent, Major, Date of Commission: June 6, 1854, Date of Rank: May 23, 1852, Residence: New York City.

- Adjutant, Lieutenant John McKeon, Date of Commission: Aug.20, 1858, Date of Rank: April 22, 1858, Residence: New York City.

- Regimental Surgeon, Captain Robert Johnson, Date of Commission: October 25, 1859, Date of Rank: October 8, 1858.

- Surgeon's Mates, Lieutenant John Fergusson, Date of Commission: October 25, 1858, Date of Rank: October 11, 1858.

- Regimental Engineer, Captain, James B. Kirker, Date of Commission: March 16th, 1857, Date of Rank: 12th January 1857, Residence: New York City.

- Regimental Quarter Master, Lieutenant Matthew O'Connor, Date of Commission: April 18, 18551, Date of Rank: April 2, 1855, Residence: New York City.

- Regimental Paymasters, Lieutenant Matthew Kehoe, Date of Commission: Oct. 25, 1858, Date of Rank: January 9, 1852, Residence: New York City.

- Chaplain: James Bagley, Date of Commission: April 18, 1855, Date of Rank: April 10, 1855, Residence: New York City.

Total on Staff: 14

"A" Company

- Captain Michael Corcoran, Date of Commission: June 24, 1854, Date of Rank: May 29, 1852.

- 1st Lieutenant Hugh C. Flood, Date of Commission: November 14, 1855, Date of Rank: October 8, 1855.

- 2d Lieutenant Theodore Kelly, Date of Commission: October 25, 1858, Date of Rank: October 6, 1858.

Enlisted 79

Total 82

"B" Company

- Captain Thomas Lynch, Date of Commission: March 9, 1857, Date of Rank: January 12, 1857.

- 1st Lieutenant Robert W. Brown, Date of Commission: June 26, 1858, Date of Rank: May 24, 1858.

- 2d Lieutenant Dennis Brown, Date of Commission: August 20, 1858, Date of Rank: July 26, 1858.

Enlisted 46

Total 49

"C" Company

- Captain John Burke, Date of Commission: March 9, 1857, Date of Rank: January 26, 1857.
- 1st Lieutenant James Cavanagh, Date of Commission: June 8, 1857, Date of Rank: March 9, 1857.
- 2d Lieutenant John Rowen, Date of Commission: June 8, 1857, Date of Rank: March 9, 1857.

Enlisted 27

Total 30

"D" Company

- Captain George Tobin, Date of Commission: October 14, 1952, Date of Rank: September 21, 1852.
- Vacant, 1st and 2d Lieutenants

Enlisted 46

Total 47

"E" Company

- Captain Maurice Keating, Date of Commission: July 25, 1856, Date of Rank: July 2, 1856.
- 1st Lieutenant Patrick Kelly, Date of Commission: March 9, 1857, Date of Rank: January 16, 1857.

- 2d Lieutenant Richard P. King, Date of Commission: June 24, 1851, Date of Rank: June 14, 1852.

Enlisted 49

Total 52

"F" Company

- Captain John Breslin, Date of Commission: March 30, 1858, Date of Rank: March 9, 1858.

- 1st Lieutenant John T. Scullen, Date of Commission: April 3, 1855, Date of Rank: March 21, 1855.

- 2d Lieutenant George Collins, Date of Commission: April 3, 1855, Date of Rank: March 21, 1855.

Enlisted 35

Total 38

"G" Company

- Captain William Malone, Date of Commission: March 9, 1857, Date of Rank: January 28, 1857.

- 1st Lieutenant John Cornan, Date of Commission: March 9, 1857, Date of Rank: January 28, 1857.

- 2d Lieutenant John Julien, Date of Commission: March 9, 1857, Date of Rank: January 28, 1857.

Enlisted 24

Total 27

"H" Company

- Captain James Kelly, Date of Commission: May 11, 1856, Date of Rank: May 7, 1856.
- 1st Lieutenant William Butler, Date of Commission: May 14, 1856, Date of Rank: March 11, 1856.
- 2d Lieutenant James Lyons, Date of Commission: December 22, 1856, Date of Rank: November 6, 1856.

Enlisted 46

Total 49

Companies "I" vacant

Company "K" vacant.

On July 24, 1859. Colonel James Ragget Ryan submitted his resignation from command of the Regiment. It was accepted by General Ewen, Commander of the Fourth Brigade. On August 26, Brigadier General Ewen presided over an election to determine the new Colonel of the Regiment. The election was held at the Division Armory on White and Elm Streets. Captain Michael Corcoran, Commander of Company "A" was voted to replace Ryan as Commander. At that time, Corcoran was second in command in the Fenian Brotherhood. In 1860, Colonel Corcoran had a dual role as Commander of the Fenian Brotherhood's Phoenix Brigade and Commander of the 69th Regiment.

Michael Corcoran

During the Summer of 1860, Queen Victoria sent the young Prince of Wales on a state tour of Canada. He was invited to visit New York, and the First Division decided to parade in his honor on October 11th. Colonel Corcoran sent Major General Sandford through Brigadier General Ewen a request to be excused from parading on this occasion on the grounds that the purpose of the parade was objectionable to him and his command. His request was refused. However, Corcoran did not march with the Regiment, and on November 20, 1860, charges were brought against him.

Because he refused to march the Regiment in front of the Prince of Wales, Corcoran became the hero of the Irish community. He was presented with the first of the Regiment's Green Flags. It had a Finian Sunburst with "Presented to the 69th Regiment" above it. Below the sunburst was written "In commemoration of October 11,

1860". The Regiment would carry this flag to the Battle of Bull Run (the first major battle of the Civil War). Corcoran's court-martial would continue until April 1861, when Confederates fired on Ft. Sumpter. Corcoran's court martial dissipated, and Corcoran was restored to Command.

Chapter Three
The Civil War

There are several causes for the Civil War. The economics of slavery and States' rights were important issues for the South. Southern States feared the North would outlaw slavery (which was the cornerstone of their economy). The election of Abraham Lincoln (without a single Southern electoral vote) was a signal to the Southern States to declare secession from the United States and to form the Confederate States of America. Prior to the War, Napoleonic tactics utilizing massed troops and stressing the attack were taught at the Nation's military academies (e.g., West Point, Virginia Military Institute, etc.). Officers who were trained at these institutions regarded the concept of the defense as ungentlemanly. These officers formed the bulk of the leadership of the Regular Army. However, pat the start of the War, the Regular Army was very small, and both sides had to rely on the Militia. Officers in the Militia usually had no formal military training and were elected by the soldiers in their unit.

The 19th Century had many technological innovations that had a major impact on the War. The railroad allowed fast movement of large numbers of troops. Rifling of rifles and artillery improved the accuracy and range of those weapons. Repeating carbines and breech-loaded rifles were a vast improvement over smooth-bore rifles, which were used by many militia units at the beginning of the War. The telegraph improved battlefield communications.

At the beginning of the conflict, the Union strategy was to attack Confederate forces located at the main rail junction at Manassas (about 25 miles west of Washington), board trains from Manassas to Richmond (about 90 miles from Manassas), and arrest the leadership of the Confederacy. After that failed, the Union's strategy was to sail the Army to Fortress Monroe and attack up the Peninsula to Richmond (about 80 miles). That failed also. The South changed its strategy of fighting a defensive war and went on the offensive. In 1862, Lee attacked into Maryland. In 1863, he again brought the Army of Northern Virginia into Union territory and attacked Pennsylvania. The South's main goal was to outlast the Union rather than conquer it. However, the South had an agricultural economy and did not have the manufacturing capabilities of the North. Furthermore, the South did not have a Navy. The Union was able to cut off supplies from Europe with its blockade of Southern ports.

The Lineage of the 69th Regiment during the Civil War was:

69th Infantry Regiment, New York State Militia (NYSM) (National Guard)

69th Infantry Regiment, New York State Volunteers (NYSV) (Federal Regiment)

69th Artillery Regiment (serving as Infantry), New York State Volunteers (NYSV), later changed to the 182nd Infantry Regiment, NYSV (Federal Regiment)

On April 20, 1861, Colonel Corcoran issued General Order Number 1, directing the Regiment to assemble on Tuesday, April 23 at 7 AM, ready to move. The men assembled at 7 o'clock, but arms and blankets did not arrive until 9 AM. It was nearly noon before the arms and blankets were issued. The Regiment's line was formed in Great Jones Street. A large crowd assembled to see the Regiment off. A silk National Color, which was made by Mrs. Charles P. Daly, was presented to the unit. Colonel Corcoran assured Judge Daly that: "The flag would suffer no dishonor as long as there was a man of the Sixty-Ninth alive to defend it." Archbishop Hughes appointed Father Thomas Mooney, Pastor of St. Brigid's Parish, Chaplain of the Regiment. Father Mooney joined the regiment about 3 P.M. and the march began.

At the head of the procession was a decorated wagon drawn by four horses and bearing the inscription, "Sixty-Ninth, Remember Fontenoy," and "No North, No South, No

East, No West, but the whole Union." The officers of the regiment were as follows:

Colonel, Michael Corcoran.

Lieutenant-Colonel Robert Nugent.

Major, James Bagley

Adjutant, John McKeon.

Volunteer Aids C. G. Halpine and John Savage

Chaplain, Rev. Thomas J. Mooney; succeeded by Rev. B. O'Reilly, S. J.

Engineers, James B. Kirker, John H. McCunn, L. D'Homergne

Surgeon, Robert Johnson

Surgeon Assistants, Drs. James L. Kiernan, J. Pascal Smith, P. Nolan.

Quartermaster, Joseph B. Tully

Paymaster, Matthew Kehoe

Sergeant Major, Arthur Tracy

Color Sergeant, Murphy.

Company "A"

Captain James Haggerty

First First-Lieutenant, Theodore Kelly

Second Lieutenants, Daniel Strayne, Daniel F. Sullivan

Orderly Sergeant, Bermingham

Enlisted 127

Company "B"

Captain Thomas Lynch

First Lieutenant, Thomas Leddy

Second Lieutenant, W. H. Giles

Orderly Sergeant, Cahill

Enlisted 114

Company "C"

Captain James Cavanagh

First Lieutenant John H. Ryan

Second Lieutenant J. Rowan

Enlisted 86

Company "D"

Captain, Thomas Clarke

First Lieutenant, Thomas Fay

Second Lieutenants James L. Dungan, Michael O'Boyle

Orderly Sergeant, M. Maguire

Enlisted 120

Company "E"

Captain P. Kelly

First Lieutenant John Bagley

Orderly Sergeant, Andrew Reed

Enlisted 100

Company "F"

Captain John Breslin

First Lieutenant P. Duffy

Second Lieutenant, M. P. Breslin

Orderly Sergeant, D'Alton

Enlisted 100

Company "G"

Captain Felix Duffy

First Lieutenant Henry J. McMahon

Orderly Sergeant, Thomas Phibbs

Enlisted 120

Company "H"

Captain James Kelly

First Lieutenant W. Butler

Second Lieutenants, James Lyons, James Gannon

Orderly Sergeant, F. Welpley

Enlisted 126

Company "J",

Lieutenant John Coonan, Commanding

Second Lieutenant Thomas Canton

Enlisted 102

It was six o'clock before the last of the relatives who had come to see their loved ones off had left the dock, and the last soldier was aboard the Harriet Lane and James Adger (the ships that would take the Regiment to war). The James Adger was a large paddle-wheel steamer with auxiliary sail. The Harriet Lane was a copper-plated steamer built by the U.S. Treasury Department and named after the niece of then-Senator (later President) James Buchanan. The ships were only designed to carry about five hundred passengers, but they were loaded with eleven hundred soldiers and a vast number of military supplies. Father Mooney kept the spirits of the men high. He worked tirelessly to make them comfortable, though there was little he could do beyond words of encouragement. He spent most of the night sitting on the deck, hearing confessions. In the morning, he set up an altar between the paddle boxes and said Mass. The ships reached Annapolis at about 8 P.M. on April 25. On April 26th, the Sixty-Ninth was quartered in one of the buildings at the Naval Academy.

The following morning, General Butler ordered Colonel Corcoran to occupy and hold the railroad between Annapolis and Annapolis Junction. The regiment hiked along the track and set up in a field near Crownsville. That night, just as the sun was setting, the sky clouded, and it began to pour. Reveille was at six A.M., and the men were tired and wet. They ate breakfast, and Father Mooney said Mass.

The Sixty-Ninth spread out along the rail line, leaving pickets at various places. The men established strong points that were named after the officers and over which flags were raised. A squad from Co. "G" dug a pit, banked it with earth, and raised the flag, giving three cheers for the Union. Above this little earthen works, which they named Fort Duffy, after their Captain Felix Duffy, they placed a board with the following inscription: "The Union Forever - Fort Duffy - Erected May 1861, by the advance patrol of the 69th Regiment, Irish Grenadiers, numbering 16 men".

The Sixty-Ninth was relieved on May 2. Half of the regiment marched to Washington that night. The other half reached the city the following day. On arrival in Washington, the Regiment received an extraordinary reception. The streets were lined with cheering people and green flags. The Regiment was assigned quarters in two buildings on Pennsylvania Avenue but were quickly to be moved to Georgetown College. Lieutenant General Scott sent ten West Point Cadets to act as drill masters for the Regiment. On May 7, 1861, President Lincoln inspected the Sixty-Ninth. The President thanked them for coming so promptly to aid the Government.

Unfortunately, the school term had not ended when the Regiment arrived at Georgetown, and the students and faculty were turned out of their quarters without ceremony when the army units arrived. As soon as their equipment was received, the Regiment set up camp in the fields. The quarters were cleaned, and the students moved back in. The government gave the College assurance that it would not be used again for quartering troops.

Camp Corcoran prior to the Battle of Bull Run

On May 8th, Thomas F. Meagher, who had been recruiting his company of Zouaves, went to Washington to talk to Colonel Corcoran about joining the Regiment. It was decided not only should the Zouaves be incorporated into the Regiment, but Major Bagley should be authorized to enlist an additional 300 men.

On May 9, 1861, the Regiment was mustered into Federal service. The regiment was formed in line, and the oath was read and explained to the men. The soldiers were told that if they did not wish to take the oath, they step out of the ranks. Sixteen stepped forward and were taken to the guard house. Later, they were stripped of all insignia and drummed out of camp.

Archbishop Hughes had assigned Father Mooney as Chaplain of the 69th Regiment. However, the Archbishop advised Father Mooney how to proceed with the Fenians. They are incompetent to receive the Sacraments and Christian burial unless they shall renounce their Fenian oath. Father Mooney was to tell each soldier individually that he is jeopardizing his soul if he perseveres in participating in Fenian activities.

Father Mooney

The Sixty-Ninth was tasked to build a fort on a hill near the Aqueduct Bridge, commanding the road leading to Fairfax Court House. The fort measured six hundred and fifty feet by four hundred and fifty feet with walls fourteen feet high. It was estimated it would take three thousand men three weeks to build. The ground was cleared. The hill leveled, and the fort was constructed by only twelve hundred Irishmen in one week.

The first of the heavy guns was placed in position on June 13th. It was a sixty-four-pound Columhiad and was named the "Hunter Gun" after Colonel Hunter, the Brigade Commander. Colonel Corcoran asked Father Mooney to bless the gun, but Father Mooney decided to "baptize" the gun. Archbishop Hughes was infuriated. On July 3, 1861, The Archbishop wrote Father. Mooney wrote a letter stating: "Reverend Dear Sir: I received yours on the 25th of August. I am glad to hear that everything is going well with the 69th Regiment. At the same time, I cannot forget that you have disappointed me regarding the advice which I gave you in Mullay's office, when you were about to start with the 69th. Your inauguration of a ceremony unknown to the Church, viz., the blessing of a cannon, was sufficiently bad, but your remarks on that occasion are infinitely worse. Under the circumstances, and for other reasons, I wish you to return, within three days from the receipt of this letter, to your pastoral duties at St. Brigid's." Father Bernard O'Reilly, S.J. replaced Father Mooney as Chaplain of the 69th.

Colonel Hunter, who was well-liked and very popular with the Regiment, was replaced by Colonel William T. Sherman as the Brigade Commander. Felix Duffy, Company "G," and Thomas Lynch, Company "B," resigned. Many of the men felt they were treated unfairly regarding their terms of service. Most felt that they should have been released on July 22, three months after they left New York. The Government held they could not be released until August 9th, three months from the date they entered Federal service at Georgetown. Many soldiers were extremely agitated. This had not been explained when they were in New York. Many threatened to desert and go home on July 22.

Colonel Corcoran took prompt action to end the trouble. He paraded the regiment on July 5 and clearly explained his position and their obligation. Colonel Corcoran said he believed reports were circulated to mislead the Regiment and discredit him. Corcoran had been a member of the Regiment, serving in almost every grade from private to Colonel. He defied any man to point to one improper act on his record. He did not come here to court political favor but to fulfill what he considered his duty. It had been said, remarked the Colonel, that Company "F" would lay down their arms on the twentieth of July, but I believe there were enough good men in Company "F" who would shoot the perpetrators of so base an act.

The Sixty-Ninth was part of the Third Brigade commanded by Colonel William T. Sherman. The Third Brigade was assigned to Tyler's First Division. General McDowell's plan for the Bull Run Campaign was simple. General Tyler's First Division was to move at 2:30 AM to make a demonstration at the Stone Bridge. Meanwhile, Hunter's Second Division and Heintzelman's Third Division were to turn the Confederates left.

LTC Robert Nugent (the Executive Officer of the 69th) fell off his horse and could not participate in the battle. Even so, Colonel William T. Sherman selected Nugent and two other officers from the Regiment for a Regular Army Commission with the rank of Captain. Captain Haggerty was appointed Acting Lieutenant Colonel. Since Major James Bagley had remained in New York and did not accompany the Regiment to Washington, Captain T.F. Meagher, Captain, was assigned as Acting Major of the Regiment.

The movement of the Union forces started late. Furthermore, it took three hours to cover the two miles between camp and the point where Hunter's Second Division and Heintzelman's Third Division were to turn north to cross Bull Run at Sudley Springs. The Sixty-Ninth and the rest of Tyler's Division reached the Stone Bridge and stopped. Confederate lookouts in Manassas could see the First Division was not moving. They also observed dust clouds (created by soldiers dragging their feet while marching) to the left of the Warrington Turnpike. The lookouts alerted the Confederate Commander, who rightly concluded that the Federal's main attack would come on his flank from the direction of Sudley Springs. He moved most of his forces to meet that threat from McDowell's Second and Third Divisions.

Colonel Burnside's men came under fire from Confederate troops posted near Sudley Spring's Road at about 10 A.M. His forces were held up for over an hour until reinforcements arrived. Confederate forces were about to be driven from their positions by Griffin's battery when (Confederate) General Bee arrived with four additional regiments. The fight was prolonged for another half hour.

The Confederate line began to wavier and fall back. Sherman's Brigade, including the Sixty-Ninth, crossed Bull Run as the Confederates attempted to keep their lines intact. Sherman noted: Early in the day, when reconnoitering the ground, I saw a horseman descend from a bluff to across the stream, inferring we should cross over at the same point. I sent a company as skirmishers across Bull Run and followed with the whole brigade, the New York Sixty-Ninth, leading. The infantry had no difficulty crossing and had little trouble ascending the steep bluff. However, the steep bluff was impassable for the artillery. I sent word back to Captain Ayers to follow if possible or, if not, to use his discretion. As we advanced, we encountered the enemy retreating along a cluster of pines. Acting Lieutenant Colonel Haggerty of the Sixty-Ninth Regiment attempted to intercept their retreat. One of the Confederates shot Haggerty, and he fell dead from his horse. The Sixty-Ninth opened fire on the enemy, but I ordered this fire to cease fire. I was determined to link up with Hunter's Division. The Brigade proceeded to the field where Union forces were engaged.

After crossing Bull Run, the 69th came under fire from the "Louisiana Tigers". During the battle, James Haggerty, who was the Acting Lieutenant Colonel, was shot and died. Recruitment efforts in New York later that month featured a flyer urging the City's Irishmen to enlist to avenge Haggerty, whose throat (the circular erroneously claimed) had been cut "from ear to ear" by a cowardly rebel. Haggerty is buried along with many of the Regiment's soldiers in Calvary Cemetery in Queens, New York. His grave site is in Section 1W, Avenue A, Grave 4/11.

Sherman's Brigade, with the Sixty-Ninth in advance, arrived on the field at about twelve thirty and assisted in breaking the enemy's lines. During the next forty-five minutes, the Irish helped Burnside's men clear the enemy at the foot of the Henry House plateau. The first phase of the battle ended here. McDowell had success but at a considerable cost. His advance had been delayed for three hours by a small force of the enemy. Burnside's Brigade had been demoralized and was, for the most part, out of action. Sherman halted his brigade while he sought out General McDowell to receive orders. Colonel Hunter, the Division Commander, was severely wounded. Sherman was ordered to join in the pursuit of the Confederates, whom McDowell believed to be still in retreat. Thomas J. (Stonewall) Jackson's Brigade formed on the heights behind the

Robinson and Henry houses, and the troops of Evans, Barstow and Bee were reforming behind Jackson. Generals Beauregard and Johnson had arrived on the field and were reorganizing the scattered Confederate troops and bringing up fresh regiments.

Unfortunately, the Federal Troops paused their advance. Both sides wore the same color uniforms. Federal Batteries, who thought they were receiving reinforcement from blue-coated Union soldiers, found themselves under fire from Confederate Virginia regiments. From their position on the Sudley Road, the Sixty-Ninth could not see what had happened on Henry Plateau. A depression that protected them from direct enemy fire prevented them from seeing what was happening. Colonel Sherman, acting on the orders of General McDowell to join in the pursuit of the Confederates, brought his brigade into action. Unfortunately for Sherman's Brigade, they were not pursuing an army in retreat but attacking a strong, entrenched, and reinforced enemy. Confederates had artillery protecting their defensive positions, and the Union troops attacked without close artillery support.

Sherman's Brigade did not attack as a unit. The regiments were sent into action one by one. Sherman, for some unexplained reason, waited until one regiment had fallen back before another advanced. The Second Wisconsin

Regiment ascended to the brow of the hill and received the severe fire. The regiment's uniforms were gray cloth and almost identical with the most of Confederate forces. When the regiment retreated towards Sudley Road, they were fired on by Union men. The regiment rallied and charged the hill a second time. Again, the regiment was repulsed and retreated in disorder. The New York Seventy-ninth was ordered to attack the brow of the hill and drive the enemy from cover. The Seventy-ninth, commanded by Colonel Cameron, charged across the hill, and for a short time, the contest was severe. They rallied several times under fire but finally broke and took cover. This left the field open to the New York Sixty-Ninth; Colonel Corcoran led his regiment over the crest of the hill. The Sixty-Ninth threw away their coats and knapsacks and formed in line of battle. They advanced slowly at a quick step, then at a double quick, and finally at a run. The firing was very severe, and the roar of cannon, musketry, and rifles was incessant. It was evident the enemy had a superior force. The Sixty-Ninth held the ground for some time. The charge became entangled with a detachment of Union Cavalry, and the full effect of the attack was nullified. Confederate Cavalry attacked the right wing of the regiment. Seeing the enemy cavalry advancing again, two Union regiments on the flank on the Sixty-Ninth broke through the 69th's lines and threw the Regiment into complete confusion.

Sherman, not knowing what was happening on the right flank, attempted to reform his regiments for a new attack up the hill. As he formed the line, he suddenly realized the only other troops on the field were Sykes' Regulars, who had fallen back and were forming square against the enemy cavalry. Sherman ordered Colonel Corcoran to do the same. The Sixty-Ninth formed a rough square as the Confederate cavalry came over the crest of the hill and charged. Sherman was mounted in the center of the formation. He gave the order to fire, and a well-directed volley scattered the attackers. Colonel Corcoran crossed the rail fence over which his men had fled and, halting the color bearer, called on the men to rally around the flag (National Color). The Sixty-Ninth's Color Sergeant was shot and killed. When another man took up the flag, he, too, was killed. The noise of the battle had drowned out Corcoran's voice, and only a few men halted. The Colonel and his party took refuge in a nearby house but before he could prepare a defense, he was surrounded and forced to surrender. The Confederates, delighted with the capture of such a well-known officer and the flag of the Regiment, made no effort to follow up the fleeing Union soldiers.

Thomas Francis Meagher

The Regiment's National Color was also captured by Confederates but was retaken by Captain Wildey of the Fire Zouaves. He killed the two Southerners who had seized it and returned the National Color to the Regiment. The Regimental Colors also fell into Confederate hands. John Keefe, one of Meagher's Zouaves, shot the Confederate who grabbed the flag and recaptured it. However, Keefe lost the flag again when he was overpowered and taken prisoner. Keefe shot his two captors with a revolver, which he pulled from his shirt and regained the Colors once more. The stories about losing and regaining Regimental Colors cannot be verified but appear in several books. Others insist the 69th never lost a flag.

Sherman's Brigade and Sykes' Regulars retreated across Bull Run and enabled the bulk of the routed Union forces to escape over the Stone Bridge. The Sixty-Ninth (without its Commander) came off the field in good order and halted on the Centerville Road to rest and await orders. The regiment was strung out along the road, trying to keep together amid the confusion of routed regiments, panic-stricken civilians, and fleeing teamsters. A Southern officer said about the 69th: Amid the few that held ground, Corcoran's Irish Regiment stood like a rock in the whirlpool rushing past them. The Irish fought like heroes and, at the end, did slowly retire. The Regiment fought valiantly at Bull Run and was one of the only Northern Regiments to leave the field in good order. Even the Southern press praised the 69th Regiment. "No Southerner but feels that the Sixty-Ninth maintained the old reputation of Irish valor (on the wrong side). All honor to the Sixty-Ninth, even in its errors.

Because Colonel Corcoran was captured, Acting Major Thomas F. Meagher led the Regiment home. The casualties of the Sixty-Ninth at Bull Run were officers, one killed, three wounded, and five prisoners. Non-commissioned officers and privates, forty were killed, eighty-five wounded, and sixty prisoners. There is some doubt as to the exact number of men lost by the regiment at Bull Run. On the return of the 69th Regiment New York State Militia from Bull Run, many veterans of the original militia regiment decided to form a new volunteer regiment for active service in the war. This Regiment was one of those raised by Thomas Francis Meagher in November 1861, and it was designated as the 69th New York State Volunteer (NYSV) Infantry but was also known as the "1st Regiment, the Irish Brigade". It was a Federal Regiment that co-existed with the Militia Regiment, which fought at Bull Run.

The returning soldiers of the Militia Regiment left their muskets in a pile at the armory. Of the 800 muskets returned from the battle, only 300 were serviceable. The others were so rusted that when they were cleaned and the rust removed, the bore was larger than originally made. The Regiment had established a great reputation for courage on the field of battle, however, the arms with which they fought so valiantly were left neglected for three months. On return from their three-month's service after the Battle of Bull Run, the 69th Regiment NYSM, while remaining in State service, formed the nucleus of the 69th New York Volunteer Infantry Regiment (69th Infantry Regiment NYSV). The 69th Infantry, NYSV was mustered into Federal service between 7 September and 17 November 1861, at New York. This regiment remained in Federal service until it was mustered out on 30 June 1865 at Alexandria, Virginia. It was the 1st Regiment of the Irish Brigade.

On 23 April 1862, the 69th Regiment New York State Militia was re-designated as the 69th Regiment New York National Guard. This Regiment was again mustered into Federal service on 26 May 1862 at New York. It was mustered out of Federal service on 3 September 1862. The

National Guard Regiment would be mustered into Federal Service again in 1863 and 1864. Again, while remaining in State service, the 69th Regiment New York National Guard formed the nucleus of another regiment, the 69th New York National Guard Artillery (serving as Infantry), which would become the 182nd New York Volunteer Infantry Regiment. This Regiment was in the brigade formed by General Corcoran after his release from Confederate prison. 69th New York National Guard Artillery was mustered into Federal service on 17 September 1862 at Newport News, Virginia, and mustered out of Federal service on 15 July 1865 at Washington, D.C.

Although Doheny was dead, Corcoran was in a Southern jail, and John Mitchell had moved to the South, many of the Irish Republican leaders who were instrumental in forming the Irish Brigade of the New York State Militia still believed in the necessity of forming an Irish Brigade. Among them was Thomas Francis Meagher. After the Battle of Bull Run Meagher worked to recruit an Irish Brigade which would serve in the federal army fighting to preserve the Union. Soon after the return of the Regiment, a grand and enthusiastic festival was held at Jones' Wood under the auspices of the Convention of Irish Societies on behalf of the widows and orphans of the soldiers of the Regiment who were slain at the Battle of Bun Run. It was estimated there were over twenty thousand in attendance. Considering that an entrance fee was charged, this was one of the grandest demonstrations that took place in support of the war. Captain Meagher, who was the main speaker, was introduced by Judge Connolly, Chairman of the Committee of Arrangements and a zealous worker in support of the Irish soldiers and the needs of their families. Captain Meagher stepped forward and was received with an enthusiastic applause. He had just returned from the battlefield, and his reception was a fit appreciation of his bravery and talent. His speech was a tribute to his brother-soldiers in battle and the justness of the American cause. He made a powerful appeal to his countrymen to rise in defense of the flag that waved over them. Meagher, who was an excellent orator, gave a vivid account of the operations of the Regiment during its service and of its noble behavior in battle. This speech induced many to join the army. Many but not all the members of the Sixty-Ninth Regiment NYSM decided to volunteer for service in a new federal regiment, the Sixty-Ninth Infantry Regiment New York State Volunteers. Meagher was offered the command of this regiment. He also received a message from General Fremont offering him a promotion to Colonel if he accepted the position of aide-de-camp on General Fremont's staff.

By the end of August 1861, there was a rumor claiming Corcoran had been transferred to Fort Sumter in Charleston, South Carolina. Lieutenant John Mitchel Jr. (a Confederate officer and son of John Mitchel of the Young Ireland Revolt) reported from his post at Fort Sumter that Corcoran was still in Richmond. Apparently, reacting to reports that Corcoran was being treated cruelly, Mitchel claimed that the Irish prisoner is treated only to cocktails, mint juleps, and other beverages, such as only Richmond can produce to perfection. He will be returned to you soon. In fact, he is treated like an honorable gentleman, taken prisoner while fighting on the side he conscientiously believed to be right. If he should be sent to our post, I shall be very happy to see him, and as Adjutant of the post, I will have our band play *St. Patrick's Day* and *The Garryowen* on his behalf. In September, Corcoran and the other Union prisoners were transferred by train to Castle Pinckney in Charleston Harbor, South Carolina. As the train approached Gaston, North Carolina, an axle on the prisoners' car broke. While the prisoners were assembled along the tracks, they were verbally harassed by local civilians.

A man yelled to Corcoran. Where is your Sixty-Ninth now? Corcoran replied. You'll see the Sixty-Ninth very soon. The man pulled a knife from his belt. Corcoran was saved when a young lady rushed between Corcoran and his would-be assailant. She said to the Southerner, you dare shed the blood of a helpless, unarmed prisoner. In the middle of November, the Union prisoners were moved to Charleston's city jail. Corcoran explained to a Confederate visitor why he would not accept parole. Corcoran said honor and patriotism stop him from doing so. Soon after, Corcoran became the center of a diplomatic crisis. A Southerner (by the name of Smith) was captured on a Confederate Privateer Savannah. He was tried and sentenced to death by a court in Philadelphia. In response, the Confederate government ordered lots be drawn from among the names of the Union prisoners in the Charleston jail to see who would be executed in retaliation for Smith's execution. Corcoran's name was selected. Thirteen other prisoners were selected to serve as hostages if President Lincoln's government hanged the thirteen other privateers in its possession. Now under virtual threat of death, Corcoran feared that he would have to suffer the ignominious doom of a convicted felon. He wrote in a letter that there could be no possible other cause for which I could be more content to freely offer up my life.

Meanwhile, the Sixty-Ninth Regiment New York Volunteers (NYSV) of the Irish Brigade, First Division, Second Corps, Army of the Potomac, was organized in New York City in accordance with orders from the War Department on August 30, 1861. It was formed by the officers and men of the Sixty-Ninth Regiment New York State Militia who served with it in the three months campaign. The officers of the Regiment were so successful in recruiting for the Federal Regiment they determined to form a brigade. The brigade was commanded by Col. Robert Nugent until March 1862, when General Thomas Francis Meagher was assigned to its command. Meagher was assisted in raising the Brigade by prominent citizens, including Archbishop Hughes, Judge Daly, Richard O'Gorman, and others. Committees were formed to raise funds, recruit and equip the new brigade. In Boston, B. S. Treanor, Esq. began raising an Irish Regiment for Brigade. A committee of women in New York began to raise funds for an embroidered stand of colors for each of the regiments in the Irish Brigade.

Volunteers came from all areas of the city but also included individuals from Albany, Utica, Buffalo, and Pittsburgh. As a company was formed, it was sent to Fort Schuyler under the command of Colonel Robert Nugent. The new 63rd Regiment offered command to Felix E. 'O'Rourke. In Boston, the new regiment was to be commanded by Colonel Matthew Murphy. Another regiment was to be raised in Philadelphia, commanded by Captain Robert Emmet Patterson. This regiment was to have a squadron of cavalry.

The 69th Regiment, NYSV, was recruited in a very short time. It was ordered to Fort Schuyler in New York. It remained there until November 18, 1861, when it left for Washington, D.C. The Regiment passed through New York City, where it was presented with a stand of colors. The colors were of the finest silk, one of which was the National American Flag, and another a green flag (First Irish Colors). The First Irish Colors bore an embroidered gold harp surmounted by a sunburst. Above the sunburst was a wreath of shamrocks; over this was a scroll with the "1st REGT IRISH BRIGADE". Beneath the harp was a second scroll that was written "RIAM NAR DRUID O SBAIRN LANN." This translates in English to "Who Never Retreated Clash of Spears."

The original field officers of the Regiment were Colonel Robert Nugent, Lieutenant Colonel James Kelly, and Major James Cavanagh. The Regiment consisted of Robert Nugent, Colonel; James Kelly, Lieutenant Colonel; James Cavanaugh, Major; James I. Smith, Adjutant; Dennis F. Sullivan, Quartermaster; Doctor I Paschal Smith, Surgeon; Father Thomas Willette (Ouellet) Chaplain.

"A" Company was commanded by Captain James Saunders and had two Lieutenants, Andrew Birmingham and Richard A. Kelly.

"B" Company was commanded by Captain Thomas Leddy and had two Lieutenants, Lawrence Cahill and John Gasson.

"C" Company was commanded by Captain Jasper M. Whitty and had two Lieutenants, Garrett Nagle and Murtha Murphy.

"D" Company was commanded by Captain Timothy L. Shanley and had two Lieutenants, John H. Donavan and Martin Scully.

"E" Company was commanded by Captain William Benson and had two Lieutenants, Terrence Duffy and David Burke.

The ranks of the 69th Regiment, NYSV, filled, and the regiment was ordered to Washington while the other units of the brigade remained training for war at Fort Schuyler. The 69th Regiment was commanded by Colonel Nugent. Prior to its departure the regiment was to be presented its flags by the ladies of New York. The silk flags and guidons were embroidered by Tiffany's New York. On November 18th, the steamer Atlas brought the entire Sixty-Ninth and officers of the other regiments in the Brigade from Fort Schuyler to the East 34th Street pier in Manhattan, so the new Colors could be presented. The troops landed about eleven o'clock and formed into columns. They were escorted by the First Cavalry and flanked by the batteries of Captains Hogan and McMahon. On arriving at Madison Avenue, the column was halted and faced to the front. The presentation of the colors took place at Archbishop Hughes' Residence on Madison Avenue. Unfortunately, Archbishop Hughes was in Europe, so the ceremony was performed by Reverend William Starrs, Vicar-General of the Archdioceses. Reverend Starrs addressed the assembled troops. Soldiers of the Irish Brigade, officers and men, the Most Reverend Archbishop of New York, before his departure for Europe, asked me to attend on this occasion as his representative. I take great pleasure in complying with his request. I regret that Archbishop Hughes is not present because I know that you would be better pleased to see him and hear his voice. However, I know his sentiments in your regard. I know his good wishes are with you. I know he has confidence in your patriotism and loyalty to the Union and the Constitution. I know that he has confidence in the fidelity of the Irish soldiers, for history has told us that the Irish soldier has always done his duty at home and abroad. Wherever his services have been employed, he has never been found wanting.

Colonel Nugent stepped forward to receive the colors from Mrs. Chalfin. Judge Daly led Mrs. Chalfin forward with the colors carried by an orderly. Judge Daly then said: "Colonel Nugent, I am requested by this lady beside me, Mrs. Chalfin, the daughter of an Irishman and the wife of an officer in the regular army of the United States, and by the ladies associated with her, to offer to your regiment the accompanying stand of colors. In committing to your charge these two flags, I need scarcely remind you that the history of the one is pregnant with a meaning in the light that it sheds upon the history of the other. This green flag, with its ancient harp, its burst of sunlight, and its motto from Ossian, in the old Irish tongue, recalls through the long lapse of many centuries the period when Ireland was a nation and conveyed more eloquently than by words how that nationality was lost through the practical working of that doctrine of secession for which the rebellious States of the South have taken up arms.

The other regiments of the Irish Brigade (the 88th Regiment and 63rd Regiment) were presented with flags by other dignitaries, and speeches were made after the presentations. At the conclusion of the ceremony, three cheers were given for the donors. The column was reformed and proceeded back to the 34th Street pier to board the Atlas for the return trip to Fort Schuyler.

It was expected that General Shields would take command of the Irish Brigade. However, Shields held the rank of major-general in the Mexican Campaign, and it would be difficult for him to take a Brigadier General post (reporting to newly appointed Major Generals with no military experience). In his reply, declining the offer, he stated that the command of the Irish Brigade should go to Colonel Meagher, who had raised the brigade and shared the honors and perils of the first battle of the war with the Sixty-Ninth. There was strong opposition to Meagher Commanding the Brigade. Many wanted an American to command the brigade. The officers of the brigade convened a meeting. And resolutions were unanimously adopted in favor of Colonel Meagher's appointment to command. A delegation consisting of Majors Quinlan and O'Neil, Dr. Reynolds, Captains Maxwell O'Sullivan, Butler, Galway, McMahon (Sixty-Ninth), Hogan, O'Donaghue, McMahon, Lynch (Sixty-third), and Quartermaster O'Hanlon was formed to discuss the recommendation with President Lincoln. The delegation was accompanied by Colonel Forney and introduced by the Honorable Preston King of New York. The recommendation of the delegation was seconded by King and Forney and Colonel Frank P. Blair of Missouri. The President complimented Colonel Meagher for his patriotism, devotion, gallant services at Bull Run, and for his services in enrolling such a fine body of men as the Irish Brigade. The President promised to give the subject his earnest consideration. The next day, the name of Acting Brigadier-General Thomas F. Meagher was sent to the Senate by the President for confirmation.

Meagher was given Command of the Irish Brigade. He was the Irish Brigade's most famous commander. He had served as Captain of Company "K," a Zouave Company in the Sixty-Ninth Regiment New York State Militia during the Battle of Bull Run. He was the senior officer (after Colonel Corcoran) and was appointed Acting Major before the battle. He also brought the Regiment home from Bull Run. Possibly for these reasons and because the Sixty-Ninth Regiment was the most famous regiment in the Irish Brigade (and the only regiment still in existence), many people think the Irish Brigade is the Sixty-Ninth Regiment. The lineage of the Sixty-Ninth Regiment does not include the other units in the Irish Brigade. The 69th Regiment and the other regiments of the Irish Brigade established headquarters at Camp California. It was situated on two hills overlooking the road from Alexandria to Fairfax, about two and a half miles from Alexandria, Virginia. The 69th's tents were located on the right of the road. The men were kept busy during the day with drills and the duties of camp-life. The Regiment spent their first Christmas at Camp California listening to music, dancing, laughing, and telling stories. Father Willett and celebrated the midnight Mass. The chapel tents were as well-decorated as circumstances would allow. In front of the open chapel tent were rude benches of hewn logs. The chapel was situated on a hill under tall cedar and pine trees. Father Dillon also celebrated Mass with Quartermaster Haverty and Captain O'Sullivan serving as altar boys. After mass, the troops retired to their tents.

On February 3rd, the Senate confirmed the President's appointment of Thomas F. Meagher as brigadier-general in command of the Irish Brigade. On the 5th of February, Meagher officially took command of the brigade. President Lincoln had replaced General McDowell with General McClellan as Commander of the Army. McClellan spent several months in1861 and early 1862 training the army for combat. In the spring of 1862, his plan was to sail the army to Fortress Monroe on the Peninsula between the York and James rivers, move up the Peninsula, and seize Richmond. His hope was the enemy would abandon its entrenched position around Manassas and Centreville to protect Richmond and Norfolk (which it did). On March 9th, he ordered the army to occupy the abandoned Confederate positions in Manassas and Centerville.

In March, the 69th Regiment NYSV moved from Camp California and headed toward Manassas. The Southerners had burned everything they abandoned, including the hospital and railroad junction. They even left unburied dead.

General French had the bodies buried. The 69th was ordered to move from Union Mills to Manassas and then to Fairfax and then Warrenton Junction. On March 16th, they found themselves at Fairfax Courthouse after marching over ten miles through snow. They settled in that evening and prepared to celebrate St. Patrick's Day. Unfortunately, their plans were interrupted when they were ordered to return to Centreville during the night of the 16th to support General French.

New York State had increased the size of its militia to meet the increasing calls for more troops by the Federal Government but the need for a draft was anticipated. On April 23, the Legislature passed an act which required all persons liable to bear arms. The preparation began on August 13, 1862. Enrollment Officers were appointed, and necessary books were prepared. Every person within the prescribed ages would be entered on the lists. In the counties of New York (Manhattan) and Kings (Brooklyn), the enrollment was placed under the immediate direction and control of General William H. Anthon. In the 1862 Adjutant General's Report, the necessity for a draft was discussed at length. The report said: "It may indeed be assumed that the right to use whatever measure necessary for the full and complete exercise of the power to "raise and support armies" is the natural coincident of the power itself, as that is deducible from the duty: with which the Government is invested to provide for the public defense; these means must include the principle of conscription or compulsory service." The concept of a "draft" would have a devastating effect on New York City within a few months.

The National Guard Regiment (69th Regiment NYSM) was mustered into Federal service on May 26, 1862, in Manhattan. The Regiment had a total strength of 1,000 members. They departed New York on May 30th for a 90-day tour defending Washington. On September 3rd, they were mustered out of Federal Service. On October 14th, the enrollment for the draft throughout the State was almost completed, and commissioners and surgeons were appointed to hear and determine on claims for exemption.

In New York City, over 200,000 individuals were enrolled for the draft, but many claimed exemption on the grounds of physical disability. After examination, 40,000 were exempted for medical reasons. There was a serious problem with bounties offered by the Federal Government and States. Many individuals who received a bounty for enlisting subsequently deserted. Moreover, New York State offered a bounty of fifty dollars in addition to the bounty and advance pay offered by the Federal Government. The problem persisted throughout the war.

The army was divided into regular corps with a Corps insignia assigned to each. Major General Sumner commanded the Second Corps. The insignia of the Second Corps was a Trefoil. The First Division of the Second Corps was commanded by Major-General Dick Richardson. The Trefoil worn by members of Richardson's Division was Red. The 69th NYSV marched to Warrenton Junction. Since the rebels had destroyed all the bridges, the troops had to wade through freezing water up to their hips. After reaching Warrenton, the regiment set up camp, but since they did not have tents, they were required to sleep in mud with little shelter. While bivouacking at Warrenton, the Sixty-Ninth was ordered towards the Rappahannock on a reconnaissance expedition. Colonel Nugent, Lieutenant Colonel Kelly, and Major Cavanagh accompanied the regiment. When they reached the Rappahannock, they found that the enemy had crossed, leaving some scouts and pickets. General Johnston, the Confederate commander, fired his artillery from the south bank of the river, shelling the Regiment. After the reconnaissance expedition, the Regiment returned to Camp California for the final time. Early the next morning, the Regiment marched to Alexandria and embarked on board the Columbia and Ocean Queen for its trip to Fortress Monroe.

Due to inclement weather, the transports were required to lay off Fortress Monroe for four or five days. Drizzling rain and sleet swept across the bay, drenching the soldiers on board. The rocking and tossing of the transport ships caused many of the soldiers to be nauseous. The weather cleared after a few days, and the transports steamed up to Ship Point and dropped anchor. The men had to disembark as best they could. Some got into the small boats, while others had to jump into the water and wade to shore. Since provisions for the Irish Brigade were not made prior to arrival, General Howard had generously ordered his Command to share their huts, fires, and rations with the Irish Brigade.

The first night was spent with General Howard's Brigade in log huts (left by the Confederates). Richmond is situated at the head of the Virginia Peninsula formed by the James River on the south and the York River on the north. Newport News and Hampton Roads are at the foot of the Peninsula, where the James River flows into the Chesapeake Bay. Across the Peninsula, the Chickahominy River flows easterly in a diagonal line from the northwest. Five roads to Richmond crossed the Chickahominy. However, rain had caused the Chickahominy to overflow its banks. The lowlands and swamps were flooded, which made travel difficult. The Army of the Potomac had approximately 50,000 men at Fort Monroe when McClellan arrived, but this number grew to 121,500 before hostilities began. The Union fleet sailed up the James River towards Richmond but was repelled. As the Union Army moved up the peninsula to Richmond, the Irish Brigade were held in reserve at Camp Winfield Scott. Each man was issued half of a shelter tent, which could be buttoned to another shelter half to form a two-man tent.

The first casualty for the 69th Regiment, NYSV, was Patrick Casey, Company "B." He died when a tree fell on him. In his pocket was a note which read, "My name is Patrick Casey, Co. "B," Sixty-Ninth Regiment, N.Y.S.V. Anyone finding this note on my person when killed will please write a note to my wife, and direct it as follows: Mrs. Mary Casey, No. 188 Rivington Street, New York". On May 4th, McClellan, threatening the Williamsburg Road, forced the enemy to evacuate Yorktown and retreat to their entrenched works at Williamsburg. As rain fell, the 69th began to put up their tents but were interrupted when they were ordered to join the battle in front of Williamsburg. The wet, muddy conditions made travel difficult, and artillery pieces often got stuck in the mud, blocking roads. At two o'clock in the morning, the regiment was halted. News came that Williamsburg had fallen to Union soldiers. Men slept in their wet clothes in the mud. The next morning, after the rain stopped, the regiment continued its movement toward Williamsburg but was subsequently ordered to return to Yorktown.

On Sunday, the 11th of May, the Regiment reached Yorktown and embarked on large transports with other units of the division. They proceeded up the York River to the White House and disembarked at Cumberland Landing. The White House was the home of the Custis family. Before marrying George Washington, his wife Martha was married to Daniel Custis. They had two children who were adopted by the President. George Washington Parke Custis was the great-grandson of George Washington. His daughter Mary was married to Robert E. Lee future Commander of the Army of Northern Virginia. Robert E. Lee lived in the Custis home in Arlington, Virginia. The house was built by George Washington Parke Custis, great-grandson of President George Washington. Lee lived there until the State of Virginia seceded from the Union. Early in the war, Lee's wife, Mary, and their daughters left Arlington. They moved south to their son's (Rooney Lee) plantation in New Kent County at White House. McClellan placed a guard on the house and ordered it to be protected. After the Battle of Antietam, the Union Army confiscated her house and property in Arlington. Since the cemeteries around Washington had reached capacity, the Union buried soldiers in the rose garden. The property would become Arlington Cemetery. You can see the Custis House (in the middle of Arlington Cemetery) from the Lincoln Memorial.

On the 19th, they reached St. Peter's Church and camped on a hill near Tyler's farm. While McClellan was preparing for the advance to Richmond, the enemy was concentrating near the Chickahominy River. McClellan was preparing roads and bridges to cross the Chickahominy swamp while McDowell was operating along the Rappahannock. Jackson fell back from Fredericksburg towards Richmond. The Confederates were massing around Richmond to strike McClellan's Army and drive them back down the peninsula. While Colonel Nugent's Regiment (69th Infantry, NYSV) was encamped on Tyler's farm, the officers of the Irish Brigade decided to hold the "Chickahominy Steeple Chase." The planning took place as a battle raged in front of Fair Oaks. The officers raced while soldiers played football. Colonel Nugent's horse "Mourne Boy" was ridden by Captain Jack Gosson (wearing a scarlet jacket and scarlet cap). Lieutenant Colonel Kelly's horse "Honest John" was ridden by Captain Saunders (wearing a blue jacket, red sleeves, and red cap). Lieutenant Colonel Kelly's other horse was ridden by Kelly (wearing a yellow jacket and red cap). It was a very colorful event, with other officers of the Brigade wearing different colorful costumes. Two horse races were to be followed by a mule race (in which the animals were to be ridden by drummer boys). The

Chickahominy Steeple Chase was interrupted by a call to arms.

Battle of Fair Oaks / Seven Pines

Cannon fire could be head in the distance, and the 69th was ordered to cross the Chickahominy at Grapevine Bridge. The regiment traveled through the swamp and hurried toward the previous day's battlefield near Fair Oaks (or Battle of Seven Pines). That night, the regiment was ordered to the front. At five o'clock in the morning, the Confederates attacked. Colonel Nugent had the Regiment fixed bayonets and prepared to engage the enemy. Confederate forces attacked across the Union lines but were unsuccessful. After several attempts to break the line, the Confederates left the field in disorder. During the action, Confederate General Joseph E. Johnston was seriously wounded. This was one of the most important things that happened during the War for the Confederacy. General Johnson was replaced by Robert E. Lee as the overall Commander of the Army of Northern Virginia.

By the end of May, the McClellan's Army had built bridges across the Chickahominy. Union forces were now facing Richmond. McClellan's Army was straddling the river, with one-third of the Army south of the river and two-thirds north. While McClellan's army was encamped outside Richmond, Confederate General Thomas J. Jackson

(Stonewall) was keeping General Banks and General McDowell's troops from reinforcing McClellan. Jackson conducted a classic military campaign of surprise and maneuver. He pressed his army to travel 646 miles in 48 days and won five significant victories with a force of about 17,000 against a combined force of 60,000. Jackson moved his army south to join Lee's Army of Northern Virginia. At the same time, Confederate General James Ewell Brown (JEB) Stuart made a bold raid around the Union Army. Under his command, he had Colonel Fitzhugh Lee, son of General Robert E. Lee, with him. Stuart was pursued by Union cavalry, Commanded by his father-in-law, General Philip St. George Cooke, who, unlike Stewart, had remained loyal to the Union.

The Battle of Fair Oaks or Seven Pines took place on May 31 and June 1, 1862. The Sixty-Ninth Regiment joined the battle on June 1st. After the Battle of Fair Oaks, Dr. Smith established a field hospital for the Regiment in a farmhouse, and Father Ouellet and the doctor tended to the wounded and dying from both sides. Instead of pressing the offensive, McClellan ordered his army to hold their positions and dig in. Richmond was only a few miles away and could be seen from the tops of the tall pine-trees in the area. The Union forces were confident Richmond would fall in a few weeks. Although the Battle of Fair Oaks or Seven Pines was tactically inconclusive it was the largest battle in the east up to that time. It marked the end of the Union offensive and led to the Seven Days Battles and Union retreat later in June. Six members of the Regiment were killed or wounded on June 1. After the Battle of Fair Oaks, Dr. Smith established a field hospital for the Regiment in a farmhouse. Father Ouellet and Dr. Smith tended to the wounded and dying from both sides.

The 69th Regiment and the Irish Brigade were on the front line of the division. Soldiers were kept very busy either building fortifications or performing picket duty. Enemy lines were not far away, and there was continual skirmishing. The lines were so close that soldiers on both sides would occasionally exchange newspapers, tobacco, and coffee.

Instead of pressing the offensive, McClellan ordered his army to hold their positions and dig in. Richmond was only a few miles away and could be seen from the tops of the tall pine-trees in the area. Union forces were confident Richmond would fall in a few weeks. Although the Battle of Fair Oaks or Seven Pines was tactically inconclusive, it was the largest battle fought in the East up to that time. The battle marked the end of the Union offensive and led to the Seven Days Battles and Union retreat in late June.

The Battle of Gaines' Mill

Lee's intention was to attack McClellan's right wing and cut off his line of retreat across the Chickahominy. On Friday morning, June 26, 1862, Confederates attacked the Union lines. Union lines faltered and collapsed. McClellan ordered the 69th Irish Brigade and French Brigade forward. They moved at double-quick into battle. The Regiment's Green flag was unfurled, and the 69th attacked, repulsing the enemy. McClellan's army, seeing the French and Meagher Brigades successful, rallied the rest of the army behind them. McClellan's troops crossed the Chickahominy while the 69th and the other regiments of the Irish Brigade held the hills guarding the passages to the bridges. Towards dawn the next morning, the 69th received the order to cross the swollen Chickahominy, destroying the bridges after they crossed. The Confederates camped that evening on the battlefield. The Union army moved back down the Peninsula toward the James River and the protection of naval gunboats.

McClellan moved his headquarters to Savage Station on Saturday night (about seven miles from the battlefield of Gaines' Mill). The Sixty-Ninth was assigned picket duty in front of Sumner's Corps. The Regiment was ordered to occupy its position until all Union forces had retired. The next morning, the Regiment joined the other three regiments of the Brigade at Meadow Station (which was about two miles below Savage Station).

Battle of Savage Station

At about four in the afternoon on Sunday, June 29, McClellan left the 69th Regiment and the rest of Sumner's 2nd Corps to protect the retreating Union Army's rear. As the 2nd Corps was preparing to withdraw, Confederate artillery fired on it. The rebels moved in force along the Williamsburg Road (having hastily repaired one of the bridges across the Chickahominy). Sumner's 2nd Corps fell back from Peach Orchard to Savage Station, where it formed into a line of battle. At about 5 PM, the enemy attacked. The Sixty-Ninth Regiment counter-attacked, and for about two hours, fierce fighting (at times hand-to-hand) ensued. The 69th and 88th Regiments charged a Virginia artillery battery. Two cannons were captured and destroyed. It was close to midnight before the wearied and hungry soldiers were ordered to fall back beyond White Oak Swamp. Due to the movement and confusion, men went for days without food. The supplies at Savage Station were burned, and the dead and wounded were left behind.

During the nightmare of which characterized McClellan's retreat down the Peninsula, the Sixty-Ninth Regiment suffered five killed, captured, or wounded. Meagher was put under arrest following an argument with his Corps Commander. Command of the brigade was transferred to Colonel Nugent. As the Regiment moved down the Peninsula, casualties increased with every battle. There were also several desertions during this time.

Battle of White Oak Swamp

The next morning, the Sixty-Ninth Regiment took up a position on Nelson's farm. They had spent the entire night in line of battle. Confederates, attempting to turn the Union flanks, attacked supply trains and artillery in the Union's rear. Lee pressed the Union forces from the Northwest, and Stonewall Jackson attacked Richardson's Division (which included the Sixty-Ninth Regiment) from the north at White Oak Swamp.

Confederate forces were unable to stop the Union's retreat down the Peninsula. When Colonel Nugent reported sick, command of the Regiment transferred to Lieutenant Colonel James Kelly. Captain Whitty and Lieutenant Burns of the Sixty-Ninth were badly wounded. The Irish Brigade held the bridge at White Oak Swamp. The Sixty-Ninth Regiment and the rest of the Brigade were held as the reserve of the 2nd Corps (which was the reserve of the Army). The Regiment was thrown into battle when things appeared bleakest. The Regiment had 14 casualties at the Battle of White Oak Swamp. At one o'clock in the morning, the Sixty-Ninth Regiment resumed its position at the rear of the army and headed toward Malvern Hill. It arrived at about 5 A.M. on Tuesday, the 1st of July.

Battle of Malvern Hill

Malvern Hill is an elevated plateau with few trees. It was traversed by several roads. The hill was a good defensive position since several ravines protected the front and the ground slopes and was an ideal position for artillery. A sheltered ravine extended on the northwest toward James River. The left and center of Union lines rested on Malvern Hill. The right of the line curved back to the James River. Union gunboats on the James River protected the flanks and covered the approaches from Richmond. The Sixty-Ninth Regiment hoped it could spend the day resting. The Regiment charged up the hill, followed by the rest of the Irish Brigade. Other Union regiments cheered them as they attacked. The Sixty-Ninth sent volley after volley into the enemy, moving slowly but steadily as they fired. Their guns became so hot they clogged. The Regiment moved coolly by the flank and was replaced by the 88[th,] who continued the attack. When the 88th became exhausted, the Sixty-Ninth Regiment dashed forward to relieve them and continue the attack. As enemy fire swept the Sixty-Ninth, the Regiment held its ground. Confederate forces made a bold attempt to hold the hill, but it was in vain. There was hand-to-hand fighting with the famed Louisiana Tigers, but they were forced to retire. Darkness prevented Union forces from following them. After a few hours' rest, the Regiment marched (in the dead of night) back to the James River. They reached the river early on Wednesday morning. Lieutenant Reynolds was killed. Captains Whitty and Leddy and Lieutenants Cahil, Donovan, Oarr, Burns, and Maroney were wounded. Major Cavanaugh had his horse shot from under him.

Lieutenant John H. Donovan of Company D, Sixty-Ninth Regiment, was shot through the right eye. The bullet exited through the ear just under the brain, and Donovan was left for dead and was captured. The next morning, Confederate General A.P. Hill ordered Union officers to surrender their side arms and when he ordered Donovan to surrender his pistol, Donovan replied he had sent them to his regiment by his servant after falling. I think, said the general, from the apparent nature of your wound, you won't have much need for it in the future. I think differently, General, Donovan replied. I have one good eye still and will risk that in the cause of the Union. Should I ever lose that, I'll fight blind! Father Thomas Willette, Chaplain of the Sixty-Ninth, remained with the wounded near Savage Station until captured by the rebels. He was later freed and returned to the Regiment.

While at Harrison's Landing, the men were issued tents and new clothing. One evening, when the officers were discussing events of the battles, Major Cavanaugh, the

Executive Officer of the Sixty-Ninth Regiment, spoke about the fact that he had run into a dying rebel officer who he knew well. Cavanaugh got off his horse and gave the officer water. He talked with the dying man about the Confederate officer's fiancé who lived in New York. The officer asked Cavanaugh to give his fiancé a locket and photograph. Cavanaugh promised to do so.

Another officer who was listening to Cavanaugh said: That was a sad case but scarcely as bad as one that I witnessed. Sergeant Driscoll, a brave man and one of the best shots in the Brigade, was in my unit. When charging at Malvern Hill, a company of Confederates was posted in a clump of trees. The Confederates kept up a fierce fire on us and charged to meet our advance. Their officer seemed to be a daring, reckless boy, and I said to Driscoll, "If that officer is taken down, many of us will fall before we pass that clump." "Leave it to me," said Driscoll. He raised his rifle, and the moment the officer exposed himself again, Driscoll fired, and the officer fell. When his company retreated, I said to Driscoll, He was a brave fellow; see if that officer is dead. I watched as Driscoll turned him over on his back. The officer opened his eyes for a moment and faintly murmured, "Father" died. I will forever forget Driscoll's frantic grief. It was harrowing to witness it. The officer was Driscoll's son, who had gone South before the war. However, the Roster of the Sixty-Ninth Regiment, NYSV does include a soldier with the name of Driscoll (although both the 63rd and 88th Regiments had soldiers named Driscoll). The officer telling the story may have been from 63rd or 88th Regiment. Both Regiments were in the Irish Brigade and officers from the Brigade would get together often.

Peter F. Rafferty was born June 12, 1845, in County Tyrone, Ireland. He enlisted as a private in Company B, Sixty-Ninth New York Volunteers, when he was 17 years old. He was awarded the Medal of Honor at Malvern Hill on 2 August 1897. Although wounded several times during the battle, he refused to leave the fight. He was shot in the mouth and lower jaw, losing part of his tongue. He was also shot in the foot. He was captured and was hospitalized in Richmond. When he was exchanged on July 25, 1862, he was paroled from the hospital in Richmond and transported to the North. He was hospitalized on July 29th at the Broad & Cherry Streets Hospital in Philadelphia and subsequently discharged for medical reasons on January 15, 1863. He died on April 30, 1910, and is buried at Calvary Cemetery, Woodside, NY.

Casualties for the Regiment at the Battle of Malvern hill were 81, killed, wounded, or captured.

On July 22, General Sumner paraded the 2nd Corp for General McClellan on a plain above Cumberland Landing.

The parade was followed by President Lincoln's review of the entire army. During Lincoln's visit to the Army, First Lieutenant James M. Birmingham, Adjutant of the 88th Regiment NYSM, was coming from a swim in the James River. The lieutenant walked over to the Sixty-Ninth Regiment's camp to visit his brother. When Birmingham turned a corner and saw the President and Generals McClellan and Sumner speaking with Colonel Nugent, he ducked behind cover and eavesdropped on the conversation. He claimed he saw President Lincoln lift a corner of the Sixty-Ninth Regiment's flag and kiss it, exclaiming, "God Bless the Irish Flag."

The Army of the Potomac remained along the James River while General Meagher and a group of officers returned to New York to recruit for the depleted Irish Brigade. The Sixty-Ninth Regiment, which began the campaign with 750 officers and men, suffered the most casualties in the Irish Brigade (from both disease and battle). Only 295 soldiers answered the Regimental roll call.

McClellan believed the Peninsula untenable unless reinforced. Throughout the whole campaign, McClellan overestimated the enemy's strength. His troops greatly outnumbered the Confederates. He withdrew his troops from the south side of the river. General Lee perceived that the theatre of action was shifting to the Rappahannock.

Union General Pope had forty thousand men on the Rappahannock, and they were about to press south. Lee made a bold and daring move. He sent most of his army to attack Union forces at Manassas. This was the Second Battle of Bull Run. However, when Lee shifted his forces toward Manassas, it led the way to Richmond, wide open for McClellan's forces. Had McClellan not been so tentative, he could have captured Richmond. Unfortunately, McClellan did not take advantage of this. He continued to request additional troops. Finally, the War Department recalled him and his army. Had an advance been made on Richmond, Lee could not have re-enforced Jackson's army at Manassas. The Administration ordered McClellan to evacuate the Peninsula, and the War Department relieved McClellan of command.

The Union army marched down the Peninsula from Harrison's Landing to Yorktown. About eight o'clock in the morning of August 16, 1862, the last of Sumner's Corps arrived at the bank of the James River. The Sixty-Ninth Regiment marched to Newport News through Williamsburg, Yorktown, and Warwick Courthouse. The Regiment embarked on transports, which took them to Aquia Creek. They traveled by rail to Fredericksburg and were ordered to report to General Burnside at Falmouth. The Regiment encamped for two days and then was ordered to Alexandria.

They traveled by rail back to Aquia Creek, where they boarded transport ships to Alexandria. Upon arrival at Alexandria, the Regiment began to set up camp near their previous headquarters at Camp California, but they were immediately ordered to Arlington Heights. From Arlington Heights, the Regiment was ordered to support General Pope's command near Manassas. The Regiment traveled to Fairfax Courthouse and Centerville arriving at Manassas after the Battle.

In August 1862, Colonel Michael Corcoran was released from Confederate prison after his capture at First Bull Run. Corcoran visited the 69th New York National Guard (NYNG), the old 69th New York State Militia (NYSM), at Fort Lyon, Virginia. The 69th NYSM had been re-designated the 69th NYNG in April and had been mustered into federal service in May. Corcoran informed his old command of his desire to form a second Irish Brigade, stating that he wanted the 69th to be the first regiment of that new brigade. Lieutenant Colonel Matthew Murphy then asked the regiment whether they wished to join, and "all answered yes." Upon their return to New York, 700 men joined the 69th New York National Guard Artillery Regiment (serving as Infantry) for three years or the war.

Corcoran was welcomed and celebrated as a hero in Washington, Baltimore, Philadelphia, Newark, New Jersey, and finally, New York City. In Washington, he dined with President Lincoln, who made him a Brigadier General. He was given command of a new Irish brigade, the Irish Legion. Many of the soldiers in the 69th Regiment, New York State Militia, joined the First Regiment in the Irish Legion (Corcoran's Legion). Since you could not have two regiments with the same name, it was called the 69th Artillery Regiment, serving as Infantry, New York State Volunteers. The name was later changed to the 182nd Infantry. The Regiment is in the lineage of the 69th.

Although Washington had not been threatened by the Confederate Army, the 2nd Corps was ordered to Washington in case of an attack. After spending a few days in Washington, the Regiment was ordered to proceed to Rockville, Maryland (about 10 miles north of Washington). The Regiment passed through Rockville and proceeded north. About two miles outside of Rockville, General Sumner received a report that rebel soldiers were threatening Baltimore. The report also said another column of approximately 30,000 Confederates were headed toward General Sumner's Corps. The Regiment formed battlelines and loaded their weapons. In Washington, rumors about Confederate threats to the city abounded. One said Stonewall Jackson's army was moving on Alexandria. People panicked. Lincoln restored McClellan to command.

In August 1862, Colonel Michael Corcoran was released from Confederate prison after his capture at First Bull Run. Corcoran visited the 69th New York National Guard (NYNG), the old 69th New York State Militia (NYSM), at Fort Lyon, Virginia. The 69th NYSM had been re-designated the 69th NYNG in April and had been mustered into federal service in May. Corcoran informed his old command of his desire to form a second Irish Brigade, stating that he wanted the 69th to be the first regiment of that new brigade. Lieutenant Colonel Matthew Murphy then asked the regiment whether they wished to join, and "all answered yes." Upon their return to New York, 700 men joined the 69th New York National Guard Artillery Regiment (serving as Infantry) for three years or the war.

While remaining in state service, the Sixty-Ninth Regiment formed the nucleus of the Sixty-Ninth Regiment New York National Guard Artillery Regiment, also known as the 182d New York Volunteer Infantry Regiment, which was mustered into Federal service on September 17, 1862, at Newport News, Virginia. In November, the Regiment was excused from attending the Brigade Assembly since it was "absent at the seat of war, for which it volunteered."

Since the Confederacy had done so well at the Second Battle of Bull Run (Second Manassas), Confederate politicians decided Lee should move his army north through

Maryland and threaten Pennsylvania and New York. At the same time, General Bragg was to invade Kentucky. Confederate leaders believed an invasion of the North was necessary to secure recognition from European Countries. This was a major change in Confederate strategy. Lee drew up plans and published Special Order 191, which spelled out the details of his plan and line of march of the Army of Northern Virginia. A Confederate Officer put the Special Order in a tobacco can and subsequently dropped it. It would be found by a Union soldier and sent to McClellan.

General McClellan proceeded to inspect the troops and fortifications on the south side of the Potomac. On September 13, the following dispatch, which spelled out in detail the Confederate plans, was provided to McClellan: SPECIAL ORDERS, No. 191

HEADQUARTERS, ARMY OF NORTHERN VIRGINIA

September 9, 1862

The army will resume its march tomorrow, taking the Hagerstown Road. General Jackson's command will form the advance and, after passing Middletown with such portion as he may select, will take the route towards Sharpsburg. Cross the Potomac at the most convenient point, and by Friday night, take possession of the Baltimore and Ohio Railroad, capture the enemy as may be at Martinsburg, and intercept such as may attempt to escape from Harper's Ferry.

General Longstreet's command will pursue the same road as Boonsboro, where it will halt with the army's reserve supply and baggage trains. General McLaws will follow General Longstreet with his own division and that of General R. H. Anderson. On reaching Middletown he will take the route to Harper's Ferry, and by Friday morning possess himself of the Maryland Heights, and endeavor to capture the enemy at Harper's Ferry.

General Walker, with his division, after accomplishing the object in which he is now engaged, will cross the Potomac at Cheek's Ford, ascend its right bank to Lovattsville, take possession of Loudon Heights, if practicable, by Friday morning, Key's Ford on his left, and the road between the end of the mountain and the Potomac on his right. He will as far as practicable, co-operate with General McLaws and General Jackson in intercepting the retreat of the enemy.

General D. H. Hill's division will form the rear-guard of the army, pursuing the road taken by the main body. The reserve artillery, ordnance, and supply-trains, etc., will precede General Hill. General Slum will dispatch a squadron of cavalry to accompany the commands of Generals Longstreet, Jackson, and McLaws and, with the main body of the cavalry, will cover the route of the army and bring up all stragglers that may have been left behind. The command of Generals Jackson, McLaws. and Walker, after accomplishing the objects for which they have been detached, will join the main body of the army at Boonsboro or Hagerstown. Each regiment on the march will habitually carry its axes in the regimental ordnance wagon for the use of the men at their encampments to procure wood, etc.

By Command of General R. E. Lee

McClellan now had Lee's entire line of march and battle plan, but he thought it was a ruse and did not act on it. Just as in the Peninsula Campaign. He was extremely cautious and completely overestimated the enemy's strength.

On the 11th of September, Jackson moved towards Hagerstown and AP Hill towards Jefferson as if going to Harper's Ferry. Lee was concentrating in front of South Mountain, which was a natural barrier to McClellan's advance. Several passes or gaps ran through South Mountain. These passes were held by a small force under the Command of General D. H. Hill. General Hood held Boonsboro, and General D.H. Hill held Turner's Gap on McClellan's main line of advance. All the passes were fortified and well-defended. This would check McClellan's advance while Jackson was attacking Harper's Ferry. On Monday, the 15th of September, the military garrison at Harpers Ferry surrendered to Jackson. On that same day, Private Timothy Donohue enlisted in B Company, Sixty-

Ninth Regiment in New York City. He would be awarded the Medal of Honor for his actions at Fredericksburg in December of that year. The Regiment was recruiting new members in New York to replace its casualties from the Peninsula Campaign. Many of the new recruits were recruited right off the boat from Ireland. Donohue had arrived from Ireland a couple of months prior to enlisting in the Regiment.

On September 13[th,] the Regiment (with the rest of the Second Corps) was on Shookstown Road near Frederick, Maryland. The advance of McClellan's army encountered the rebels at South Mountain, but since the Second Corps was held in reserve, the Regiment did not arrive on the battlefield until most of the fighting was over. That night, the Regiment bivouacked in an open field. Since McClellan's army drove the Confederate forces from the mountain pass at South Mountain, Lee moved his forces towards Sharpsburg, crossing Antietam Creek. Lee formed a line of battle on the west bank. McClellan's army followed closely with the Second Corps in the lead and the Sixty-Ninth Regiment and the rest of the Irish Brigade in the advance.

In New York City on September 13, 1862, the 69th New York Volunteer Artillery Regiment was ordered to Camp Scott, Staten Island. The Regiment was able to enlist new recruits due in part to the high bounties offered for enlistment in the Corcoran's Legion. In September, for example, the National War Committee pledged an additional $50 on top of the regular enlistment bounty for those who joined the Corcoran's Legion in the next ten days. Additionally, the 69th New York was authorized a veteran Bonus for all members of that organization who joined the new 69th Regiment serving in Corcoran's Legion. Several soldiers would desert the Regiment from Camp Scott.

Corcoran's Fenian membership was probably a strong impetus for his fellow Fenians to join his Legion. Indeed, for them, the impending liberation of Ireland was more important than the war to save the Union. To the Fenians, Corcoran was not only a fellow patriot but also their chieftain in the Gaelic tradition of old. For instance, Corcoran, along with Michael Doheny and John O'Mahoney, were responsible for organizing the Irish Republican Brotherhood in the United States in 1859. Consequently, Corcoran was able to attract recruits from not only New York but also from other States and Ireland. Corcoran hoped that his Legion would swell into an Irish Division, with units being raised among the Irish communities in Boston, New Haven, and Philadelphia.

On September 15th, General Richardson arrived with the First Division on the other side (east bank) of Antietam Creek. Since it was late in the afternoon and the rest of the

Second Corps had not yet arrived, the First Division was not ordered to continue the pursuit.

General Sumner's Second Corps was the advance of the Union Army. General Richardson's First Division was the advance of the Second Corps. General Meagher's Irish Brigade was in the advance of the First Division. Since the Sixty-Ninth Regiment, NYSV was the first regiment of the Irish Brigade, and it was the lead element of the Brigade. Therefore, if Sumner, Richardson, or Meagher were ordered to cross the Antietam that evening, the Sixty-Ninth Regiment would have been the first to engage the enemy. General Richardson halted and deployed his division on the other side of Antietam Creek. That night, Union and Confederate artillery exchanged fire over the Antietam Creek.

The exchange of artillery fire continued the morning of the 16th. Union Forces spent most of the morning preparing for their attack. At about four in the afternoon on Tuesday the 16th, General Hooker's Corps was ordered to cross Antietam Creek at the upper ford and establish a position on the enemy's left flank. He crossed without opposition and established his position. Artillery fire was exchanged.

The 69th Artillery Regiment mustered into Federal service on September 17, 1862, at Newport News, Virginia. The bloodiest battle in American history was fought on the same day in Sharpsburg, Maryland. It is normally considered three separate engagements: the cornfield, the sunken road or bloody lane, and Burnside Bridge. The battle commenced with a desperate struggle in Miller's cornfield (near the Dunker Church). Hooker's Corps and Confederate forces fought for possession of a cornfield (first engagement). Possession of the cornfield changed several times. Each side would attack, and the opposing side would withdraw. The opposing force, which had been driven from the cornfield, would re-group and counterattack. This happened several times. By the time this phase of the battle was over, not a stalk of corn was left standing in the field. It is in the second engagement of the day (the Sunken Road or Bloody Lane), that the Sixty-Ninth Regiment and the Irish Brigade would participate.

Lieutenant Colonel James Kelly, Commander of the Sixty-Ninth, NYSV, stood listening to the roar of battle. Two miles away across Antietam Creek, the Union First and Twelfth Corps were attacking Lee's Army. A misty drizzle blocked Kelly's view of the fighting, but musket fire and distant cheers signaled the Union attack. Behind Kelly, heavy Union artillery opened fire on Confederate positions (which were over a mile away). The noise was deafening but familiar. Kelly had been fighting the Rebels for over a year (first as a Company Commander with the old Sixty-Ninth

New York State Militia at the first Bull Run battle, then during the Peninsula Campaign). He became Commander of the Regiment in August when Colonel Nugent was sent home on sick leave.

The Sixty-Ninth mustered about 320 men out of the more than one thousand who had enlisted in the last twelve months. Recruits came from all walks of life and from many States. Company D was made up of members from the Twenty-third Illinois, an Irish regiment that had fought in the recent campaign in Missouri. The 23rd Regiment had been disbanded after the battle of Lexington, and Captain Timothy Shanley (along with a hundred other Irish patriots) answered Meagher's call to join the Irish Brigade. Shanley was still recovering from a wound he received during the Peninsula campaign and was looking for a chance to avenge his injury.

The roles of the Sixty-Ninth contained several close relatives. Newly promoted First Lieutenant Andrew Birmingham of Company "A" had been First Sergeant of the Militia Company "A" and had fought at First Bull Run. Lieutenant Birmingham had been a lawyer in New York City prior to enlisting in the 69th. H is brother Richard was a Sergeant, and his cousin William (a miner from northwest New Jersey), was a private in the company. William was seriously wounded at Malvern Hill and was hospitalized.

Due to shortages in officer positions, several officers were assigned acting positions. Major James Cavanaugh was assigned as Acting Lieutenant Colonel. (Known as the "Little Major" (due to his short stature), Cavanaugh was a lion in battle). Captain Felix Duffy of Company "G" was the Acting Major of the Regiment. Duffy missed the first battle of Bull Run since he was sent home due to some misunderstanding. (Duffy liked to carry an Enfield rifle into battle to have a crack at the enemy).

Lieutenant Patrick Kelly (a father of five) commanded Company "G" after Duffy was assigned Acting Major.

Company "K" was commanded by First Lieutenant John Conway; Conway had joined Company "K" (Commanded by Captain James McMahon) in October 1861. Conway commanded Company "K" throughout the Peninsula campaign. His young friend, Lieutenant Peter Kelly, served as his second in command.

Captain James McGee commanded Company "F." At Antietam, Company "F" was the Regiment's Color Company. A well-known Irish patriot and a comrade of Meagher's during the Young Ireland Revolt in 1848. McGee was a writer for the *Irish American* newspaper before joining the Sixty-Ninth. McGee was a large, robust man. During the Peninsula Campaign, McGee was a tiger on the battlefield.

Company "F" carried two flags into battle, the National Color and the Green Regimental Color (First Irish Color).

The Sixty-Ninth Regiment occupied the right of the Irish Brigade. The Regiment approached the Strasburg Road, which at that point was about three feet lower than the surrounding ground (the Sunken Road). Rebel forces were positioned on a Sunken Road and brought heavy fire on the troops as they advanced. The sunken road was a country lane connecting the Hagerstown and Boonsboro Pikes. It ran generally west to east below a small rise south of the Mumma and Roulette farms. Over the years, farmers' traffic had worn the road down between three to five feet below ground level. The road was bordered by snake rail fences. For much of its length, the road was set back some distance from the rise, providing a "reverse slope" position that protected the Confederates from long-range Union artillery and rifle fire. A large, plowed field fronted the road, and a cornfield and orchard bordered it behind. The Confederates packed the road with men from Generals D. H. Hill's and R. H. Anderson's divisions.

The Confederates were surprised to see the Regiment and Irish Brigade emerge from the cornfield. They changed the direction of their fire to engage the Irish Brigade. Soon, "minie balls" began to strike the troops who were near the rail fence. Men quickly knocked off the fence rails, moved forward about fifty yards, and dressed their lines. Riding to the front line with his staff, Meagher called for volunteers to tear down the next fence so it would not hold up the advance. Volunteers ripped the rails away from their supporting posts but lost half their number to the Confederate fire.

Fathers Thomas Willette (Chaplain of the Sixty-Ninth) and Father William Corby (Chaplin of the Eighty-eighth) were mounted nearby. Seeing the danger the men faced, the Chaplains galloped along the battle line, calling out the Catholic prayer of Absolution and forgiving the sins of every man.

At Lieutenant Colonel Kelly's command: "Sixty-Ninth! Forward March!" the three men of the Color Guard strode a half dozen paces in front of the line. Lieutenant Colonel Kelly, Major Cavanaugh, and Captain Duffy took their positions behind the Regiment's line. Moving as one, the Sixty-Ninth stepped off towards the enemy. The men began to chant the Irish battle cry, "Faugh-a-Ballagh!" Its cadence set the pace for the advance. Meagher rode back to Lieutenant Colonel Kelly. "It will be Fontenoy again, Colonel, Fontenoy!" Meagher yelled, "We shall march to the top, give them two volleys, and then go in with the bayonet."

The Sixty-Ninth passed by one of Kimball's regiments, which had been stopped by enemy fire during an earlier attack (at Sunken Road). The soldiers of Kimball's regiment, who were lying on the ground, cheered the Sixty-Ninth as it marched by. As they passed Kimball's line, a fold in the crest gave the Sixty-Ninth its first view of the sunken road. The Confederates hidden in the road saw the Regiment and opened fire. The bullets tore into the Sixty-Ninth's right. This fire struck down Captain Duffy, leaving the right wing without a field-grade officer.

Chanting "Faugh-a-Ballagh!" the Sixty-Ninth surged over the last few yards to the crest. The Rebels, hidden in the sunken road, caught sight of the Regiment's Colors as they emerged over the top. First, they saw the finials and streamers, then the flags themselves, emerald green and red, white and blue. Then, the battle line appeared as if on parade. The Rebels rose up, leveled muskets, and fired.

Captain McGee was shocked to see his two Regimental Flags fall to the ground. The survivors of the color guard immediately picked up the flags while the Sixty-Ninth reformed their ranks. The Regiment presented a solid front to the enemy. Company officers ordered their men to open fire. A volley lashed into the Confederates. Dozens of them fell while the rest ducked behind the shelter of the road bank.

Even more surprising to the Confederates, the Sixty-Ninth stood its ground. The Regiment poured a volley of fire into the enemy. Their position on top of the rise gave the Sixty-Ninth a slight height advantage. They could fire directly into the enemy's lines and up and down the sunken road.

The Sixty-Ninth Regiment was equipped with .69 caliber smoothbore muskets. Most military men thought the large caliber musket ("Pumpkin Slinger") was obsolete. It was not accurate at ranges above one hundred yards. Furthermore, the musket was designed for close-in fighting. It used a special "buck and ball" round consisting of a .64 caliber round lead ball and three .30 caliber buckshot. Every round fired a powerful shotgun-like blast of lead into the Confederates. The ranges at the sunken road were between thirty and fifty yards. At that distance, the large caliber musket was a devastating weapon.

Eight color-bearers carrying the Regiment's green flag, the "First Irish Colors," were shot. The flag was riddled with bullets. It fell to the ground when the soldier who was carrying it was shot. General Meagher cried out, "Raise the Colors and follow me." Captain James McGee rushed forward, and raised the Colors, and cried, "I'll follow you!" As he raised the flag, a bullet hit the flag staff and broke it in two. The flag fell once more. McGee raised the broken staff and Colors and waved it, cheering the regiment on. McGee draped the flag over his shoulders and strode towards the Rebel line.

General McClellan was watching the advance of the Irish Brigade from the crest of a hill. When the "First Irish Colors" went down, one of his Aides said, "The day is lost, General, the Irish fly!" McClellan relied heavily on his "green flags." He had used the Irish Brigade to stop Rebel attacks at Fair Oaks, Gaines Mill, Savage Station, White Oak Swamp, Glendale, and Malvern Hill. McClellan, seeing McGee raising the "First Irish Colors," replied. "No, no! Their flags are up! They are charging!"

Confederates fired lethal volleys at the approaching Sixty-Ninth. Lieutenant John Conway, leaning into the fire as if into a hailstorm, led Company "K" forward. A bullet smashed into his body and knocked him to the ground. Sergeant Richard Bermingham of Company "A" was shot in the chest. Captain Timothy Shanley of Company "D" felt a minie ball tear into his shoulder. The regiment seemed to melt-away under the concentrated Confederate musketry. Seeing that it was impossible to go further, Meagher called off the attack, and the Sixty-Ninth fell back to the top of the rise.

When the bayonet charge faltered, some of the Confederates jumped out of the sunken road to counterattack. They misjudged their enemy. The Regiment turned and delivered a volley into the exposed Rebels. Most of them fell dead or wounded. The see-saw battle continued in this way for more than half an hour. The Sixty-Ninth's front was slowly shrinking. As the Regiment was whittled away, the men moved to the center, dressing on the colors. Every time a regimental flag went down, another brave soul snatched it up.

Low on ammunition, muskets fouled by black powder residue, officers and sergeants wounded or dead, the privates fought on. Colonel Kelly was wounded. Major Cavanaugh took command of the Regiment. He stood in the center of the Sixty-Ninth's line (by the color bearers), encouraging the remaining men to keep up their fire. A Confederate soldier shouted from the sunken road, "Bring them colors in here!". One of the soldiers from the Regiment shouted back, "Come and get them, you damned rebels!" Infuriated, the two men carrying the Sixty-Ninth's flags ran forward several yards and began to wave them in the Confederates' faces.

Major James Cavanagh submitted the after-action report of the battle. The report provides a description of the Regiment's involvement at Antietam. Kavanaugh noted that Lieutenant Colonel James Kelly, Commander of the Regiment, was wounded shortly after the Regiment's involvement in the battle. Cavanaugh assumed command of the Regiment. Captain Felix Duffy, Acting Major, was also mortally wounded in the early part of the engagement. The Regiment remained upon the field in the front line until it had expended all its ammunition, and the Brigade was relieved by General Caldwell's Brigade.

Capt. James E. McGee, Commander of Company "F," distinguished himself by his coolness and bravery. His command had been almost entirely decimated. McGee picked after the green flag after the bearer had been wounded and held it aloft throughout the battle. Captain James Saunders, Commander of Company "A," and Captain Richard Moroney, Commander of Company "I," bravely cheered on their men throughout the battle. Lieutenant Terrance Duffey of Company "G" and First Lieutenant John T. Toal of Company "H" rallied their commands, which had become so greatly reduced in numbers. Of the many officers who entered the field, the above are all that were left. The remainder were either killed or wounded during the engagement.

There was a great loss of officers and men. Cavanaugh noted Captain Felix Duffy, Lieutenant Patrick J. Kelly, Lieutenant Charles Williams, and Lieutenant John Conway. I feel that our regiment has sustained a great loss, and one the recollection of which will be ever green in my memory. For those officers who have been wounded, Captains Shanley and Whitty, both disabled for the second time, and Lieutenants Nagle and Patrick Kearney. Among the non-commissioned officers who particularly distinguished themselves First Sergeants. Murtha Murphy, Company "C," Michael Brennan, Company "B," Bernard O'Neil, Company "C," and Soucoth Mansergh, Company "H," are most worthy of a commission. Among the enlisted who also distinguished themselves, I also recommend Patrick O'Neil of Company "C," John Kelly of Company "K" and Sergeant Major Patrick Callahan. Cavanaugh also noted the Regiment had 40 new recruits who were of great assistance.

The Sixty-Ninth lost 44 killed and 152 wounded during the battle at the sunken road (a loss of sixty-one percent of its strength). The wounded were carried back to a field hospital set up near the cornfield. Lieutenant Andrew Bermingham of Company "A" sat comforting his brother Richard. Nearby lay Lieutenant Colonel Kelly with a terrible wound through his mouth. Captain Shanley (just returned after recovering from his Malvern Hill wound) sat wounded with a rifle ball in his shoulder. This wound would prove fatal.

Among the dead was First Lieutenant Patrick Kelly of Company "G," who lay near the crest of the rise. Captain Felix Duffy (the irascible Commander of Company "G") was one of the first to fall. He lay eighty yards from the top of the rise. The body of Lieutenant John Conway, Commander of Company "K," lay on the field in front of Bloody Lane, surrounded by a dozen of his men.

About one hundred and twenty recruits had joined the Irish Brigade the day before the battle.

They were assigned to provost-duty but requested to be allowed to participate in the engagement. Seventy-five of the new recruits were either killed or wounded. Private Timothy Donohue, who enlisted in "B" Company, may have been one of the recruits who escaped harm. He had enlisted only a few days before in New York City, and whether he made it to the Antietam Battlefield is unknown.

Confederate Forces left the field and headed south. McClellan did not pursue. The Regiment crossed the Potomac at Harper's Ferry and encamped on Bolivar Heights. President Lincoln reviewed the Army at Sharpsburg. During a meeting with McClellan, President Lincoln urged him to pursue the Rebels. General McClellan had very little respect for President Lincoln. He did not think Lincoln was worthy to give him military advice. McClellan did not pursue the Rebels and press the battle. Lincoln once again relieved McClellan of Command. McClellan was replaced by General Burnside. The Sixty-Ninth Regiment (along with the rest of the Irish Brigade) moved to Warrenton, Virginia.

On November 8, 1862, following orders issued by Corcoran, the Artillery Regiment 69th Artillery Regiment, serving as Infantry, New York State Volunteers) broke camp at 1 PM and marched to Clifden Landing. They embarked on the steamers Cahawaba, City of Bath, and Pocahontas for the trip to Fortress Monroe, Virginia. The Irish soldiers in new uniforms embarked without incident, but due to inclement weather, the ships were unable to depart for two days. While waiting for the weather to clear, Colonel Murphy discovered that a well-known politician of the 6th ward was on board selling liquor to his men. In front of the officers of the 69th, Murphy exposed this politician as a corruptor of discipline and forced him to return of his soldiers' money. The Politician was then put ashore amid the jeers and shouts of the men.

Before their departure, the Artillery Regiment was presented with a green battle-flag by Judge Charles P. Daly on behalf of Richard O'Gorman. Richard O'Gorman had represented Corcoran at his court-marshal in 1860 for refusing to parade the 69th NYSM for the Prince of Wales. (O'Gorman had also presented the 69th New York State Militia with the Green Prince of Wales Flag, which it carried at First Bull Run). The flag for the 1st Regiment of the Legion was green, embroidered with the Harp and the Fenian Sunburst. The words, in Irish, "First in the Van and Last in the Retreat" above. Colonel Murphy accepted the flag on behalf of the Regiment and said that those words would be their battle cry.

There was a dispute between the 69th Regiment NYNG and the 69th Artillery Regiment over which unit should receive $10,000, which was offered by New York City, to any militia regiment that volunteered into the Federal Army for either 80 days or three years. Major Bagley argued the Sixty-Ninth Regiment, N.Y.S.N.G., should receive it because several hundred of the old members served in the first three months of the war. Colonel Murphy argued the money should go to the 69th Artillery since they volunteered to serve in Corcoran's Legion. The money eventually went to the Artillery Regiment, but the dispute eventually led to the change of the name of the Artillery Regiment to the 182d Infantry regiment, NYSV. The 182nd was reorganized as Infantry, and officers from each company were deemed overstrength since artillery regiments had four officers in each company while infantry regiments only had three.

In mid-November, the Irish Brigade moved to Falmouth, Virginia. Recruits who recently enlisted joined the Regiment there. If Timothy Donohue had not joined the Sixty-Ninth Regiment just before the Battle of Antietam, he most certainly joined the Regiment in Falmouth.

Winter had set in. Cold and bleak winds whistled over the fields of Virginia. The soldiers (imagining that they had gone into winter quarters) prepared comfortable huts. However, General Burnside, the new Commander of the

Army of the Potomac, had other ideas. He wanted to attack and defeat the rebel forces at Fredericksburg. Burnside reorganized the Army into three Grand Divisions. Each Grand Division had two corps assigned. (During the Civil War, a corps had two or more divisions assigned. Each division had two or more brigades. The brigades had two or more regiments assigned. Each regiment normally had five or more companies.) After the battle of Antietam, General Darius Couch took Command of the II Corps, replacing General Sumner, who was given command of a Grand Division.

On the 11th of November, Sumner's Grand Division arrived at Fredericksburg. Sumner (and General Burnside) demanded the surrender of the Confederate forces in the town. Since the pontoon bridges to cross the Rappahannock had not arrived, the Union Army was forced to remain on the opposite side of the river from the enemy. The enemy was fortifying the hill across the river on Mayre's Heights. The bridge equipment did not arrive for three weeks. Had Burnside been able to cross the river when he first arrived, he would have faced little opposition. Unfortunately for the Union, the Confederate Army was reinforced and prepared for the attack.

Meanwhile, Corcoran was forming his new Brigade, the Irish Legion (sometimes called Corcoran's Legion). On

November 17th, Mathew Murphy enrolled to serve three years and was mustered onto the 69th Artillery Regiment (1st Regiment of Corcoran's Legion) as the Colonel. Murphy had been the Lieutenant Colonel of the 69th Regiment, NYSM. James Bagley was elected the Colonel of the Militia Regiment while Corcoran was in captivity. Bagley was probably made Colonel because of his connections with Tammany Hall. Bagley had not volunteered for Federal Service with the Militia Regiment (Bull Run), the Irish Brigade, nor Corcoran's Legion. Mathew Murphy was one of the Fenian leaders. He had commanded the Phoenix Brigade (a secret unit controlled by the Fenians) after Corcoran. The leadership of the Artillery Regiment consisted of Colonel Matthew Murphy, Lieutenant Colonel Thomas M. Reid, Major Theodore Kelly, Adjutant William Fogarty, Quartermaster John Fahy, Surgeon John Dwyer, and Assistant Surgeon James T. Fahie. Except for Lieutenant Colonel Reid, the staff was from the 69th.

With the high bounties and the approach of the first draft in November 1862, recruiting officers had little trouble finding recruits for the Artillery Regiment. However, the harsh demands of discipline, the boring routine of camp life, and the lures of family and friends in nearby New York City caused many recruits to slip out of Camp Scott at night. Of the 1,100 men who enlisted in the Artillery Regiment, 265 deserted at Camp Scott (on Staten Island) before the Regiment was mustered into service. At Newport News, the Artillery Regiment continued to drill and train. Colonel Murphy persisted tirelessly to ensure his soldiers were prepared for war. Corcoran continued to maintain strict discipline. He understood the value of training once on the battlefield. Corcoran prohibited the sale of liquor in camp, declaring that any found would be destroyed. The Regiment began Thanksgiving Day 1862 with Mass celebrated by Father Dillon, followed by a grand review.

On December 2, the First Irish Colors of the 69th Infantry, NYSV, along with the other green flags of the Brigade, were to be returned to New York City by Captain McGee. McGee turned over custody of First Irish Colors to Daniel Devlin, Esq., City Chamberlain and Chairman of the Executive Committee of the Irish Brigade. McGee received a new set of Colors for the Regiment. Invited on the occasion were Archbishop Hughes, Honorable Judge C. P. Daly and Judge H. Hilton of the Common Pleas, and numerous dignitaries. Officers from the Irish Brigade (who were on sick leave or recruiting duty) were also present, including Lieutenant Colonel James Kelly, Captains Leddy, Whitty, Nagle, Carr, and Moroney., and several others.

Fredericksburg, Virginia, is approximately midway between Washington and Richmond. General Lee had established very strong defenses, which, added to the natural geography of the area, made his positions almost impregnable. The Confederate army was arrayed with General Longstreet's Corps, Ransom's, McLaws', and Picket's divisions on the left of Mayre's Heights and Anderson's division on the right. The Sixty-Ninth Regiment would attack Anderson's position. There were several Irish regiments in Anderson's Division. Confederate artillery covered both Marye's and Lee's Heights.

Fredericksburg

Battle of Fredericksburg

Union artillery opened fire on Confederate positions at about 9:15 in the morning of December 13, 1862. In response, Confederate artillery shelled the town of Fredericksburg (which had been evacuated on December 11th when Confederate forces withdrew). The Sixty-Ninth Regiment and the rest of the Irish Brigade would attack uphill from the town to Mayre's Heights.

The Regiment had lost so many officers during the Battle of Antietam in September that Captain Thomas Leddy, who commanded Company "B," was the most senior Captain in the Regiment. Because of this, Leddy was appointed Acting Major of the Regiment and transferred to the Regimental Staff. Lieutenant Andrew Bermingham was transferred from "A" Company to command Company "B" before the battle.

Leddy had joined the Sixty-Ninth Regiment NYSV on September 10, 1861, to serve three years. He was mustered in as Captain of Co. B on October 15, 1861. Leddy was wounded on December 13, 1862, during the battle. He left the Sixty-Ninth Regiment NYSV to join the Veteran Reserve Corps on June 9, 1863.

Bermingham had joined the Sixty-Ninth Regiment NYSM also to serve three years. He was mustered in as Private in Company A on October 18, 1861. He received a commission as a Second Lieutenant on December 26, 1861.

Bermingham was promoted to First Lieutenant on July 2, 1862. He was wounded in action during the battle on December 13, 1862, and died of his wounds on December 17, 1862.

Since the First Irish Color was returned to New York, and the Second Irish Color had not yet been presented to the Regiment, the soldiers placed sprigs of boxwood in the hats. Early in the morning, the Irish Brigade was drawn up in line of battle. Colonel Nugent awaited the order to advance.

French's Division was first to attack up the heights, followed by Zooke's Brigade. Both attacks failed. On the command "Irish Brigade, advance, Forward, double-quick, guide center," the Regiment marched through a cornfield under tremendous fire. Huge gaps are opened in the ranks, but they closed quickly, and the Regiment moved forward again. When the Regiment crossed the first fence on the heights, the enemy withdrew to its secondary breastworks behind a stone wall. From there, they fired relentlessly upon the Regiment. The Regiment (and the rest of the Irish Brigade) continued to a second fence. Enemy fire grew even more intense, but still, the men moved forward. The bodies of fallen Union soldiers impeded the advance.

They stormed Mayre's Heights with sprigs of green boxwood in their caps. The Irish Brigade rushed the center enemy line. An Irish regiment from Georgia gave them a cheer and then mowed them down with rifle fire. Not a man reached the stone wall. The regiment almost ceased to exist, but the enemy found the body of n Sixty-Ninth man nearest the stone wall. Cavanagh (Acting Lieutenant Colonel) shouted: "Blaze away and stand it, boys." Then, Major Cavanagh was shot in the hip.

Captain Thomas Leddy, Acting Major, who had arrived only the day before the battle from Washington, was wounded severely in the left arm. He had just recovered from a wound received at Malvern Hill. Lieutenant Callaghan, who had been detailed to command Company "H" from another company, was wounded in four different places. Second Lieutenant David Burke was severely wounded in the left shoulder. First Lieutenant Bernard O'Neill, Commanding Company "D," was severely also wounded. Captain O'Donovan, who lost his eye at Fair Oaks, was hit by a piece of shrapnel in the left breast. Lieutenant Bermingham (the new Commander of Company B) had both thighs broken.

The ranks of the Regiment were disseminated. Among the wounded was Timothy Donohue of Company "B." Donohue was wounded carrying a wounded officer (probably Lieutenant Bermingham) from the field. Timothy Donohue was awarded the Medal of Honor for his actions at Fredericksburg.

His citation reads:

"DONOGHUE, TIMOTHY - Rank and organization: Private, Company B, Sixty-Ninth Regiment New York Infantry. Place and date: At Fredericksburg, Va., 13 December 1862. Entered service at: ------. Birth: Ireland. Date of issue: 17 January 1894.

Citation: *Voluntarily carried a wounded officer off the field from between the lines; while doing this, he was himself wounded".*

Timothy Donohue had a brother, Patrick, who may have been awarded the Victoria Cross (the highest military award for heroism in Brittan) for carrying a wounded officer from the field during the Indian Mutiny in 1857. The Donohue brothers were both born in the small Irish village of Neenah in County Tipperary, Ireland, Patrick in 1820 and Timothy in 1825. Timothy came to the United States in 1862 and enlisted in the Sixty-Ninth Regiment on September 15th. Some historians believe two families in Neenah had sons named Patrick. They believe Timothy's brother Patrick was not the one who was awarded the Victoria Cross. However, many of Timothy Donohue's decedents believe Timothy's brother Patrick was awarded the Victoria Cross. Family members claim relatives had the medal many years ago.

Patrick Donohue married Mary Anne Edwards, whose husband, Thomas Edwards, had died.

Thomas Edwards and Mary Anne Edwards had two daughters named Eliza and Anna. Thomas Edwards died before Anna was born, and she and her older sister were raised by her mother and stepfather, Patrick Donohue. In 1845, Anna's older sister, Eliza Julia Edwards, married Edward John Pratt. Eliza's grandson, William Henry Pratt, is better known as film star Boris Karloff. Patrick's other stepdaughter, Anna, married Thomas Leon Owens or Leonowens. Anna worked as a governess for the King of Siam. The book "Anna and the King of Siam" and the play "The King and I" are based on her life.

Despite the heavy casualties, the Regiment continued its movement forward. Men held their hands before their faces as though they were walking through a driving hailstorm, but instead of ice, the Regiment was facing shells and bullets. Less than a hundred yards from the Rebel lines, the Regiment and Irish Brigade charged on. Amazingly, a cheer went up from the Confederates sheltered behind the stone wall. They cheered the gallantry of the attack as though they had never seen anything like it. Then, the men in gray leveled their muskets and poured a sheet of fire into the Brigade.

Wounded or not, most of the Irish went down. A few hardy souls pressed forward and dashed over the last fifty yards to the wall. But they were quickly shot down. When the battle ended, the Rebels would note that the Union men closest to the wall wore sprigs of boxwood in their caps.

The official After-Action Report of the Battle of Fredericksburg was written by Captain James Saunders who (since all the senior officers were either killed or wounded reads) Commanded the Regiment. It reads: Camp near Falmouth, December 22, 1862. In compliance with general orders received December 21, I hereby certify that the Sixty-Ninth Regiment New York Volunteers entered the battle of Fredericksburg on December 13, 1862, commanded by Col. Robert Nugent, and 18 commissioned officers and 210 rank and file, in which the above-numbered regiment lost 16 commissioned officers and 160 rank and file, leaving Captain James Saunders, Lieutenant Milliken, and Lieutenant L. Brennan to bring the remnant of the regiment off the battle-field.

Most serious casualties lay on the battlefield all night. The hillside in front of Marye's heights was strewn with bodies. It was an unusually cold December night, and the moans of the wounded could be heard over the wind. The Northern Lights could be seen in the sky which is extremely unusual that far south.

Confederate General George Picket (who would lead the fatal charge against the Union center during the Battle of Gettysburg) commanded the Division defending Marye's

Heights. Picket said of the Irish Brigade: "The brilliant assault on Marye's Heights of their Irish Brigade was beyond description. … We forgot they were fighting us, and cheer after cheer at their fearlessness went up all along our lines."

During the battle, the new green flags arrived from New York. Captain Martin arrived from Washington with supplies to celebrate at their presentation to the Brigade. The presentation was held in the theater in Fredericksburg. Generals Couch, Sturgis, Wilcox, and Hancock (and many other guests) were invited. Confederate artillery continued to fall on the town. The party began, and the Second Irish Color was presented to what was left of the Regiment. General Hancock, who had witnessed the charge against Marye's Heights, said that only Irishmen could enjoy themselves after this day. The party ended when the shelling got too close to continue. The Regiment returned to its former quarters at Falmouth, Virginia, and celebrated the Christmas and New Year holidays there.

On Monday, December 29, 1862, the Artillery Regiment was ordered to break camp. They then sailed to Norfolk. The Regiment marched through Norfolk to the rail station, where they boarded a train for Suffolk, Virginia. Suffolk had been occupied by Federal troops since May of 1862. Suffolk had railroads to Petersburg and Norfolk, Virginia, and Weldon,

North Carolina, running through the town, it controlled the land approaches to the mouth of the James River (north of the Great Dismal Swamp). Suffolk also sat alongside the main lines of communication with costal North Carolina. Union Major General John J. Peck took command of the town in September of 1862. He immediately started building works. These works, supported by forts, took six months to build and stretched fifteen miles.

Upon reaching Suffolk, the Regiment bivouacked on the tracks, lying on the cold ground. The next several days were spent on fatigue duty. Soldiers worked to complete the defenses of Suffolk and dug rifle pits. Several of the 69th Companies were pressed into service to garrison network forts. Garrison's life, however, soon became monotonous and routine.

Neither Corcoran nor Murphy had resigned from key leadership positions in the Fenian Brotherhood. In addition, they entertained visits from John O'Mahoney, the Head Centre of the Fenian Brotherhood. These were hardly social visits.

On January 16, 1863, a Requiem Mass was held in Saint Patrick's Cathedral in New York City for the repose of the souls of the dead of the Irish Brigade since the beginning of the war. The Mass was attended by General Thomas Francis Meagher (accompanied by Mrs. Meagher), the Staff of the

Irish Brigade, Colonel Nugent, Colonel of the Sixty-Ninth NYSV, and many officers of the Sixty-Ninth Regiment, NYSM. Father Willette, Chaplain of the Sixty-Ninth NYSV, celebrated the Mass. Father Maguire was the deacon, and Father Wood was the sub-deacon. The Very Reverend Dr. Starrs, Vicar General of the Archdiocese, performed the absolution (since Archbishop Hughes was absent). Father McNearney was the Master of Ceremonies. After the Mass, John Savage read a poem he wrote for the occasion.

The Artillery Regiment would get its first taste of battle in January. On the evening of January 29, a Rebel Brigade with several artillery batteries under Confederate General Prior advanced across the Blackwater River. On January 30, at 1 AM, the Regiment marched to Blackwater. Corcoran's command was not only the Legion but also the 11th Pennsylvania Cavalry, 13th Indiana, 6th Massachusetts, 167th Pennsylvania, 130th New York, and three batteries of artillery.

Battle of Deserted House

As the 69th troops left Suffolk, they began singing but were ordered to stop so they would not signal the Rebels of their approach. The road was muddy and uneven. Men would fall or lose their shoes in the mud. At 5 AM, the Regiment surprised a Rebel bivouac at the Deserted House (about 10 miles from Suffolk). The Regiment came under intense Rebel artillery fire. The 69th was ordered into a sunken road to escape the bombardment.

At about 5:15 am, Corcoran ordered an advance. However, Corcoran ordered 800 paces rearward to reduce casualties since they bore borne the most casualties). Later the 69th was ordered forward to support a Battery of the 7th Massachusetts Artillery. After pushing the enemy back and repelling two counterattacks, the Regiment was able to have breakfast. That afternoon, the Regiment pushed five miles further (to Pocosin's Creek), only to find the enemy had fled.

On the evening of January 30th, the Regiment headed back to Suffolk. It arrived early on the morning of January 31st (after marching 32 miles in 24 hours). The 69th New York lost 3 Killed and 10 wounded. The Regiment suffered its baptismal fire and acquitted itself well. The 69th and Colonel Matthew Murphy played an especially distinguished role.

After the fight at Deserted House, life once again settled down into the usual dull routine of camp life. In February, Corcoran departed to visit New York and Albany. While in New York, Corcoran testified at a Court of Inquiry called by Major Bagley and the Officers of the 69th National Guard. This Court was to determine which 69th Regiment was the real 69th National Guard. The Court settled the dispute by designating the 69th Regiment serving on active duty with

Corcoran's Legion as the 182nd New York Volunteer Infantry Regiment, although this designation was often ignored. For the purposes of distinguishing the three Regiments in the lineage, it will be referred to as the Artillery Regiment.

In mid-February, General Meagher went to see President Lincoln to ask his permission to allow the Irish Brigade to return to New York to recruit new members. The President greeted Meagher warmly and said he would consider his request. Meagher returned to his headquarters near Fredericksburg. On February 19th, Meagher wrote the Secretary of War and asked to be allowed to return to New York to recruit replacements for the decimated Irish Brigade. The letter pointed out that decimated regiments from Maine, Massachusetts, and Connecticut had been ordered home to enable recruiting.

On St. Patrick's Day, 1863, the Irish Brigade decided to again hold a steeplechase. The course was laid out, and the seating was erected. An announcement was sent to all officers in the Army of the Potomac. In March (along with the rest of the Army of the Potomac), the regiment received identifying corps badges. As members of the II Corps' First Division, the men of the Brigade were assigned a red trefoil to wear on their hats.

The Artillery Regiment celebrated Saint Patrick's Day by decorating the camp and holding a parade. This was the first St. Patrick's Day parade ever held in Suffolk, Virginia. The Regiment formed for a parade at 12:30. They returned to camp around 5:30 PM and were dismissed. Food and beverages were sent to every regiment of the Legion. A dinner was held for the Officers of the Legion and their guests which continued until the early morning hours.

There are differences and similarities between the two Federal Regiments. The NYSV Regiment (Irish Brigade) had seen active fighting since it was formed. It was already assigned to a Division and Corps. The Artillery Regiment had been formed a year later. Since the structure of the Divisions was already decided, and the Artillery Regiment was part of a brigade, it was more difficult to assign it to a division than it would have been if it was an individual regiment. Individual regiments could be used to replace regiments in brigades that were understrength without affecting the structure of a division. Corcoran's Irish Legion would have to replace a brigade, which would cause a major change in the division's structure.

The NYSV Regiment's soldiers came primarily from Irish neighborhoods in the Lower East Side (around the armory). The Artillery Regiment's soldiers came from almost every neighborhood in Manhattan. Their identity was not that of a neighborhood but of nationality. (Historically, the National Guard is made of immigrants, and the makeup of National Guard units reflects the population of the city or town). Many soldiers in the Artillery Regiment enlisted to receive bounties rather than to train to free Ireland.

The NYSV Regiment had few desertions before 1863. The Artillery Regiment had over 27% desert while on Staten Island. The NYSV Regiment had many professional officers, while the Artillery Regiment's officers normally rose through the ranks. Furthermore, many members of the Artillery Regiment were Fenians, while the NYSV Regiment leadership identified more with the Young Ireland movement. The NYSV Regiment was in continuous battle, and it received a lot of press coverage. The Artillery Regiment was in the backwaters of Virginia and received much less press coverage. Many of the national newspapers originated in New York, and the interest of New Yorkers was the battles against Lee and his Army of Northern Virginia. Corcoran called his brigade the Irish Legion rather than the Second Irish Brigade mainly because he did not want to limit his command to a brigade. He wanted to command an Irish division.

While both Regiments were primarily Irish Catholic, Catholicism played a major role in the Artillery Regiment (e.g., Colonel Murphy issued orders that it was only proper that officers accompany their men to divine services). Recruiting for the Irish Brigade was much easier than for Corcoran's Irish Legion. While the NYSV Regiment saw battle from its initial deployment to the end of the war, the Artillery Regiment would have to wait until 1864. Meagher and the NYSV Regiment allowed consumption of alcohol. In fact, Meagher was accused of being drunk at Antietam. Corcoran and Murphy placed strict controls upon the men and strictly regulated alcohol. The sale of "strong liquors" was absolutely forbidden.

With respect to the third regiment in the lineage of today's 69th Infantry Regiment (69th Infantry Regiment National Guard), leadership under Major Bagley appears lacking, and the Regiment lacked discipline. This is evidenced by the way unit members left their weapons in a pile without cleaning them after Bull Run. During the Annual Inspection on October 28, 1863, the Militia Regiment is listed with 442 present and 221 absent. The inspector noted the 69th paid little attention to drill and company officers didn't understand their duties or failed to give any evidence of it.

Matthew Murphy left command of the Artillery Regiment and assumed command of the Irish Legion on April 9, 1863. Corcoran was now Commanding the 1st Division, 7th Corps. In early April, the paymaster paid the soldiers, and most of the money they received was sent home to families. Elements of General Ambrose Burnside's 9th Corps, Army of the Potomac, arrived at the Suffolk in early April. However, more importantly, Confederate General James Longstreet arrived with two divisions of the Army of Northern Virginia.

Richmond had detached General Longstreet in early February and put him in charge of the Department of Virginia and North Carolina. Brigadier General Roger Pryor, who had been soundly beaten by Corcoran's Legion at the Battle of the Deserted House, informed Longstreet there were large stocks of hogs and corn in the Northeast North Carolina. Seeing an opportunity to seize these invaluable stores, Longstreet moved toward Suffolk on April 11. He laid siege, but it appears he had no intention of taking the town.

Upon learning that Longstreet's troops were advancing upon Suffolk, the Artillery Regiment was ordered to prepare for battle. Corcoran alerted his troops around 3 AM. As Colonel Corcoran approached the hospital of the 155th NYV, he was stopped by an intoxicated Lieutenant Colonel Kimball of the 9th Regiment NYSV ("Hawkin's Zouaves"). Kimball demanded the countersign and refused to let Corcoran and his staff pass. After Corcoran had asked several times to pass, Kimball made what appeared to be a move for his revolver. Corcoran promptly shot him. Kimball died a short time after. Corcoran was once again court-martialed. He requested a Court of Inquiry, which found the killing unjustified. Corcoran was censured but no action was taken on the charges.

Later that morning, the enemy drove the Legion's pickets from South Quay Road and Edgarton Road, beginning the "Siege" of Suffolk. The "Long Roll" was beaten by the drummer boys, and the Regiment manned the breastworks. The Legion was deployed to the right of Fort Dix. Here, the Legion formed for battle with the Artillery Regiment on the right, the 164th and the 170th on the left, and the 155th in reserve.

General Corcoran took the offensive on April 24, leading an expedition up the Edenton Road to Bern's Farmhouse. Corcoran was determined to eliminate the advanced rebel Sharpshooters who were killing his troops. Corcoran led 5,000 Infantry, 400 Cavalry, and 2 Batteries of artillery forward. A skirmish ensued, and Confederate General George Pickett's Division was driven from their rifle pits. Corcoran's men burned the buildings which the Confederates had used for cover. The Legion, on the right of the line, was only lightly engaged and suffered only a few casualties. After burning the buildings, Corcoran's troops returned to Suffolk. On May 2nd, the Rebels ended the siege of Suffolk.

The ranks of the 69th Regiment, NYSV (Irish Brigade), were thinned by the battles of 1862. Probably due to this, they were (for the most part) spared in the next major clash with Lee's Army, the Battle of Chancellorsville on May 2nd and 3rd. Things had remained quiet until the end of April when the Union Army under General Hooker, Commander of the Army of the Potomac, tried to out-flank the Army of Northern Virginia. General Hooker was the one who was outflanked, and his army suffered great losses at Chancellorsville when Stonewall Jackson's troops slammed into his right flank on the morning of May 2, 1863. The fighting would go on for two days, and Hooker was solidly defeated. The NYSV Regiment only suffered eight casualties.

After the Battle of Chancellorsville, the strength of the NYSV Regiment was so low that it was reduced to the strength of a little more than a company. The entire Irish Brigade only had a few hundred men. Meagher submitted his resignation probably to force a favorable answer to his request to have the Irish Brigade stand down for recruiting purposes. Meagher received a curt answerer from Washington addressed not to the Commander of the Irish Brigade but to Brigadier-General T. F. Meagher, United States Volunteers. Sir- Your resignation has been accepted by the President of the United States, and it will take effect on this day.

Patrick Kelly (who was a private in the Sixty-Ninth Regiment New York State Militia) at the Battle of Bull Run was now the Commander of what was left of the Irish Brigade. The Sixty-Ninth Regiment was commanded by Captain Richard Moroney. The Regiment consisted of only 75 men. The AG Report for 1863 notes that on June 12, 1863, the regiment was consolidated into two companies with James J. Smith listed as Adjutant, Dennis F. Sullivan listed as Quartermaster, Captain James E. McGee, Commanding Company "A" with First Lieutenant Bernard S. O'Neil and Second Lieutenant Luke Brennan and Company "B" commanded by Captain Richard Moroney with First Lieutenant John D. Mulhall and Second Lieutenant Soncoth Maneergh. In a few weeks, General Lee would begin his move north to Pennsylvania. The Army of Northern Virginia would meet the Army of the Potomac in the little town of Gettysburg on July 1st.

Twenty-six-year-old Private Michael McIntyre of Company C, Artillery Regiment, who had enlisted for three years in the Regiment on September 16, 1862, in New York, was wounded in action on May 16, 1863, at Carrsville.

The next few weeks, the Artillery Regiment spent on the offensive attacking and capturing several buildings from rebel sharpshooters, ripping up railroad tracks, and destroying everything that could be of use to the enemy. The Regiment then headed north to Fairfax, Virginia, where it would spend the next 10 months. With the termination of Federal operations at Suffolk, the Regiment and Legion were transferred to the Department of Washington, 22nd Corps, and placed in Corcoran's Division, whose primary mission was guarding the Railroad connection between Alexandria and the Army of the Potomac at Falmouth.

General Lee met with President Jefferson Davis and Secretary of War James Seddon to lay out his plan for the invasion of the North. Davis considered dispatching portions of Lee's army to help relieve General Pemberton in Vicksburg (which was being attacked by General Ulysses S. Grant). After securing permission for the invasion, General Lee returned to his Army in late May 1863 and began his move north. President Davis hoped the invasion might compel Grant to abandon his Vicksburg assault. On May 10th, the Confederate Army began its move. By June 23, advance elements of Lee's force were in Pennsylvania. As Lee moved the Army of Northern Virginia north, it was spread out over fifty miles. He was unaware of the location of the Army of the Potomac (since General J.E.B. Stewart had failed in his mission to keep him informed of their actions). On learning the closeness of the Union Army,

General Lee ordered his army to consolidate near Gettysburg, Pennsylvania.

When General Lee marched north in 1863, the Governor of Pennsylvania asked for assistance to protect his State from the possibility of invasion by the Confederate Army. New York, fearing the Confederates may march through Pennsylvania into the lightly defended center of the State (Buffalo, Syracuse, Utica, and then on to Albany and New York City), agreed to send troops to Harrisburg. New York National Guard Regiments began to depart for Harrisburg in June. The Militia Regiment was scheduled to depart on June 22[nd,] but they were sent instead to Baltimore on orders from the Secretary of War.

Draft Riots

On July 13, 1863, draft riots erupted in New York. The rioters were incensed at what they perceived as an inequitable conscription law that essentially exempted the wealthy, who could buy a $300 exemption or pay substitutes to go in their places, who were predominantly Irish laborers. Colonel Nugent of the NYSV Regiment (who resigned his field commission after being wounded at Fredericksburg) had reverted to his regular army rank of Captain. He was assigned as Provost Marshal in charge of New York City's draft. Although he was considered an Irish war hero, a mob attacked Nugent's house and burned it to the ground. The rioters noticed portraits of Nugent, Thomas Meagher, and Michael Corcoran in the house and slashed the likenesses of Nugent and Meagher but left the picture of Colonel Corcoran untouched. The mob also hurled the tattered battle flag of the NYSV Regiment out the window and stole the Nugent's sword. The flag was picked up and saved by firemen from Engine Company No. 45, and later, police discovered the Nugent's sword in the possession of a boy (although the jewels in the hilt were missing).

The Militia (National Guard) Regiment was in Baltimore under the Command of James Cavanaugh when the riots broke out. The regiment officers quickly drafted a series of resolutions expressing regret and indignation concerning the mob's actions. They attributed the excesses of the rioters to thieves from other cities and volunteered to return home to repress the insurrection.

The Adjutant General's Report for 1863 notes the draft would take place in New York City. The militia of New York City and Brooklyn were then in Pennsylvania and Maryland and were not available to subdue any riots. The Adjutant General went to Washington in the hope of having the draft postponed until a sufficient military force could be returned to the City. The next morning, riots broke out. The Secretary of War immediately directed a temporary suspension of the draft and ordered four regiments belonging to the city to return without delay. The National Guard Regiments and the City Police eventually quelled the riot.

Battle of Gettysburg

On realizing from his spies the Union Army had followed the Confederate Army north, Confederate General Longstreet, the First Corps Commander in Lee's Army of Northern Virginia, urged General Lee to head south to a good position between Washington and the Union Army. The move would force the Union to attack a strong Confederate position. Longstreet had commanded the troops at Bloody Lane at the Battle of Antietam and the Sunken Road on Mayre's Heights at the Battle of Fredericksburg. He saw the advantages of the defense. However, this was contrary to military doctrine at the time. War should be fought in a gentlemanly manner. Lee did not like the fact that Longstreet utilized spies and the defense was ungentlemanly. On the other hand, Longstreet foresaw how battles would be fought in World War I. Lee decided to attack even though the Union had more troops and was in a better position on the field.

On July 1st, elements of the two armies clashed as more and more units from both sides approached the town. At dawn on July 2nd, the Sixty-Ninth Regiment NYSV and what was left of the Irish Brigade halted near the Union defensive line at Cemetery Ridge. The Second Corps moved into position on Cemetery Ridge between Major General Sickles' Third Corps and components of the First and Eleventh Corps. Confederates, meanwhile, had established themselves on a ridge about a mile to the southwest (beyond which lay a wheat field and a peach orchard). About midday, General Sickles led the Third Corps (about 10,000 men) from Cemetery Ridge, Little Round Top, and Big Round Top toward the Peach Orchard. The resulting gap left the Second Corps' left flank vulnerable. The situation worsened when Sickles' men retreated under attack from Lieutenant General James Longstreet's Confederate Corps. The First Division was ordered to prepare to support General Syke's Fifth Corps in defending against Longstreet's attack. At about 4:30 in the afternoon, Colonel Kelly, Commander of the Irish Brigade, asked Father William Corby, Chaplain of the 88th Regiment, to give the men general absolution. Father Corby mounted a large rock and gave the Brigade General Absolution with the sounds of battle all around him. At Rocky Knoll, the NYSV aided in driving the enemy back and took several prisoners.

The Confederates (despite two days of desperate assaults) had failed to take the Union position on Cemetery Ridge. On July 3rd, Lee ordered a desperate assault on the center of the Federal lines. (This was the famous Pickett's Charge). Some of the Confederates reached the Union lines but were either killed or captured when they did. A Confederate Brigade (Wilcox's) advanced opposite the Regiment's position. It disappeared into a depression in the field about 150 yards away from the NYSV. The Regiment stood ready to receive them. After a short time, the Confederate Brigade hoisted a white flag. The Sixty-Ninth helped gather up the prisoners. The Regiment had 20 casualties at Gettysburg.

The NYSV Regiment skirmished with A.P. Hill's Corps in the Battle of Mine Run. It also acted as rear guard for the ammunition wagons after the battle. Before going into winter quarters at Stephensburgh, a recruiting drive and the return of some of the wounded brought the Regiment up to minimum strength. Many recruits signed up, but many of them were never able to be accessed into the Regiment. The Regiment was reorganized into six Companies. Father Willette also rejoined the Regiment. On October 14th, John Pendleton, who was wounded at Antietam, was captured at Auburn, Virginia. He died at Andersonville Prison in Georgia the following July 2nd. On November 28th, Colonel

Robert Nugent was mustered out of the Regiment. He would return to Command the Regiment on October 30th, 1864.

In October 1863, Corcoran was assigned to guard the railroad between Centreville and Manassas. The Artillery Regiment was assigned an area near Centreville (within the 30 miles assigned to the Legion). Confederate Major John S. Mosby, who in early 1863 was authorized to form and take command of the 43rd Battalion, Virginia Cavalry, Partisan Rangers (Mosby's Rangers, i.e., a guerilla organization) attacked the area often with his raiders. The task of guarding this section of the railroad was exceptionally unpleasant for the many Fenians in the Regiment. Many of them had been guerilla fighters in Ireland (including Corcoran). The men in the Artillery Regiment fully understood the futility of the mission, but they felt useless. Corcoran wrote to the President and requested another command. Shortly after the letter was written, the Irish Legion was transferred into the 3rd Division, 5th Corps. Morale in the Legion improved.

In November, the first National Convention of the Fenian Brotherhood was held in Chicago. The two leading officers of the Irish Legion, General Corcoran and Matthew Murphy, were elected to the Central Council of the Brotherhood. In addition, Corcoran, Murphy, and Francis Welply (of the 69th Artillery Regiment) were signatories to a document making the society an open organization. Prior to the convention, the Fenians were a secret revolutionary society, which placed its members at risk of excommunication from the Catholic Church. The document was approved (although these three were signed by Proxy). The Irish Legion was the only military unit to have three representatives at the convention (indicating a significantly higher Fenian sympathy and membership than in any other unit in the Army of the Potomac). No one from the Irish Brigade attended.

There were many desertions in 1863, but there was also a recruiting drive (for the NYSV Regiment) in New York City throughout the fall and winter. Many recruits signed up but many of them never were accessed into the Regiment. In December, there was a drive to have members of the Regiment who had enlisted for three years re-enlist (even though their term of service had not yet expired). Those who reenlisted would receive a reenlistment bonus and 30-day furlough. Most of the Sixty-Ninth Regiment reenlistments took place in December. The peer pressure to reenlist was great. Thomas Fitzgerald reenlisted on December 23rd and deserted on February 4, 1864, less than six weeks after his thirty-day furlough.

1863 was another eventful year for the NYSV Regiment. General Meagher requested the Regiment be allowed to stand down for recruiting purposes. He resigned when his request was denied. The Regiment suffered casualties in Chancellorsville and Gettysburg. Colonel Nugent left the Regiment, and Father Willette returned. At the close of the year, the Regiment was encamped in winter quarters north of the Rapidan River.

As Christmas 1863 approached, visitors came to spend the holidays. Among them were the wives of Generals Meagher and Corcoran. On December 22, Corcoran and Meagher headed for Fairfax enroute to Washington to meet them. Corcoran mounted Meagher's spirited horse (which had won the Irish Brigade Horse race on St. Patrick's Day 1863) and challenged Meagher to a race. Meagher accepted, and Corcoran took the lead. As he rounded a bend on the dusty road, Corcoran had a seizure and was thrown from the horse. Corcoran was carried back to his quarters; he died two and a half hours later.

On Christmas Eve, 1863, Corcoran's body was removed from his quarters and escorted by the 69th Artillery Regiment and the 164th Regiment, along with a battery of Artillery and Squadron of Cavalry, to the railway station for the journey north. Corcoran was buried on December 27th at Calvary Cemetery in Queens, New York. Among the pallbearers were Generals Meagher and Dodge, Colonels Matthew Murphy, John O'Mahoney (Head Centre of the Fenian Brotherhood), J.R. McIvor, Hugh C. Flood, ex-

Colonel McEvilly and Lt. Colonel Reid representing the Artillery Regiment. The Honor Guard and Escort was the first regiment of the Phoenix Brigade (99th NYSNG). In tribute to Corcoran, the Officers of the Irish Legion resolved to wear black crepe on their left arms for 30 days as a badge of mourning.

On January 2, 1864, under the Command of Captain Richard Moroney, about fifty enlisted veterans of the Sixty-Ninth Regiment NYSV arrived in New York City and were greeted by their relatives and members of the Sixty-Ninth Regiment New York National Guard. A meeting was convened at Whitney House to plan a reception. General Meagher and all the officers of the Irish Brigade who were in New York City would attend. A grand banquet was for the enlisted veterans and discharged wounded of the Regiment. It would be held on January 16th at Irving Hall. That day at noon, the NYNG Regiment assembled at City Hall under the Command of Captain Maroney. The Regiment was reviewed by the mayor. The Regiment marched up Broadway, accompanied by a band, to the banquet hall. The hall was decorated with the war-worn flags of the Irish Brigade. Around the galleries, names of the engagements in which the NYSV Regiment participated were displayed on shields, "Yorktown," "Fair Oaks," "Gaines Mill," "Savage's Station," "Peach Orchard," "Glendale," "White Oak

Swamp," "Malvern Hill," "Antietam," "Fredericksburg," "Chancellorsville", and "Bristow Station." On a trophy was inscribed "Gettysburg". General Meagher and the principal officers of the Irish Brigade entered the hall, accompanied by a group of dignitaries. General Meagher made a speech followed by the men toasting the General. A toast was then proposed to dead comrades and soldiers of the Irish Brigade. Other toasts followed. Colonel John O'Mahoney was then introduced, and he made a speech. He concluded by toasting to the memory of General Michael Corcoran.

The Irish community also mourned Corcoran's death, particularly by the Fenians. Michael Corcoran was not only the former military commander of the Fenian Brotherhood but one of its three founders. The Secretary of War was going to replace Corcoran with General Meagher, but General Halleck wanted General Tyler to take the position.

Steady progress was made in recruiting for the NYSV Regiment during the months of January and February 1864 due to the efforts of Colonel Nugent, Captain McGee, Adjutant Smith, and their assistants. The NYSV Regiment was rapidly reaching minimum strength. The Regiment added several new companies. With the expiration of the veteran's furlough, the Regiment returned to their winter quarters in Virginia in early February.

The Irish Legion continued the dreary routine of trying to capture Mosby's Raiders and the routine of camp life. On January 20, 1864, a ball was organized by the Sergeants of the Regiment. This was originally to have been a Christmas Ball, but it was postponed because of Corcoran's death. The Ball celebrated the first anniversary of the Battle of the Deserted House.

St. Patrick's Day 1864 was celebrated in typical Irish Brigade fashion, opening with a Mass, followed by a banquet and celebration. Lieutenant-Colonel James Kelly rejoined the Irish Brigade as Commander (having been relieved from duty at Ann Arbor, Michigan). He would only Command for a short time. After Colonel Kelly's departure, Colonel Thomas A. Smyth (of the First Delaware Regiment) was appointed to the Command of the Irish Brigade. March and April were uneventful, but May would open a new campaign. St. Patrick's Day in the Artillery Regiment was also celebrated with normal elaborate festivities. The National Guard Regiment, Commanded by Colonel Bagley, marched in a parade in New York City.

Battle of the Wilderness

At the beginning of May 1864, Robert E. Lee clashed with General Ulysses S. Grant in the Battle of the Wilderness. This was the first of a series of engagements over the next six weeks in which Grant tried to outflank the

Confederates and take up a position between them and Richmond. In each case, Lee was able to counter Grant's move. The Union lost almost 55,000 men, while the Confederates lost less than half that number.

On the first day of the Battle of the Wilderness, the Irish Brigade was assigned to the Second Corps. The Corps was commanded by General Winfield Scott Hancock. The NYSV Regiment was heavily engaged (although four-fifths of its members were recruits). The Regiment behaved with great steadiness and gallantry.

General Lee felt his best chance against the numerically superior Army of the Potomac was to strike while they were passing through the Wilderness. Lee began to concentrate his army for the attack. He expected the battle would be like the Battle of Chancellorsville, which was fought on the same ground. Lee believed if he defeated Union troops in the Wilderness, they would limp back to Washington as they had done so many times before. Lee misjudged the tenacity of Grant. Even though Grant was lost in the wilderness, he kept moving his army south. On May 5, the NYSV Regiment marched down the Catharpin Road to Brock Road into the Wilderness towards Todd's Tavern. It was still armed with smooth-bore muskets. Fighting continued for several days. The Regiment suffered its heaviest casualties on May 5th.

During the battle, the NYSV Regiment lost 44 soldiers killed, wounded, or captured.

With the opening of Grant's spring campaign and the abandonment of Falmouth as his principal supply base, defending the railroad became unimportant. Consequently, the Artillery Regiment was ordered to Alexandria and, from there, southwest to Grant's new supply base at Belle Plain. On May 17, the Regiment was ordered to report to the Army of the Potomac Headquarters at Spotsylvania, west of Fredericksburg. The Regiment was reassigned from the 6th

Corps to the 4th Brigade, 2d Division, 2d Corps. The Artillery Regiment and the NYSV Regiment were now in the same Corps and would both wear II Corps hat device, the red trefoil. The Red Trefoil appears on the distinctive unit insignia of today's 69th Infantry. In May, at Spotsylvania Court House, the Artillery Regiment joined the first line of attack on the Rebel works. The Regiment advanced on the division's left flank. It plowed into Lee's fortifications and pressed 500 yards to the main battle line, waiting for the rest of the Brigade to come up. The Regiment was ordered to hold this advance position (which they did until ordered to fall back to Po River.

The Battle of the Wilderness was almost immediately followed by the Battle of Spotsylvania, which occurred on May 12th. The NYSV Regiment had been one of the last

Union units to march out of the Wilderness. On May 8, as Federal forward elements were sparring with the Rebels at Spotsylvania, the Irish Brigade marched down to Todd's Tavern, arriving there around 11:00 AM. They then moved forward two miles before digging defensive earthworks. The Regiment skirmished with the enemy that night and then marched until May 11[th,] when they reached Spotsylvania.

Grant ordered General Hancock to lead II Corps in a massive assault on "the Muleshoe," a salient in the Confederate line. On the night of May 11, II Corps marched behind the army's rear. They passed quietly to their attack assembly area. The attack was scheduled to begin the following morning. As the NYSV Regiment approached in the early morning fog, the Confederates opened fire. However, due to the dampness of their powder, their volley wasn't effective. The Union Army pushed forward. The army captured two Generals, twenty cannons, and over two thousand enemy soldiers. General Lee wanted to personally lead a counterattack at the Muleshoe or Bloody Angle. He was convinced this would not be wise. General Gordon led an attack that drove the Union Army back to their original lines.

The NSV Regiment had 81 soldiers, and the Artillery Regiment had 31 casualties during the Battle of Spotsylvania.

North Anna River

The Artillery Regiment remained on the Po River until May 20th. On May 23, the Regiment was ordered up to support Smyth's Brigade. It assisted in holding the Rebel fortifications at the North Anna River. During the Action, Sergeant Major Joseph Keele earned the Medal of Honor. His citation reads: "Voluntarily and at the risk of his life carried orders to the brigade commander, which resulted in saving the works his regiment was defending." The Regiment had 21 casualties during the battle.

On the night of May 20th, the NYSV Regiment marched to Milford Station. On May 23rd, they marched to the North Anna River crossing it only to re-cross it on May 27th. On May 29, the Regiment reached Pamunkey Creek, where it remained till June 1st. On June 1st, the Regiment began their march to Cold Harbor. On June 3rd, they attacked the enemy's line. Although the Regiment succeeded in reaching the Confederate rifle pits, fierce rifle and artillery fire forced it to fall back. When the Brigade Commander ordered the Regiment back to its own entrenchments, it was cut down by enemy artillery. After finally reaching their entrenchments, they remained there until the night of June 12th, when they withdrew to the James River.

While the standoff continued along the banks of Topotomony Creek, General Philip Sheridan's Cavalry

Corps encountered Rebel cavalry and infantry on May 31 at Cold Harbor. The Rebels were driven from their positions. Lee counterattacked, but Sheridan's Cavalrymen held until reinforced by the Federal 6th Corps and later by General Baldy Smith's 18th Corps. The two Corps attacked on June 1st and took the Southern rifle pits. Grant felt that an assault at 4:00 a.m. June 2 would destroy the Southern position. Hancock's 2d Corps was ordered to Cold Harbor but arrived after 7:00 a.m. The attack was postponed 24 hours, during which Lee's Rebels dug in and prepared a series of trenches and works. Any hope of Union success was gone.

At 4:00 a.m. June 3, the Artillery Regiment attacked at Cold Harbor, charging on the Division's extreme left. The Regiment advanced to within 50 yards of the enemy works but was unable to take the Southern position because of both a deep ravine and the heavy fire. Nevertheless, the Regiment (along with the rest of the Irish Legion) managed to hold their position for more than an hour. Finally, the Regiment fell back 150 Yards to the crest of a hill and dug in.

At Cold Harbor, the NYSV Regiment had 42 casualties, and the Artillery Regiment had 82. On the night of June 12, 1864, the Regiment, along with the 2d division, 2d Corps, secretly moved to the James River and crossed at Windmill Point. After a brief rest, the Corps advanced on Petersburg.

Petersburg

General Grant decided he would attack Petersburg, which was an important railroad junction on the way to Richmond. Late in the evening of June 16, the Regiment captured one of the enemy's breastworks after hand-to-hand fighting and heavy from the enemy. For the next two days, the Regiment attacked enemy lines, and a few members of the Regiment managed to get inside the enemy's defenses; they were either killed or captured. The Regiment suffered heavy losses and was ultimately pushed back. On June 10, Confederate General William Mahone launched a counterattack that struck the left and rear of the 1st Division, Second Corps. The force of this brilliant counterstroke caused the Irish Brigade, including the NYSV Regiment, to break and run. Panic soon spread to the 3d division. In addition, most of the 2nd Brigade and 2nd Division were surprised and captured. As night fell, the Irish Legion was ordered to charge and retake the lost ground. The Rebels let them come close to their positions before they opened fired. For two hours, the wounded of the Legion kept coming in, and many were left to die in front of the Rebel position.

After casualties to the Union Army numbered more than 10,000, Grant ordered a halt to the assaults and prepared for a lengthy siege of Petersburg. The siege lasted many months.

The Artillery Regiment was sent to Deep Bottom as a diversion for the offensive of the Petersburg Mine. Union soldiers dug a long tunnel under Confederate fortifications at Petersburg. On July 30, they exploded over 300 pounds of gunpowder under Confederate fortifications (the Petersburg Mine). Union forces charged into and around the crater caused by the explosion. Most of the soldiers milled in confusion in the crater. Confederates quickly recovered and launched several counterattacks. Union forces were repulsed with severe casualties. The Artillery Regiment returned to Petersburg and remained until it returned to Deep Bottom on August 14th, where they participated in another diversion on August 18th. The Regiment suffered 8 casualties at Deep Bottom.

The National Guard Regiment was mustered into Federal service on July 6, 1864, at New York and mustered out of Federal service on October 6, 1864, at New York.

Ream's Station

The Artillery Regiment returned once again to Petersburg on the August 21st. The Regiment received orders to march for Ream's Station, which was reached on August 23. On August 24, the Union II Corps moved south along the Weldon Railroad, tearing up track. On August 25, the Artillery Regiment was ordered to hold a line of rifle pits just south of Ream's station. In the early evening,

Confederate General Henry Heth attacked the front and both flanks of the 2d Corps. Around 6:00 PM. The 1st Division broke and ran. The Artillery Regiment held its position and withdrew only when it appeared they risked capture. Confederates captured 9 guns, 12 colors, and many prisoners. II Corps was shattered. Maj. Gen. Winfield Scott Hancock withdrew to the Union line near the Jerusalem Plank Road. Regiments that lost their colors in the action were forbidden to carry them again. The NYSV Regiment had 45 casualties, and the Artillery Regiment had 58. Reduced to only 116 members and under the command of Captain M. Doheny, the Artillery Regiment was engaged in fatigue duties, with the rest of the 2d Corps around Petersburg for the next two months.

Boydton Plank Road – Hatchers Run

On October 26, the Artillery Regiment was ordered to march towards Hatcher's Run. The next day (October 27, 1864), the Regiment was ordered out as skirmishers while the rest of the Irish Legion held a line of earthworks. Around 2:00 PM, the Regiment attacked along with the entire Brigade. The enemy withdrew across Hatcher's Run. The Regiment followed across Hatcher's Run and dug in. They repelled several counterattacks by Confederates before being ordered to withdraw. Casualties for the Artillery Regiment at Boydton Plank Road were 15

On October 30, 1864, Rebels raided the NYSV Regiment's picket line at night. The picket line had manned posts about twenty yards apart connected by trenches. The picket line was manned by two officers, three sergeants (who were acting lieutenants), and 230 enlisted men (190 of whom were recent recruits). Posing as picket relief, Confederates infiltrated the left wing and proceeded down the picket line, capturing prisoners as they went. Another group of Rebels approached the right wing of the line, which was commanded by Lieutenant Murtha Murphy. Murphy ordered his men to open fire. This dispersed the Confederates, but Murphy was wounded in the head.

Many soldiers in the NYSV Regiment were captured. The after-action report of the affair concluded that ten of the NYSV Regiment's recent recruits (who had deserted to the enemy) had informed the Rebels of the picket line's dispositions. The deserters may have been Confederate soldiers who enlisted in the Regiment. One of the deserters was John Nichols. He enlisted as a substitute for a New York draftee to serve three years. Nichols was mustered in as private in Company "A" on September 22, 1864. He deserted but was subsequently captured and hung.

On October 31, 1864, the National Guard Regiment assembled on Washington Square for its Annual Review and Inspection. The Inspector noted the Regiment, with a muster roll of nearly 500 members had only 240 officers and men present (this included 24 band members). Only one company (of the eight companies present) had the minimum number of soldiers required to continue in State service. Nearly as many members of the regiment were absent (from the most important event of the year) as were present, showing an indifference to their duty to the State and Country. The inspector recommended consolidating the companies, making only five.

2nd Hatcher's Run

In November, the Artillery Regiment and the Irish Legion were ordered to defend the Dunn House Battery and Battery No. 9 (on the Petersburg Lines). As the Second Corps took to the field again on December 7th, the Artillery Regiment and Corcoran's Legion were left behind to hold off any enemy advance. Later in the month, General Gibbon ordered each Brigade Commander to rank the Regiments in their Brigades. The Artillery Regiment was deemed as the crack regiment of the Irish Legion.

The Artillery Regiment was once again ordered to Hatcher's Run in February of 1865. On the morning of February 5th, the Regiment deployed to the left of the Armstrong House, holding the right of the brigade's line. The Irish Legion dug in while the Regiment moved out on picket duty. At about 4 PM, Rebels attacked from the woods, and the Regiment was driven back. After dark, the fortifications were improved, and an abatis was thrown up in front of the line. Colonel Murphy (Commander of the Artillery Regiment since its formation) was mortally wounded during the engagement. He died of his wounds on April 16, 1865, in the Field Hospital at City Point, Virginia. There were only three casualties at Hatcher's Run in February 1865. However, the most serious was the loss of Colonel Mathew Murphy who was only 23 years old.

On February 5, the NYSV Regiment marched back to Hatcher's Run and built entrenchments while under enemy fire. Several Confederates deserted and surrendered to the Regiment. On March 17, 1865, the Regiment and Irish Brigade celebrated its last Saint Patrick's Day in the Federal Army. It was not as an elaborate celebration as the previous ones. Among the guests were General Meade and many Corps and Division commanders. As in years before, the day began with a High Mass, which was celebrated by the Regimental Chaplain, Father Willette. As in the past, the officers of the Brigade held a grand steeplechase. This one was marred when Lieutenant Michael McConville fell from his horse and fractured his skull. McConville had enlisted in the Company "F" of the Sixty-Ninth Regiment NYSV in October 1861. He had just been commissioned Second

Lieutenant by Colonel Nugent on February 9, 1865. He died from his injuries on March 26th.

As the Petersburg Campaign ended, Lee's Army of Northern Virginia was exhausted from a winter of trench warfare on a 40-mile front. Grant's well-equipped and well-fed army was growing in strength. On March 29, 1865, the Union Army began an offensive. The attack broke the Confederate defenses southwest of Petersburg. It also cut the supply lines to Petersburg and the Confederate capital. Union victories at the Battle of Five Forks on April 1, 1865, and the Third Battle of Petersburg (often called the Breakthrough at Petersburg) on April 2, 1865, opened Richmond to imminent capture. Lee ordered the evacuation of Confederate forces from both Petersburg and Richmond. Confederate government leaders fled west from Richmond that night.

While Lee was abandoning Petersburg, the Artillery Regiment was at Crow's Farm. The Regiment and the Irish Legion were detached to guard the cavalry train. They were not re-attached with the Division. On April 6, the Regiment (along with the Division) pursued the retreating Rebels for three days before encamping at Clover Hill on April 10, 1864. The Regiment stayed there until the end of the war. The Regiment participated in the Grand Review and remained in Federal Service until July 15, 1865, when they were mustered out. The first time an Adjutant General's Report listed the regiment as the 182nd Infantry Regiment was in 1864, but it always crossed referenced it as the 69th Regiment National Guard Artillery.

In February 1865, Lieutenant Colonel James J. Smith took Command of the NYSV Regiment. Finally, after months of fighting around Petersburg, Lee abandoned both Petersburg and Richmond, moving his army west toward Appomattox Courthouse. The Regiment participated in battles at Hatcher's Run, Five Forks, Sutherland's Station, South Side Railroad, Amelia Springs, Farmville, and Appomattox. The NYSV Regiment was present at the surrender of General Lee and the Army of Northern Virginia.

Both the NYSV and Artillery Regiments participated in the Grand Review of the Army of the Potomac. The NYSV Regiment returned to New York City and was mustered out of the Federal Army at Hart's Island, New York Harbor, on July 2, 1865. Of the almost 1,000 men who joined the Sixty-Ninth Regiment New York State Volunteers in 1861, less than 40 remained. The Artillery Regiment remained in Federal Service until July 15, 1865, when it was mustered out of Federal Service. The Regiment was first mentioned in the New York Adjutant General's Report in 1864. It was listed as the 182nd Infantry Regiment, but it was cross-referenced as the 69th Regiment National Guard Artillery.

The last survivor of the Sixty-Ninth Infantry Regiment New York Volunteers (NYSV) was Henry Mingay, who died April 23, 1947, in Glendale, California. Henry was born on Dec. 3, 1846, in Philby, England. He was the fourth son of Richard and Ruth Mingay. When Henry was four, his family emigrated to New York. Henry left school in 1860 to become a bootblack and printer's devil in a newspaper of Saratoga Springs, New York. When the Civil War broke out, Henry was refused enlistment because he was too young. But he got by on his second attempt and was sworn into the Sixty-Ninth Regiment. He saw action in all the regiment's battles and was mustered out as a sergeant. He was wounded in the right arm. Later he was commissioned a first lieutenant and was later advanced to captain. He left New York for Colorado in 1885 with his wife and family and went into the printing business. In 1914, the Mingays moved to Monrovia, Tujunga, and finally to Glendale. His wife Emma passed away in 1924. His daughter Edith died in 1933. At the age of 98, Henry married Aimee Cleveland Hennessey (who was 30 years younger) in August 1945. He was photographed standing between James Cagney and Pat O'Brien during the promotions for the movie "Fighting Sixty-Ninth Regiment" in 1940.

Most people associate the NYSV Regiment as the Irish Brigade (Meagher's Irish Brigade). It is not. Meagher's Irish

Brigade comprised the 69th NYSV, 88th NYSV, 63rd NYSV and the 28th Massecuites. Only one of those regiments is in the lineage of the 69th. The 69th Regiment during the Civil War should rather be considered as the 69th Irish Brigade composed of the 69th Infantry, New York State Militia (NYSM), the 69th Infantry Regiment, New York State Volunteers (NYSV), and the 182nd Infantry Regiment (Artillery Regiment). Instead of being under the command of a Brigade Commander who set the direction of the Brigade, the 69th Irish Brigade had an overriding mission to free Ireland from England.

Chapter Four
Post-Civil War

After Meagher resigned from his position in May 1863, he returned to New York. In December 1863, the Army rescinded Meagher's resignation and assigned him to various positions but none to commanding troops. After the Civil War, he was appointed Secretary of the Montana Territory and Acting Governor. In 1867, at Fort Benton, Montana, Meagher fell (or was pushed) overboard from a riverboat on the Missouri River. His body was never found. There are many theories relating to his death or murder.

Both the NYSV and Artillery Regiments were absorbed into the National Guard Regiment. The Regiment retained its Irish orientation, and most of the leadership was born in Ireland. The Regiment also retained its Irish Republican orientation, much to the dismay of the State. In a newspaper article in 1898, the New York Tribune called for the disbanding of the 69th Regiment. It read the regiment should be wiped out just because it is distinctively Irish. Throughout its history, members of the Regiment would identify themselves with Irish Republican causes.

The 69th regiment was inspected on October 17, 1865, at Tompkins Square. There were 373 members present and

259 absent. Once again, the Brigade Inspector commented unfavorably on the Regiment. It was the inspector's opinion that the number present at the inspection was the real strength of the regiment. He believed the absentees were continued on the rolls from year to year just to keep the apparent strength of the Regiment higher. The inspector noted the armory could easily be broken into and it was not a safe for storage of State property. The inspector reported that in 1864, 500 new Springfield muskets were issued to the regiment, but only 370 can be found in the armory. He believed the soldiers were taking the arms home.

In 1866, James Cavanaugh served as the Lieutenant Colonel of the Regiment. He would be promoted to Colonel in 1867 and serve as Commander of the Regiment until 1893 (when he was retired on December 1st). The State promoted him to Brevet General. This was the first time the State appointed someone a Brigadier. Cavanaugh is by far the longest-serving Commander of the Sixty-Ninth Regiment (having Commanded the Regiment for over 26 years). He is also one of the longest-serving officers in the Regiment (having spent almost thirty-three years with the unit).

The Sixty-Ninth Regiment was inspected on October 23, 1866. The Regiment had 347 present and 155 absent. The arms and equipment were in good order. In 1867, Colonel Martin T. McMahon, who Commanded the regiment in

1866, was given a brevet promotion to Major General. That left the Commander's position vacant. It was filled by Colonel Cavanaugh. In 1869, the Fourth Brigade was disbanded, and the regiment was transferred to the First Brigade.

The 69th Infantry Regiment and especially its Commander, Colonel Cavanaugh, participated in Irish Republican. In 1870, the Irish Republican Army recruited out of the 69th Armory for General O'Neill. Colonel Cavanagh's name appears in the Fenian Brotherhood's financial ledger. Colonel Cavanagh led the Guard of Honor escort for Charles Stewart Parnell's (Land League) departure from New York City in 1880. Colonel Cavanaugh offered the post of Inspector of Marksmanship for the 69th to one of his associates, William Hearns. (Hearns was a member of the Fenian Brotherhood, Irish Republican Brotherhood, Irish Republican Army, and Irish American Republican Association. The Fenian Brotherhood commissioned Hearns to conduct a clandestine mission to assess the state of the Fenian Brotherhood in Ireland in the 1870s. He was accused of blowing up a ship in Waterford harbor).

Not only was the Commander of the Regiment involved in Irish Republican activities, but unit members too were involved in extremely active roles in Irish Republican causes. In June 1889, members of the 69th appeared (in uniform) with the Legion of St. Patrick and attended the encampment of the Irish American Military Union at Brommer Park. Second Lieutenant Neil Breslin, "B" Company 69th, was a member of Clan na Gael. Breslin's daughter unveiled the Irish Republican Brotherhood (IRB) monument in 1907 (which suggests Lieutenant Breslin was a prominent member of both the IRB and Clan-na-Gael). Patrick K. Horgan, who Commanded Company "C" in 1879, is believed to be a member of the "Dynamite Party," Irish Skirmishers, Irish Nationalists Aid, and the Defense Association. He is believed to have attended the Great Dynamite Convention of 1888, as well as participating in the Dynamite War and the explosion in the Local Board Offices of London (March 1883). He was an advocate of political assassination and a member of the Irish Invincibles. Horgan associated with numerous Irish revolutionaries, including O'Donovan Rossa (Phoenix Club, Fenian Brotherhood, Invincibles, "Dynamite Party"), Professor Mezzeroff (Irish Skirmishers), and Thomas Gallagher, an operative during the "Dynamite War".

Not every officer in the Regiment felt a duty to Ireland.

Edward Duffy

Edward Duffy was the Company Commander of "E" Company. In 1875, Duffy was promoted to Major. As he moved up the ranks within the Regiment, he would fight against its Irish Republican leanings. He would eventually win. Although the New York State probably wanted to rid itself of militia organizations with ties to foreign countries, Cavanagh was a war hero and the most senior Colonel in the State. The State did not want to sully the reputation of one of its senior officers and one of the State's most decorated war heroes. That all changed when Cavanagh retired in 1893.

Colonel James Cavanaugh (known as the "Little Major" during the Civil War) commanded the Regiment from 1867 until 1893. James Cavanaugh was born in Ireland and enlisted as a Private in Company "E," 69th Infantry Regiment, N.Y.S.M, in the Fall of 1852. He was promoted to First Lieutenant on March 9, 1857. He was promoted to Captain on January 13, 1859, as the Commander of

Company "C." Cavanaugh was the Commander of Company "C" in 1860 when Colonel Corcoran refused to parade the Regiment for the Prince of Wales. He Commanded Company "C" at Bull Run. Upon his return to New York, he helped Colonel Nugent organize the Sixty-Ninth Regiment, New York State Volunteers. He was assigned as Major of the Regiment and accompanied it until he was wounded at the Battle of Fredericksburg. At the Battle of Malvern Hill, on July 1, 1862, Major Cavanaugh had his horse shot from under him. At Antietam, Lieutenant Colonel James Kelly (Command of the 69th Regiment) was wounded and carried from the field. Acting Lieutenant Colonel Cavanaugh took command and led the charge at Bloody Lane. Major Cavanaugh stood in the center of the Sixty-Ninth's line by the color bearers, encouraging his remaining men to keep up their fire. Cavanaugh again took command of the Regiment at Fredericksburg after Colonel Nugent was wounded. Cavanaugh was shot in the hip during the battle. He was medically discharged from Federal Service on May 16, 1863, for disability. He then joined the 69th New York State Militia. Cavanaugh commanded the Militia Regiment when on active duty in Baltimore in 1863 when the Draft Riots broke out in New York City. In 1866, he served as the Lieutenant Colonel of the Regiment. He would be promoted to Colonel and Commander in 1867 and served in that role until 1893 when he was retired on December 1st. On his retirement, he was promoted to Brevet General by the State.

Colonel Cavanaugh is buried in Calvary Cemetery, Woodside, N.Y. He was 61 years old when he died. His grave is in Section 7 Range 13 Plot CC Graves 5/8. There are 9 burials in this grave-holding. He died in New York City on January 7, 1901. The burial took place on January 10, 1901.

Colonel Edward Duffy was born in Ireland. He was appointed Colonel of the 69th Regiment on April 13, 1898. He enlisted as a Private in Company "E," 69th Regiment, on June 3, 1867. He was promoted to Corporal on May 14, 1868, Sergeant on December 10, 1868, and First Lieutenant on March 14, 1871. He was promoted to Captain, as Regimental Adjutant, on December 31, 1874, and Major, 69th Regiment on December 10, 1875, Lieutenant Colonel on March 25, 1896, and Colonel, April 13, 1898.

Duffy commanded the Regiment when it was Federalized on May 2, 1898, for the Spanish-American War. Duffy volunteered 100% of the Regiment for the War, and 100% of the soldiers went. He served on active duty as Colonel until January 13, 1899. He was the Regimental Commander when the new armory was opened in 1906. A large portrait of him hangs in the Duffy Room in the Armory. The room was named in his honor.

Duffy and Cavanaugh would compete fiercely over the management and future direction of the Regiment. Cavanaugh was a Fenian and believed the Regiment should play a role in Ireland's struggle against England. Duffy did not. Cavanaugh was often criticized for his leadership. Duffy was often praised by State Inspectors.

In 1875, the General Inspection noted the Regiment had suffered from the dereliction of an incompetent adjutant, who was replaced by Captain Duffy. In the report, Duffy's service as Adjutant was characterized as great. In Marksmanship proficiency, Duffy was always one of the highest scorers of the Regiment.

On February 12, 1883, Colonel Cavanagh ordered an election to be held for choosing a Captain for Company "C." Cavanaugh directed First Lieutenant William Purcell, who Commanded the Company, to issue the proper notices to the troops. An incident occurred, which brought charges and counter charges and the arrest of Lieutenant Purcell. This was followed by an investigation by the State. Since Lieutenant Purcell was late for the election, Colonel Cavanaugh accepted a roster from the company clerk. When Lieutenant Purcell arrived, he presented Colonel Cavanaugh with a different roster which Cavanaugh refused to accept. Charges claiming Purcell had enlisted people to ensure he would be re-elected. This led to the arrest of Purcell. Major

Duffy and several officers called for the removal of Colonel Cavanaugh and sent a letter to the Adjutant General. The subsequent investigation conducted by the State was critical of Cavanaugh but did not find cause to remove Cavanaugh.

The report from the State Investigation also noted problems with Cavanaugh's leadership (e.g., does not possess as full knowledge of State military law and regulations as is necessary in a Commanding Officer, his enforcement of discipline is in the main fair, one of his actions while legal, was discourteous and arbitrary, general efficiency of the command is fair. That the general drill of the regiment is fair. That the books and papers are fairly kept. That the discipline, with exceptions noted, is fair, etc.). The report mentions a field officer (not by name but obviously Duffy) circulated a petition to remove Cavanaugh among the officers of the Regiment. The investigation found the evidence produced shows Colonel Cavanagh has become aware of the errors he committed, that no improper motives governed his action, that on the contrary, his desire to secure the best interests of his Regiment led him into the course pursued, and that the Regiment under his command has been improving in discipline and efficiency; therefore, further action in the matter is deemed neither to be warranted nor to be conducive to the best interests of the National Guard.

In 1889, the armory was located on 6th Street and Third Avenue. The regiment occupied the second and third floors. The General Inspection noted the armory is utterly unfit for occupancy. It is too small for such a large and prosperous organization.

In 1892, the Regiment was activated for the Quarantine Riots on Fire Island. During Colonel Cavanagh's tenure the regiment experienced a period of stability of leadership. Besides the regimental staff, the commands of the companies remained relatively constant. However, during Cavanagh's reign, the Regiment kept its Irish Republican leanings. Although much of the Irish Republican activities were conducted secretly, there are strong indications that Cavanagh was intimately involved in the Irish Republican movement. The State could do little to purge the unit of its Irish Republican Orientation. Cavanaugh was too powerful. However, when Cavanaugh retired, the State acted immediately. The Regiment was reduced to a battalion. This is clear evidence the State was particularly unhappy with the Regiment. The AG Report indicated there were cliques within the regiment. The group that was most identified as Irish Republican was purged. All the Field and Staff Officers of the Sixty-Ninth Regiment (except Major Edward Duffy) and all Officers of Companies "B," "E," "F," "G," and "H" were rendered supernumerary (over strength) on December

6, 1893, and disbanded. The Sixty-Ninth Regiment was reduced to a battalion of five companies. It was designated the Sixty-Ninth Battalion and assigned to the First Brigade. The only companies that remained in the organization were Companies "A," "C," "D," "I," and "K." Companies "B," "E," "F," "G," and "H" were disbanded.

Three days later (on December 9, 1993), Lieutenant Colonel James Moran, Major William O'Meagher, Surgeon, Captain Hugh Coleman, Captain William Cushing, Captain Hugh Joseph Kelly, Chaplain, Captain Paul Francis Leonard, Captain Patrick J. Morgan, Captain Thomas Mortimer, Captain Stephen P. Ryan, First Lieutenant Charles Mahon, First Lieutenant James John McCoy, First Lieutenant William McLoughlin, First Lieutenant John Murphy, Adjutant, First Lieutenant John E. O'Brien, Second Lieutenant Patrick Monahan Drew, Second Lieutenant Denis J. Feery, Second Lieutenant Patrick Hayes, Second Lieutenant Walter Charles McGee, and Second Lieutenant John J. Scanlon were rendered supernumerary (over strength and not authorized), and discharged.

The Irish Republican orientation of the Regiment (before the reorganization to a battalion) can be clearly seen by the actions of the officers and soldiers who were discharged. The former Executive Officer Lieutenant-Colonel Moran, all the Officers and soldiers who were discharged from the 69th (along with members of the Clan-na-Gael) formed a new regiment called the First Regiment of the Irish Volunteers. Lieutenant-Colonel Moran was the Commander. The Clan-Na-Gael was involved in every revolutionary undertaking looking to free Ireland from British rule.

The 69th Infantry Battalion was quartered in the 69th Regiment Armory on 8th Street and Third Avenue. Duffy was appointed Battalion Commander. In January 1995, the Battalion was called out to aid civil authorities during the Brooklyn Trolly Car disturbance. Duffy was praised in the General Inspection Report for improving the unit. The 69th Battalion was reconstituted as the 69th Infantry Regiment two years later (September 4, 1895). In 1895, Duffy was made a supernumerary. Colonel George Moore Smith took Command of the Regiment. Smith served in the 7th Regiment for his entire career prior to becoming Commander of the 69th. The unit members did not appreciate the appointment of Smith. Furthermore, the Officers of the Regiment saw it as an attempt to denationalize the Sixty-Ninth, destroying its Irish heritage.

War with Spain

The United States declared war on Spain in the Spring of 1898. On April 27, the President called for volunteers, and the regiment was selected to enter the United States Volunteer service for two years. At the time, the Sixty-Ninth

Regiment's strength was thirty-one officers and 529 enlisted men. The Regiment consisted of ten companies. It began to recruit and organize two additional companies. On May 2, 1898, the Regiment was ordered to report at the foot of 34th Street and the East River at 10 A.M. to take a boat to Long Island City. From there, it went by the Long Island Railroad to the Camp at Hempstead Plains. Recruiting was continued to replace the men rejected by the medical officers. Shortly after the departure from the City, orders were issued for the Sixty-Ninth to prepare for the muster into Federal Service. On May 19, 1898, the Regiment was mustered into Federal service as the Sixty-Ninth Regiment, Infantry, New York Volunteers. Many visitors from Manhattan, including a large delegation from the Friendly Sons of St. Patrick, gathered to witness the ceremony. When the men took the oath which made them members of the United States Volunteer Army, a cheer rang through the field. After the muster ceremony, the Friendly Sons of St. Patrick presented the Regiment with a new stand of Colors. The stand consisted of the National and State Flags and the historic green flag of Ireland.

On May 24th, the 69th received orders to leave Camp Black and to report to General John Brooke in Chickamauga, Georgia. On Friday, May 27th, the Regiment arrived at Chickamauga National Military Park. The Regiment was assigned a camp site about two miles from Lyttle Station on the Southern Railroad. Tents were pitched that evening, and the regiment was issued thirty wagons and one hundred and twenty-one mules. While at Chickamauga, the Regiment was attached to the Second Division, Third Army Corps.

On Monday, May 30, 1898, Major-General Brooke ordered the Regiment to proceed to Tampa, Florida, and report to General Carpenter. The Regiment struck camp at Chickamauga on June 2 and took a train from Rossville Station, Georgia, to Tampa, Florida. It arrived on June 6, 1898, and pitched tents camp at Palmetto Beach. It was assigned to the Second Brigade, Third Division, Fourth Army Corps.

The soldiers had not received their military pay and allowances. In the middle of June, the Friendly Sons of St. Patrick collected approximately $2,000 for the soldiers. In a letter to John Crimmins, the Treasurer of the Friendly Sons, Colonel Duffy expressed his appreciation and thanks on behalf of the whole Regiment. The money sent by the Friendly Sons was spent on fresh meat. In comments to the New York Times, Crimmins complained about the current situation in the Regiment. He said while the Friendly Sons were willing and ready to do all they could for the soldiers in the field, they should not have to call on individuals for aid. Furthermore, it is a shame that the troops cannot get their pay from the State, and still a greater shame that they must come under incompetent men in charge of the War Department.

While in camp at Palmetto Beach, recruiting parties were sent north. They returned to the Regiment with 303 recruits. On July 24, 1898, the Regiment broke camp at Tampa and traveled to Fernandina, Florida, arriving the next day. The Regiment camped about half a mile north of the town. On August 12th, the Regiment received orders to proceed to Huntsville, Alabama. The Regiment broke camp and, in the evening, took a train for Huntsville. The Regiment was separated into two groups when it left Fernandina, but at Montgomery, the railroad found it necessary to form three sections (because of the heavier grades the trains must climb). On leaving Montgomery, Companies "E" and "G" occupied the first five cars of the first section. When the train was about eight miles west of Birmingham (near the town of Newcastle), five cars left the rails while at a high rate of speed and were dashed to pieces. The wreck occurred in a "cut" (a portion of the track with embankments on both sides).

The railroad cars were thrown against the side of the embankment with such force they flew high into the air and landed upside-down. Private Peter Farley, Company "G," was killed instantly. Sergeant Frank Glennon, Company "G," was severely injured and died enroute to the hospital.

In addition, twenty-six soldiers and one civilian teamster were injured. The injured were transported to Birmingham and admitted at Wilson and Brown Infirmary (a private institution).

On Monday, August 29th, the Regiment reached Huntsville and was ordered to camp in a beautiful farming valley about a mile west of the town. The soil was a red shale and was covered with a short, thick growth of grass. The water was from a spring, which was one of the principal attractions of this part of the State. During a review of the troops at Huntsville, the regiment made such an impressive showing that the Secretary of War mistook the men for Regulars rather than Volunteers.

In mid-October, Colonel Duffy reported on other aspects of the regiment's situation. He noted that forty-five men were in the hospital suffering from typhoid fever (contracted in Tampa). In addition, he had granted 220 furloughs because soldiers were homesick. Duffy also reported that he discharged about eighty of his men because their families depended on them. As to reports the regiment would be sent to Cuba or Puerto Rico, Duffy said the men were ready to do their duty. In November, the Regiment was assigned to the Second Brigade, First Division, Fourth Corps. The Regiment was mustered out of Federal service on January 31, 1899.

Veterans of the Irish Brigade assembled on October 29, 1910 to dedicate the statue of Father Corby of the Irish Brigade. Note the young girl wrapped in the American flag and the defiant pose of the young lad in the front row sticking his tongue out at the photographer! (Courtesy of Adams County Historical Society)

On January 7, 1901, Colonel Cavanaugh died. In 1902, a site was selected for a new armory on land obtained from the County. The new armory would be located between 25th and 26th Streets on Lexington Avenue. The cornerstone was laid in 1904. On October 12, 1906, the Sixty-Ninth Regiment was directed to take possession of its new armory on Lexington Avenue. The Sixty-Ninth Regiment Armory replaced thirty-two tenements and apartment houses that had occupied the site since the mid-nineteenth century. The competition for the design of the Sixty-Ninth Regiment Armory was won by the firm of Hunt & Hunt in 1903. The Sixty-Ninth Regiment Armory is an unusual example of what might be termed "Beaux-Arts Military" architecture.

The armory strongly reflects the Hunt brothers' training in the academic design principles of the Ecole des Beaux-Arts. The armory's symmetrical composition, monumental attic, grand arched entrance, and clearly articulated parts are characteristic of a later, more refined stage of the Beaux-Arts tradition. The bold use of form, clear expression of function, and inclusion of gun bays gives the armory a decidedly military character. The design represents a significant departure from the popular neo-medieval fortress mode identified with earlier armories.

Chapter Five
World War I

On 28 June 1914, a Serbian nationalist assassinated Archduke Franz Ferdinand, heir to the Austro-Hungarian throne, in Sarajevo. That event set in motion a series of treaties and alliances, which quickly embroiled the world in the first global war. Although Kaiser Wilhelm I, Emperor of Germany, King George V, monarch of England, and Czar Nicholas, ruler of Russia, were first cousins, these treaties and alliances set off what may well be termed as the most disastrous family argument in history.

Casualties were high on both sides. Both the Germans and the French Allies dug elaborate opposing trench lines from the North Sea to Switzerland. Despite continued heavy losses on both sides, the lines could not be advanced more than ten miles in either direction for years. The first two years of the War saw the introduction of several new weapons systems, the machine gun, fragmentation artillery shells, and poison gas. To minimize the impact of these systems, improvements were made in defensive systems. The machine gun could fire rapidly and used belt-fed ammunition. It made infantry and cavalry attacks across no man's land (the space between the opposing trenches) very costly. To more safely cross no man's land, the British introduced the Mark 1 Tank. Soon, all combatants adopted tanks. Tanks provided more protection against small arms fire, but they were slow and vulnerable to artillery. Artillery shells were filled with ball bearings (fragmentation munitions). The shells were designed to explode in the air and would cause severe head wounds. To protect soldiers' heads from shrapnel, steel helmets were introduced. Finally, the use of poison gas was the impetus to develop protective masks. Another horrific weapon which was developed and used during the first two years was the flamethrower. Little could be done to protect troops from this weapon, but its range was limited. America observed these developments closely and realized changes in military policy and training were necessary.

1916

In 1916, Congress debated eliminating the National Guard and transferring its functions to the State Police. The outcome of these debates was the Federalization of the National Guard. New York State increased recruiting and stressed training of its units. The National Guard doubled in size. In New York, a Military Training Commission composed of the President of the University of the State of New York, the Commander of the New York National Guard, a member appointed by the Board of Regents of the University of the State of New York, and a fourth member appointed by the Governor, was established. All males between the ages of 16 to 19 years (with certain exceptions) were provided military training prescribed by the Commission. The training was not more than three hours each week during the school year. New York established State Military Camps for field training. Events on the Mexican Border provided the excuse to increase the size of our military and improve the training of our military forces without signaling we were preparing to enter the War in Europe, thereby upsetting voters who believed the U.S. should remain neutral.

Mexican Border

Poncho Villa's men crossed the border into New Mexico, killing seventeen Americans. A punitive expedition, led by Gen. John Pershing, was ordered, and National Guard troops from nearly every state poured into Texas. In New York, Governor Whitman mobilized the Sixth Division and by 27 June, the first units were on their way to McAllen. The Regiment was Federalized on July 6, 1916, and departed for the Mexican Border on July 11. It was transported to McAllen, Texas, and arrived on July 19th. The War Department assigned Regular Army Officers to National Guard organizations. Colonel William Haskell was appointed Commander of the Regiment.

Haskell graduated from West Point Military in 1901. He was commissioned Second Lieutenant, Cavalry and assigned to the 9th Cavalry Regiment. He was promoted to First Lieutenant and assigned to the 4th Cavalry Regiment. He was later to be detailed to the Signal Corps. He was assigned to the 14th, 8th, and 7th Cavalry. He graduated from both the Infantry and Calvary Schools. Haskell graduated from the Command and Staff College in 1905. He was assigned Commander of the 69th on July 31, 1916. Once in command, Haskell transferred outsiders into the Regiment. Haskell's friend from Squadron A's Troop C, Latham Reed, was slotted to replace Phelan as Lieutenant Colonel. The 69th Infantry had 54 Officers and one thousand eleven enlisted soldiers on the Border.

Although the 69th New York saw no significant military action during its months along the border, its officers and men gained valuable experience for what was soon in store for them in France. When the United States declared war on Germany only a few months later, almost all the men who had served under Colonel Haskell in Texas went overseas with the Regiment. One of the men who had accompanied the 69th to Texas and who would later accompany it to Europe was Chaplain Father Duffy. Father Duffy was born in Cobourg, Ontario, Canada, in 1871. He was one of eleven children of an Irish father and an Irish Canadian mother. He completed his university education in Toronto. Duffy attended St. Joseph Seminary in Troy, New York. He was ordained in 1896. Father Duffy would become one of the most important and influential figures in the Regiment.

Another significant individual in World War I was Joyce Kilmer. Alfred Joyce Kilmer was born in New Brunswick, New Jersey, on December 6, 1886. He was named after two priests at Christ Church in East Brunswick, Alfred R. Taylor, the Curate, and the Rev. Dr. Elisha Brooks Joyce, the Rector who baptized him in the Episcopalian Faith. The Kilmer family were parishioners of Christ Church, the oldest Episcopal parish in East Brunswick. In 1913, Kilmer converted to Catholicism. Kilmer was the son of Dr. Frederick Kilmer, a chemist for the Johnson & Johnson Company credited with developing one of its best products, baby powder. His mother was Annie Kilburn, who doted on her son with an almost suffocating love. Kilmer studied at Rutgers University, then went on to Columbia, and in 1908, married Aline Murray, a poet and writer.

In 1917, Joyce as a private in the Seventh Regiment, New York Army National Guard, but he wanted to transfer to the 69th Regiment. He was already a famous poet. His most known work being "Trees." On 16th August, the transfers were marched from the Seventh Regiment Armory on Park Avenue down to the Sixty-Ninth Regiment. Kilmer was among the 355 soldiers transferred from the Seventh to the Sixty-Ninth.

In 1917, the United States had a standing army of fewer than six thousand officers and not more than one hundred and twenty thousand men. The National Guard had almost as many troops (101,174 citizen-soldiers under State control). 66,594 National Guardsmen had seen service on the Mexican border. New York was the only State to provide a division during the Mexican Border Punitive Campaign. President Woodrow Wilson's policy of neutrality continued until 1917, when Germany's policy of unrestricted submarine warfare threatened America's commercial shipping. It provided the excuse to enter the War. On April 6, 1917, the U.S. declared war on Germany. When war was declared, nearly every National Guard regiment was undermanned. It would take months before these State Militias were ready to sail for France. Each regiment in the State wanted to be the first to reach the wartime strength of 2,002 soldiers (later expanded to thirty-six hundred). At the Sixty-Ninth's armory on Lexington Avenue, a major recruiting effort was conducted. The character of the Sixty-Ninth was changed. Three days after the regiment returned from Texas, a disappointed Colonel William Haskell was mustered out as Commander and assigned to his previous duties as Inspector-Instructor of Cavalry. Lieutenant Colonel Latham Reed (the transfer from Squadron A) took over as

Acting Commander. No one knew if Reed would get the post permanently.

World War I posed an ideological problem for the predominantly Irish 69th. On Easter Monday, 1916, Ireland rebelled against British rule. The British began a round of executions of the rebel leaders. Feelings ran high on both sides of the Atlantic, and President Wilson's failure to call for a halt to the executions led to stiff opposition from Irish Americans at the polls in 1916. Despite this, when Wilson took America into the war in April 1917, the 69th was the first National Guard regiment to recruit up to full strength.

With the summer of 1917 fast approaching and the nation astir with war fever, the ranks of the Sixty-Ninth were soon swollen with enough soldiers to form a full regiment of 2,002 men and officers. The only vacancy left was at the top. Who would be Colonel? Latham Reed was unpopular among most of the officers. The old guard in the Regiment feared the appointment of a complete stranger, another non-Irish, non-Catholic outsider. The War Department moved slowly, perhaps because it had to make another decision that would affect every regiment in New York City. Word reached New York that a new division of National Guardsmen was to be organized, and once completed and trained, it would be the first of the country's militia to sail for France. The new division dubbed the "Rainbow," New York would have the honor of furnishing one of its infantry regiments.

Several of the city's regiments were worthy of selection. Certainly, the Seventh Regiment had earned the right as the oldest National Guard regiment in the country. The Sixty-Ninth also had an inside track. Its Civil War record, when Gen. Robert E. Lee called the regiment the "Fighting Sixty-Ninth," gave it a more than even chance on its selection. Once Secretary of War Baker had made the decision to form the Rainbow Division, he named General Mann to command it. Colonels Michael Lenihan and Robert Brown were promoted to Brigadier General and selected to command the Division's Eighty-third and Eighty-fourth Brigades.

The Sixty-Ninth was visited by Martin Sheridan, arguably America's finest athlete. Sheridan was a police detective and member of the Irish American Athletic Club. Sheridan won nine Olympic medals, five of them gold. He was born in County Mayo. During the 1918 Olympic Games in London, the U.S. team marched past the king of England. Although the modem Olympic Games were still new, tradition held that all countries parading before the host country's head of state dip their flags. The American flag was held by a shot-putter, Ralph Rose. Sheridan convinced Rose and the American team that "This flag dips to no earthly king!" The next day, as teams from more than thirty countries marched past King Edward VII (who, in 1860, when he was the Prince of Wales, had been snubbed by Michael Corcoran's Sixty-Ninth Regiment), all flags dipped respectfully. But when the American contingent strode by, Rose held the Stars and Stripes high with one hand. Since then, the United States has never dipped its flag at the Olympic Games.

After their meeting with Sheridan, the Regiment went to the Polo Grounds for a Sunday baseball game between the New York Giants and the Cincinnati Reds. The game was sponsored by the Friendly Sons of St. Patrick for the benefit of the Regiment's needy families. After the game, the Regiment traveled by train to Hempstead Plains. The Camp Mills was one hundred twenty acres on what is known as Hempstead Plains. It had been built over the site of another training area, Camp Black, where troops headed for Cuba in 1898 and received training.

Several of the older veterans of the Sixty-Ninth were familiar with the site because they had been sent there when the Regiment had been mustered into service during the Spanish-American War. Army engineers reconstructed Camp Mills as a place to train thousands of soldiers in modem warfare. Camp Mills was named in honor of the late Albert Mills, a Congressional Medal of Honor recipient during the Spanish-American War. Although temporarily blinded, Mills rallied his men. Afterward, he was assigned as the superintendent of the U.S. Military Academy. Before he died in 1916, he drew up plans for federalizing the National Guard.

The 69th Regiment (now the 165th Infantry) was the first contingent of the Forty-second Division to arrive at Camp Mills. (When the 69th was Federalized, New York State formed the 69th Regiment, New York Guard, to take their place). Units from Wisconsin and Ohio (which, along with the Sixty-Ninth, would complete the Eighty-Third Infantry Brigade) had been delayed but were expected within the week. Transfers from New York's other regiments were due in a few days. Their arrival would mean trouble, and so would the arrival of the 167th Infantry, the old Fourth Alabama. The Regiment had last met the Fourth Alabama on the battlefield at Bull Run and Gettysburg.

After the first night, Father Francis Duffy remarked the Old 69th was tenting on the Hempstead Plains, where Colonel Edward Duffy and the old 69th encamped in 1898 when getting ready for service in the Spanish War. It is a huge regiment, now bigger than the whole Irish Brigade ever was in the Civil War. And the Regiment was getting bigger, and so were its problems. Men from other regiments poured into Mills, many of them angry because they had been transferred from their own regiment without their consent.

They had enlisted with friends and expected to stay with them. Getting unceremoniously transferred to the Sixty-Ninth was not part of their plans. Bitter feelings were everywhere, even among the men of the 165th, who felt many of the new soldiers were inferior physically and mentally.

Several regiments transferred their problem soldiers rather than their best. Soon, the regiment reached full strength of enlisted men (three thousand six hundred). However, the Regiment was still short of the required number of officers. On 28th August, two hundred soldiers from the 165th deserted. Three-quarters of them fled back to the Fourteenth's encampment at Sheepshead Bay.

The 167th Infantry (the old 4th Alabama) arrived at Camp Mills on 28 August. What happened when they reached Hempstead Plains almost started a second war between the states. The soldiers from the 69th began to jeer at the Southern boys, calling them boll weevils. A fight broke out between the two regiments. A few days later, two companies of the 167th broke past their own guards and attacked the guards of the 165th. The fight between the New Yorkers and the Alabamians raged for several minutes and ended with the Southerners being forced back to the Alabama camp. The fights between the two regiments were referred to as the last battle of the Civil War.

The Alabamians were ready to fight anyone, especially blacks, and within days of their arrival, several of them went into nearby Hempstead and attacked every dark-skinned person they saw. Later, an epidemic of measles, mumps, and meningitis broke out in the 167th, and the soldiers were quarantined. That quarantine made them testy. The ban was not lifted for six weeks. The epidemic proved costly, and a handful of the 167th soldiers died.

Oliver Ames was among a group who, as soon as they were commissioned, joined the 165th Infantry. He was a graduate of Harvard University and came from a family that had changed the course of American history. It provided much of the management, funding, and tools for the construction of the first transcontinental railroad. Ames' great-grandfather was president of the Union Pacific Railroad. Members of his family served as the Governor of Massachusetts, Congressman, and U.S. Senators. The Ames family traced their descendants back to the Mayflower and were related to former President Theodore Roosevelt.

At Harvard, Oliver joined the "Harvard Regiment" made up of over one thousand student-soldiers (precursor of the Reserve Officer Training Corps (ROTC)). Ames went to an Officer's Candidate training camp in Plattsburgh, New York, in 1917. Two other Princeton men who on the Mexican border transferred into the Sixty-Ninth Regiment, Charles Baker and Van S. Merle-Smith.

In 1917, training in Plattsburgh was divided regionally. The first officer candidates came from New York City. The first contingent of fourteen companies arrived on 12 May. The second group started two days later. Out of the total number who graduated, eleven were assigned lieutenants in the 165th Infantry. The group included Basil Beebe Elmer, son of a prominent professor at Cornell University (where Basil recently earned his degree), Harper Silliman, the grandson of the publisher of Harper's magazine, Howard Arnold, son of the president of Arnold, Schiff & Company, (manufacturer of parasols), (Arnold was one of the few Jewish officers in the regiment), William Given Jr. (also a Yale man), Francis Joseph McNamara, Beverly Becker, Henry Crawford, Philip Lacy, Raymond Newton, Horace Stokes, (son of the head of the publishing house of Frederick A. Stokes & Company), and Arthur Bunnell, (a Williams College graduate).

As more and more officers filled the ranks of the 165th, daily drills intensified. Other units of the Rainbow Division arrived, including the 166th Infantry from Ohio (the old Fourth Ohio Regiment) and the 150th Machine Gun Battalion from Wisconsin (three companies of the old Second Wisconsin), completing the make-up of the Eighty-third

Infantry Brigade. Michael Lenihan was fifty-two years old. He graduated from West Point and had known Generals Ulysses Grant and Philip Sheridan. The 165th Infantry approved of him. He was Irish and a devout Catholic. Sometimes Lenihan would surprise Father Duffy by serving as an altar boy at morning mass. The troops genuinely liked him and called him "General Mike."

The 166th Infantry Regiment was a relatively new National Guard unit. It was headquartered in Columbus, Ohio, and commanded by Col. Benson Hough, affectionately called the "Old Man." On 9 September, the 166th arrived at Camp Mills. The 150th Machine Gun Battalion arrived at Mills a few days before the 166th.

From-the moment the 165th departed its armory to train at Camp Mills, Major William Donovan (Wild Bill), a former Columbia University athlete, was determined to whip the men of the First Battalion into physical shape. He attempted to train his men for open warfare by all kinds of unique approaches. The soldiers began to call him Wild Bill (a name he was called at Columbia for his athletic ability) after he led them on a cross-country run for four miles. His men admired him all the same, for he was the fastest man in the unit. In another instance, Donovan divided his battalion into two sides of five hundred men each. He had them take off their shirts and attack each other. The maneuver will be just like a great football game, he informed his operations officer. I am having the men go through this thing shirtless so that they will get accustomed to the impact of flesh against flesh. There is a lot of that ahead of them.

Donovan had a pair of tough officers and an eccentric sergeant to assist him. The sergeant was Jay Casey of "C" Company. He pushed his men forward in training by cracking a bullwhip over their heads. The "B" Company Commander, Captain Tom Reilley (a football coach at New York University and Columbia), taught the men the rudiments of running and hurdling. In "C" Company, Donovan had Captain William Kennelly, a real-estate tycoon (who once had been listed as among New York's handsomest bachelor millionaires). Donovan ordered over two hundred boxing gloves and was anxious for them to arrive so he could begin teaching them the finer points of pugilism.

Donovan believed soldiers must learn it's possible to fight even if they are hurting. Donovan wanted every man to be able to stand up and take punishment like a real fighter. He felt the boxing would do just that. He wanted his men to be sluggers who laugh at pain and bruises. He was trying to prepare them for that day ahead when they would need every ounce of their endurance and courage. Another of the Battalion's professional boxers was "D" Company's Richard O'Neill. He was only eighteen when he enlisted in the Sixty-Ninth in June of 1916. He was one of thirteen children. The O'Neills lived near the Johnson family (Norwegians and non-Catholics). The Johnsons had a beautiful daughter, Estelle, and she was O'Neill's girlfriend. Richard decided to join the Sixty-Ninth because he believed there was something special about the old Sixty-Ninth. Another reason was that "D" Company's First Sergeant, Edward Geaney, was his brother-in-law. O'Neill was awarded the Medal of Honor.

When President Roosevelt heard about the First Battalion's instruction in the art of self-defense, he invited all the commanding officers to his home at Sagamore Hill for a party. The officers were Donovan, Kennelly, Reilley, Captain George McAdie ("A" Company), and Captain James McKenna ("D" Company). Captain George McAdie, Commander of "A" was Scottish. Father Duffy described him as "my kind of Scott-like a volcano, rugged to outward view, but glowing with fire beneath. Roosevelt was comforted because he saw in them good fighting stuff. He admitted to his son, Archie, that the Major (Donovan) could have easily been a Lieutenant Colonel. Physical fitness was one of the priorities that Major General William Mann (42nd Division Commander) and Colonel Douglas MacArthur (Chief of Staff) had set for the division, and Donovan had followed through on that priority the moment he set foot in camp.

While the First battalion strained and sweated under Donovan's regiment, it seems that the Third Battalion was having it easy. So much so that Corporal Martin Hogan found camp life "routine." In his memoirs, he used routine in three successive sentences to describe what went on. He also noted the Regiment had almost no marksmanship training at Camp Mills. Hogan believed the amount of training the Rainbow Division received before deploying was very greatly exaggerated.

The Third (Shamrock) Battalion's "I" Company had a boxer who could have defeated any of Donovan's boys in the ring. Big Mike Donaldson from Haverstraw, New York, worked in the brickyards along the Hudson River. He was built solid as a ship with shoulders as wide as anyone's in the Regiment. As a young man, he fought the middleweight champion Stanley Ketchell. Big Mike so impressed the great middleweight that, according to local legend, Donaldson wound up as his sparring partner. Donaldson also had one thing that no other man in the old Sixty-Ninth had. He knew Duffy longer than anyone. In 1897, Donaldson went to St. Peter's Church in Haverstraw. St. Peter's Haverstraw was Father Duffy's first parish. Although he stayed there less than a year, Father Duffy remembered the powerful youngster who, along with O'Neill, the other prizefighter in "D" Company, would distinguish himself in battle. Duffy wrote he had an old friend in Camp, Mike Donaldson. Mike was an altar boy of mine in Haverstraw not long after I was ordained. We both left there. I went on to teach metaphysics, and Mike went into the prize-ring. He became much more widely and favorably known to his fellow citizens than I can ever hope to be.

If anyone was Big Mike's antithesis, it was the poet Joyce Kilmer. After weeks of wrangling and wondering, his transfer from the old Seventh Regiment to the 165th Infantry came through. However, it was at a time of terrible suffering for Kilmer. His daughter, Rose, died of infantile paralysis. Kilmer wrote in a letter to Father Duffy when he arrived at Camp Mills, I am, as you know, a member of the 165th Infantry, U. S., (formerly the 69th New York) as I have transferred from Company "H" and exchanged 8 hours a day of violent physical exercise almost deadening to the brain (but useful for me, after my grief), to Headquarters Company for exacting but interesting statistical work. I have been assigned Senior Regimental Statistician, but despite this title, I am still a Private. At the time of Rose's death, Kilmer's wife, Aline, was in the hospital awaiting the birth of another child, a son named Christopher. He was born three weeks after Rose's funeral. A week after Joyce settled in with his new Regiment, his parents visited him at Camp Mills.

"Orders at last," Father Francis Duffy wrote in his diary on 28 October. Orders for the Division's departure. The men left from the ports of New York, Hoboken, and Montreal on different dates. The first contingent, including the Division Headquarters and the 166th Infantry from Ohio, left on the night of 18th October with only a little training in weaponry and barely enough uniforms to go around. Winter was coming, and the soldiers still needed sweaters, mufflers, and winter socks. The boots which were issued were of inferior quality. The Division Chief of Staff, Douglas MacArthur, sailed on the Covington for St. Nazaire. By the time the 165th left Camp Mills, it was the end of October. Father Duffy recalled how Major William Donovan's First Battalion slipped out quietly in the night, bound for Montreal. Duffy accompanied Donovan's men to Canada and then returned to sail a few days later from Hoboken.

Before the Regiment departed Long Island, families and friends came to Camp Mills for a last good-bye. A farewell dance was held at the Garden City Hotel. Officers and their wives or sweethearts danced slowly around the crowded ballroom. At eleven PM, a bugler strode into the ballroom and blew "Taps." Colonel Charles Hine then ordered the orchestra to play "Send Me Away with a Smile." When the song ended, "Taps" was played again. Duffy noted in his diary the throats of the soldiers tightened, and the women cried.

The last Battalion to leave Camp Mills was the Third Battalion (Shamrock Battalion), commanded by Major Timothy Moynahan. Father Duffy liked Moynahan and described him as the ideal Irish soldier, born-trim, erect, handsome, active in his movements, commanding, and crisp in his orders. A vivid, interesting character in our drab modern life. He has one fault: a flaring Irish temper when military discipline is violated, or high ideals belittled. The Shamrock Battalion boarded the "America," a captured German transport originally named "Amerika." The entire "Rainbow" Division sailed across the North Atlantic in different convoys. Like the 69th, many of the regiments in the Division were split up and sailed on different ships.

France March

The ships used separate sea-lanes to avoid German U-boats. Transports headed for Brest while others sailed to Liverpool. In the end, they all met in France. Donovan sailed on the "Tunisian," a passenger liner and not a troop transport. Most of the crew were teenagers. Donovan detailed his men to the galley to help serve food. Donovan insisted on boxing lessons for all his men, and they spared together every afternoon. During the time the Forty-Second Division was sailing to France, events in Russia were changing the course of the war threatening the chances for Allied victory. The Bolsheviks gained control in Russia. With Germany's assistance, Lenin returned to Russia and assumed power. He negotiated a separate armistice with Germany. This allowed Germany to shift divisions from the eastern front to the west. The German military now had numerical superiority over England, France, and Belgium (136,000 officers and three and a half million men).

Germany planned a massive offensive to end the war before the American forces would be deployed. From 24th October until 12th November, a combined Austrian and German army inflicted severe casualties on the Italians at Caporetto. The dismayed Allies realized they needed a Supreme War Council to provide unity of command. General Ferdinand Foch was named Commander-in-Chief of Allied forces.

The Forty-Second Division landed in France early in November. The Division was sent to the training area at Vaucoleurs. It was billeted in the surrounding villages (Broussey, Naives, Sauvoy, Vacon, and Villeroy-sur-Meholle). The towns were about forty miles west of the Luneville Sector (twenty-five miles south of the Argonne Forest). The arrival of the Rainbow Division gave General John Pershing a total of 125,000 men on the ground in France. The Allies (especially France) wanted to use the American soldiers as fillers for their weakened divisions. Pershing disapproved of the concept. He wanted to keep his divisions together.

The First Battalion arrived in Liverpool on 10th November. The rest of the Regiment steamed through a thick fog into Brest. They were held on the transports for over a week. Donovan and the First Battalion took a train from Liverpool to Southampton, and from there, they sailed across the English Channel to Le Havre. They boarded a cramped French troop train for the 250-mile trip to Vaucoleurs. The Battalion arrived on November 15th in the training area at Vaucoleurs. When the rest of the Regiment finally landed at Brest, they boarded troop trains with the famous "40 Hommes 8 Cheveaux" (40 men, 8 horses) painted on the sides of the boxcars. The men called the boxcars "hommies" and "chevoos."

The training area was close enough to the front lines that the soldiers could hear the rumble of artillery. In early December, as training intensified, so did the weather. On the 19th of December, Major General William Mann was replaced as Commander of the Rainbow Division by Charles Menoher. A rumor Colonel Hine would be next because a report criticized his failure to prepare his men for battle. The Division's uniforms (including hob-nailed boots) were in wretched condition. Equipment (including clothing) had to be shipped overland by train and was slow to reach his troops. Rumor had Lieutenant Colonel Latham Reed would be relieved as well.

The division was ordered to the Seventh Training Area at Rolampont. It was sent be sent to Grand (about fifteen miles southwest of Vaucouleurs), until after Christmas. The

165th Infantry's departure date was the day after Christmas. The march to the village of Longeau, south of Rolampont, was an eighty-mile trek through the foothills of the Vosges mountains to the banks of the Marne River. It would be long, cold, and legendary.

Father Duffy celebrated a midnight Mass on Christmas. Although the church in Grand was small, Duffy felt most of the Regiment could squeeze into it. The church was seven hundred years old, with a watchtower made of stone seven-feet thick. Joyce Kilmer and Private Frank Driscoll (an ex-Jesuit novice from Duffy's old parish in the Bronx) helped get the Church ready. Duffy placed the Regimental colors, along with the French Tricolor, in the front of the Church near the Altar. He asked the Regimental band and a few French violinists to provide the music. Knowing he couldn't hear everyone's confession or communion by himself, he asked the church's curate, another priest, and the chaplain from an artillery unit to help. When the church was ready, Father Duffy asked one of the soldiers how he felt about a French priest (who couldn't speak English) hearing his confession. The soldier said it was fine since all he could do was give me a penance, but you'd have given me hell.

On Christmas Eve, a heavy snow fell in the Meuse Valley. During the Mass, Brigadier General William Lenihan and Colonel Charles Hine and their staffs sat in the Sanctuary. After Father Duffy's sermon, the soldiers sang "The Little Town of Bethlehem," "The Snow Lay on the Ground," and "Oh, Come All Ye Faithful," Communion (even with three priests) took hours. The Mass was over at 2 AM. Father Duffy was pleased the Regiment celebrated Christmas in high and holy fashion.

On the morning of December 26th, the Regiment broke camp for its long march to its final training area. Snow swirled around, shivering soldiers as temperatures plummeted to near zero. The Regiment would remember the march as their Valley Forge. Things started out badly but got much worse. The food and supplies were carried by three-ton French wagons pulled by mules. The route was treacherous, with steep grades. The mules were not shod for winter, and many were not even broken in. To make matters worse, many of the harnesses didn't fit the mules. When the convoy reached a steep incline (over 3 miles long), the wagons got stuck in the snow and could go no further. By the time the convoy reached the village where the troops were billeted, the soldiers were already marching out.

The troops were issued hobnailed boots, which soon deteriorated. The boots absorbed water and shrunk when they dried. The Regiment had to cross the Vosges Mountains in a blizzard without eating breakfast. Noon mess was a slice of bread and hardtack. After the Regiment had marched a few miles, their hobnailed shoes began to fall apart. Kilmer described how desperate the march was. He wrote soldiers would crush their bleeding feet into their frozen, broken hobnails. In the morning, without breakfast, they would start out with a song on their lips. They had to climb the foothills of the Vosges Mountains through a blizzard. At noon (shifting their feet about to keep the blood moving), they would (if it was one of the lucky days) have a slice of bread or two pieces of hardtack for noon mess. At night, they would sleep instead of eating supper.

As the frozen, tired soldiers trudged through the deep snow, the wind whipped against their numbed cheeks. The mess wagons could not keep up with the marchers and arrived in the villages hours after the men had found their billets and crashed for the night. The mule-drawn mess wagons kept falling farther and farther behind. The first day, it was six miles; the next day, ten. For the men on foot, there were no reserve rations. It meant the soldiers went hungry. When the wagons finally clattered into the villages where the men were billeted (in attics or barn lofts or in stables, stretched out on cold stone or wooden floors or on smelly straw), it was after midnight. Most of the men were too tired to eat. They waited until four in the morning when breakfast was served (which was only rice mixed with a syrup, bacon, bread, and coffee). The tramping soldiers begged for food from the French villagers who lined the way to watch the first Americans soldiers pass by. They were ragged, shivering, and starving. Each day's march covered between fifteen and twenty miles.

Donovan was at a field officer's school for five weeks and missed the long, miserable march. Colonel John Barker took Command of the Regiment. While Donovan was still at school, Barker arrived in Longeau. He was forty-six years old and a graduate of the U.S. Military Academy at West Point. He was a hero of the Spanish-American War and the Moro uprising in the Philippines. He earned three silver stars. When Pershing reached Paris in the summer of 1917, Barker was there to greet him. One of the first things Colonel Barker did upon taking Command of the 165th Infantry was call for an investigation of the deplorable conditions. He appointed Major George Lawrence (Medical Corps) and

Major William Stacom (Second Battalion Commander) to investigate the plight of the men and report back to him. Doctor Lawrence found that the enlisted men had been without a change of clothing, including underwear, for two months. 40% of the men had worn-out shoes and there were none to be issued. Barker forwarded Lawrence's report through the chain of command to the Division Commander. Major Stacom stated the condition of the clothing was poor. In his report to the new Division Commander, Colonel Barker focused on four things: living conditions, clothing, cleanliness, and morale. The shoes were unserviceable and ill-fitting. The men were filthy, although showers had been erected for them. He complained too many men had long hair. He felt morale was not too bad but noted that the lack of clothing and facilities for general cleanup following a painful march had taken much out of the men. The Regiment was ill-equipped in all areas.

Once again, events in Ireland would impact the Regiment. In 1916, the Irish would again rebel against English rule. The English responded with their typical draconian measures. They shot 16 of the leaders and imposed additional hardships on the Irish people. The rebellion, which began on Easter Monday, 1916, was not popular with the Irish. When the 1,000 rebels marched on Dublin, there were over 100,000 Irish fighting in the British

Army in France. However, the assignation of the leaders of the Easter Rebellion galvanized the Irish against English rule. The rebellion spread to the entire country.

In early 1918, the Regiment received new weapons and uniforms. The uniforms were a big problem. The uniforms were shipped from the British zone. When the crates were opened, the troops found the new uniforms were British with brass buttons with the crown of England imprinted on them. Soldiers threw the uniforms on the ground. In 1918, Ireland was at war with England, fighting for Irish freedom. Father Duffy, who declared himself an Irish Republican, was in "H" Company area the day the British uniforms were issued. He saw soldiers destroying the uniforms and warned them not to destroy government property. Duffy approached Colonel Barker, who was unconcerned. He said to Duffy they would have no problem wearing British shoes, would they. "No," the Priest quickly shot back. "They'd have the satisfaction of stamping on them."

Barker was shocked by the Chaplain's sharp reply. He felt Pershing had dumped him into a nest of Irish malcontents. They were dressed in filthy rags and worthless shoes, but they grumbled about new uniforms. Duffy explained to Barker the Regiment did not have divided loyalty or dubious reliability. Duffy said there were soldiers in the Regiment who left Ireland to avoid service in the

British Army. But as soon as the United States went to war, these men, though not yet citizens, volunteered to fight for America. Duffy said we have our racial feelings, but these do not interfere with our loyalty to the United States. He asked Barker how he would feel if he was issued a German helmet and told to wear it. Barker slammed the table angrily at the thought of wearing a German helmet. He assured his Chaplain that the men would receive American uniforms. Some of the Irish soldiers in the Regiment had built a bonfire to burn the uniforms. Duffy calmed them down. The button mutiny was quelled when officers and men struck a compromise. The British buttons were cut off and replaced by American buttons. This settled the men down.

New officers arrived to bolster the 165th Infantry. Among them was Lieutenant Basil Elmer and his friend, Lieutenant Oliver Ames. Elmer was promoted to Captain and told to organize the Regiment's Intelligence Section. Lieutenant Oliver Ames was assigned to Major Donovan's First Battalion as Adjutant. The relationship between Donovan and Ames grew stronger with each day. The Major worked the young Adjutant hard. Donovan's pace was fast and furious. He kept Ames up until one or two every morning. The Intelligence Section under Lieutenant Elmer was small. The staff was an eclectic group.

Among them were John Livingstone Mott, Leonard Beck, Edwin Titterton, and Bill Levinson (who spoke French fluently). Watson, Beck, and Titterton were Seventh Regiment transfers. Captain Elmer assigned a member of the Intelligence Section to accompany each night patrol outside the wire. The section was a close-knit group. They performed dangerous work but no more than necessary. Captain Elmer turned a blind eye when they slipped into a nearby village for a glass of wine or a beer. Joyce Kilmer didn't join the group for several months, but when he did, the tight-knit group resented his intrusion. They disliked the fact they were still Privates First Class while Kilmer was a Sergeant. Furthermore, the group believed Kilmer took his rank too seriously.

In mid-February, while training in the Rolampont area, the Forty-second Division received orders attaching it to the French VII Army. Officially, the Division was part of the First U.S. Army Corps under Major General Hunter Liggett. The French Army had dug in along a front from the village of Luneville to the village of Baccarat. The 165th reported to the 164th French Division. The sector assigned to the Regiment was about thirty kilometers southeast of Nancy and included Luneville and a subsector called Chussaille-Rouge Bouquet. Getting there meant the Regiment had to re-cross the Vosges Mountains, a trek of more than one hundred thirty miles. This time, however, the men rode in trains. The trains left Langres on February 16th and arrived in Luneville the following day.

Before boarding the troop train to Luneville, Private Tom Shannon and his friend Private Frank Hays (both of "I" Company) got into serious trouble. Shannon had his story portrayed in the 1940 movie "The Fighting 69th" (James Cagney played Shannon in his role as Jerry Plunkett). In the villages around Langres, local priests sold a home-brew liquor called "Palestine." Shannon had no idea the potency of the homebrew would lead to a court-martial, which, if found guilty, could mean his execution by firing squad. The Commander of Company "I," Captain Ryan, posted guards to keep his men out of the priests' distilleries. The guards were ordered to stop soldiers from dealing with the priests who sold the liquor.

On February 15th, Private Hays went to buy liquor from one of the priests. He didn't have enough money, and the priest refused to give it to him. Hays went back to his billet and complained to Shannon. Shannon (who had three convictions for being absent without leave) grabbed his rifle and went to see the priest. Shannon, who was already drunk, staggered into the street. The Corporal of the Guard heard the bolt of a rifle snap shut and saw Shannon aiming his rifle in the direction of the priest. A bullet winged past the priest, who quickly gave Shannon the liquor. Captain Ryan arrested Shannon and requested a court-martial be convened. The Officers of the Court found Shannon guilty and sentenced that he be dishonorably discharged.

Father Duffy intervened on Shannon's behalf, pleading that he stay in the Sixty-Ninth. In the movie, Shannon is portrayed by James Cagney as a wise-cracking coward whose fear in the front lines led to the death of several men. Plunket dies a hero's death. The movie is roughly based on Father Duffy's book, "The Father Duffy Story". The one truth in the way the movie portrayed the incident was that Shannon did die a hero's death. During the Battle of the Ourcq River, Shannon was killed when he advanced under heavy machine-gun fire.

Rouge Bouquet

Rouge Bouquet Chaussailles was a subsector about 10 miles east of Luneville. It was a wooded area with twisted trenches. The floors of muddy trenches were covered with wood planks so soldiers wouldn't sink in the mud. The trenches had deep dugout shelters shored up by timber, which could accommodate about 40 men. The Regiment was ordered to Camp New York (in the forest around Croixmare) prior to entering the trenches (under French supervision). The Regiment's stay in the trenches was to be brief, only to orient them to trench warfare. Each battalion would spend ten days in the trenches along with French units. The first unit in the trenches was the Donovan's First Battalion.

On the morning of February 27th, Donovan entered the trench complex. Rain and sleet fell on the soldiers. Trees toppled by shellfire lay across the trenches. The soldiers of the First Battalion experienced their pounding of artillery. Donovan established his command post and a first-aid station. Company Commanders cautioned their men to keep down, be quiet, and not let curiosity get the best of them. The German artillery assault was relentless. Soldiers of the Second and Third Battalions were held in reserve.

On 5th March, Oliver Ames sent an intelligence report to Company Commanders in the First Battalion. The report informed them the 42nd Division had first combat deaths. During the night of March 4th, 1918, a heavy bombardment hit the 168th Infantry. One Captain, one Corporal, and 5 Privates were killed, and 10 soldiers were wounded. The report stated that after the artillery bombardment, Germans attacked the 168th's position. The enemy was repulsed, but no prisoners were taken. The First Battalion suffered its own casualties while in the trenches, but no one was killed.

Major William Stacom's Second Battalion relieved Major Donovan's First Battalion. Companies "E," "F," "G," and "H" left for Camp New York on March 1st. The men carried two days' of rations and one blanket each. Like the soldiers of the First Battalion, the troops were on edge. Father Duffy stood in the muddy square and put his arm around each man as he passed. The sub-sector assigned to "E" Company was Rezonville, Patte d'Oie and Rocroi. Company "E" relieved the soldiers of Company "A." Rocroi was an eight-hundred-yard front which ran up hill to an observation post.

Along that stretch of trenches, there were four dugouts. Three of them were in poor shape (only held together by rotting timber). Not only were the dugouts in disrepair, but they had also been constructed on the forward face of Rocroi hill (within sight of enemy guns) instead of being located on the reverse slope. The "A" Company Commander assigned Sergeants to each "E" Company platoon to escort the soldiers to their posts and brief them on their duties. The Germans, who were just across no-man's land, watched and waited. Sergeant O'Connell of "A" Company was assigned to assist the First Platoon. He explained to Lieutenant Norman's (Platoon Commander's) soldiers how they should hold their positions in case of attack. O'Connell divided Norman's platoon, assigning thirty men to Dugout Number One (the largest of the underground shelters) and fifteen men to Dugout Number Two.

The air in Dugout One stank of dank earth, stale mustard gas, and sweaty men. When O'Connell got the Platoon organized, he reported back to Lieutenant Norman. Norman took down notes and seemed pleased. As Norman and O'Connell headed to the platoon command post, O'Connell noticed the men were now outside. They were airing their straw bed sacks on top of the trench wall. Sergeant O'Connell advised Lieutenant Norman he'd better tell his men to remove the bed sacks and get back inside the dugouts immediately. Snipers were in the woods and could easily pick them off. Norman did and invited Sergeant O'Connell to eat lunch with his platoon. O'Connell accepted. After lunch, O'Connell ran into Sergeant Spencer Rossell (another Company "A" non-commissioned officer), who had been assigned to assist the Second Platoon. Sergeant Rossell told O'Connell he was heading to the YMCA store for candy and cigarettes. O'Connell asked Lieutenant Norman if he could accompany Rossell. Norman said yes. Leaving with Rossell saved O'Connell's life.

Around two o'clock in the afternoon, the Allied artillery fired on the German defenses. The men of the First Platoon dashed out of their dugouts to view the spectacle. An hour later, the Germans fired back. Lieutenant Norman, who had been momentarily buried in debris and was slightly wounded, ordered his platoon back inside the dugout. The men grudgingly went, heading down the steep stairway which descended forty feet beneath the ground. The German artillery bombardment lasted through the afternoon and into the evening. With each explosion, the dugout shuddered, rotten timbers quaked, and dirt fell from above. Private Drain looked anxiously at the shaky earthen ceiling. Not liking what he saw, he slipped under a bunk stacked against the dugout wall. Sergeant Helmer watched Drain disappear under the bunk. Lieutenant Norman reminded his men that when the shelling ended, they were to go up into their positions in the trenches. No sooner had he issued his order a huge shell hit the dugout roof. The explosion was enormous. It rocked the ground above the dugout. Rotten beams gave way, and the ceiling fell. Tons of earth fell into the dugout. Sergeant Helmer found himself in the doorway of the forward entrance.

When Sergeants O'Connell and Rossell reached the YMCA store, they found it was closed. Heading back to their command posts, they ran into Lieutenant Arthur

Cunningham, who informed them that the telephone lines in that sector had been destroyed. Over the horrific noise of exploding shells, O'Connell heard from a platoon sergeant about the destruction of Dugout Number One. Sergeants O'Connell and Rossell ran into the trenches to where "E" Company was stationed.

O'Connell discovered that at Dugout Number Two, all fifteen men were alive but dazed. All right, O'Connell said to one of the "E" Company NCOs, you hold all the men here and have them ready so that when the barrage lifts, they will take the positions to repel any possible enemy attack. O'Connell worked his way to the demolished dugout. There were a few men outside, and they said that Norman and his men were dead. However, inside Dugout Number One, half the soldiers survived the cave-in, but there was no way out. The two entrances were blocked. The survivors moaned and wept. Sergeant Helmer from "E" Company was half buried in the front stairway. He had enough air for him to breathe, but he was pinned by a broken hunk of timber that had fallen on his leg. Dirt drifted down on him, slowly filling the dugout below.

Helmer realized that his body shielded Private Raymond and Private McCormack from the rising dirt that slid down the dugout entrance. One of the heavier beams had dropped on Private Ellinger's shoulders. He prayed aloud and struggled to hold it up so it wouldn't fall on the men trapped below him. Unable to hold the beam, dirt covered his face, and he suffocated and died. Deeper into the dugout, Lieutenant Norman, his stomach pierced by a fallen timber, was curled up on a bunk. Some of the frightened survivors huddled around him in the pitch dark. The stench of earth and gas-filled their nostrils. We are fighting for a good cause, Norman said. Let us die like men. Under his bunk, Private Drain (his leg broken) encouraged the men. He said they'd be saved. The men outside would not let them suffocate. In no time, they'd be dug out and brought up into the fresh air.

Major Marion Battle, the Division's Assistant Adjutant, was in the Battalion's Command Post along with Major Donovan (who was carrying his blackthorn stick, one of the Regiment's several traditions) when word reached them that Lieutenant Norman's platoon had been wiped out. Donovan asked for permission to go there and make an accurate assessment of the damage. He also wanted to assist in rescue attempts. Major Battle refused to let him go. Majors were not expendable, he said. Instead, send a Lieutenant. When Major Battle left, Donovan said to Major Stacom that he was going to Rocroi. Major Stacom said he should. On reaching the sub-sector (amid the constant enemy shelling), Donovan told the men to find entrenching tools. He put together a rescue party and started digging.

Helmer recalled the lack of air took its toll inside the dugout. Choking dust and gas stench filled the suffocating darkness. Pinned at the stairwell, Helmer prepared to die. As each of his comrades died, Helmer saw something in the pitch dark that he kept to himself for years. He swore that a faint purple light rose slowly from the body of each dead soldier toward the ceiling of the dugout, where it disappeared. Above the cave-in, men dug furiously. The shelling was constant. Helmer had resigned himself to the fact that he and everyone entombed with him were going to die. Helmer felt the deadly grip of dirt around his body loosen and fall away. He was almost free. He thought his only chance was to cut off his trapped foot. He had a pocketknife that could do the job. But Private Raymond refused to be rescued until he found a way to free Helmer's foot from under the timber. The timber was lifted, and Helmer was dragged out of the dugout. Helmer thought his nightmare was over as he and three men were sent back to the Company Command post. A shell exploded next to him, killing Private Edward Kelly and wounding Private Stephen Navin. After escorting Navin to a medical clearing station, Helmer reached the Command Post and reported to Cavanaugh. Then he broke down, his body trembling. He wept uncontrollably. After he pulled himself together, Helmer went back to try to save the soldiers still trapped.

Constant shelling thwarted the rescue effort. With each explosion, the ground shook, and more of the walls of the dugout collapsed. Helmer prayed that at least Drain be saved. As he rejoined the men digging at the entrance, he could see the row of bunks under which the private had crawled. He yelled at the rescuers that they had to get Drain out first. But Drain, still clinging to the hope that everyone would be saved, yelled back, don't bother with me, get the other fellows. Another shell then rocked the ground, and an avalanche of earth closed the opening, entombing the men once again. From beneath the tons of earth came the muffled, despairing whisperings of the few men still alive. Donovan shouted down to them; we will get you out. We will get you out. But Donovan knew that nothing more could be done and that this would be their tomb.

Twenty-one men were killed in the cave-in. The dead who had been pulled out of the dugout were buried in a small cemetery in the village of Croixmare. The rest were left were they died. Father Duffy was grateful that before the soldiers had gone into the trenches, he'd heard their confessions. He went to the caved-in dugout, read the services for the dead, and blessed the spot where his boys were now entombed.

Joyce Kilmer immortalized the incident in his poem "Rouge Bouquet."

In a wood, they call the Rouge Bouquet
There is a new-made grave to-day,
Built by never a spade nor pick
Yet covered with earth ten meters thick.
There lie many fighting men,
Dead in their youthful prime,
Never to laugh nor love again
Nor taste the Summertime.

For Death came flying through the air
And stopped his flight at the dugout stair,
Touched his prey and left them there,
Clay to clay. He hid their bodies stealthily
In the soil of the land, they fought to free
And fled away.

Now over the grave, abrupt and clear
Three volleys ring:
And perhaps their brave young spirits hear
The bugle sing:
Go to sleep! Go to sleep!
Slumber well
where the shell screamed and fell.

James P. Tierney

Let your rifles rest on the muddy floor,
You will not need them anymore.
Danger's past; Now, at last, Go to sleep!"
There is on earth no worthier grave
To hold the bodies of the brave

Than this place of pain and pride
Where they nobly fought and nobly died.
Never fear but in the skies.
Saints and angels stand.
Smiling with their holy eyes
On this new-come band.

St. Michael's sword darts through the air
And touches the aureole on his hair
As he sees them stand saluting there,
His stalwart sons;

And Patrick, Brigid, Columkill
Rejoice that in veins of warriors still
The Gael's blood runs.
And up to heaven's doorway floats,
From the wood called Rouge Bouquet,
A delicate cloud of bugle notes

That softly say: "Farewell! Farewell!
Comrades true, born anew, peace to you!
Your souls shall be where the heroes are
And your memory shines like the morning star.
Brave and dear, Shield us here. Farewell!"

On St. Patrick's Day, Father Duffy commemorated the fallen at Rouge Bouquet and said Mass was near the Third Battalion. They were experiencing their first stint in the trenches. In the afternoon, Duffy recited Joyce Kilmer's "Rouge Bouquet" at the site of the cave-in. As the Chaplain read the final words of the poem, a bugler standing next to him played "Taps" while in the woods another bugler echoed the song. Since that time, one of the Regiment's most precious traditions is to read the Rouge Bouquet at funeral services for members of the 69th Regiment Family.

A raiding party from the First Battalion was set to enter no-man's land while the Germans prepared to give the Third Battalion its first taste of mustard gas. The French selected Donovan's battalion for the 165th's first raid into no-man's land. The mission was simple. Take prisoners, gather information, and blow-up dugouts. Corporal Bob Foster of "D" Company fastened a green flag with harp and Erin Go Bragh to the barrel of his rifle. A French observer said the flag was inappropriate. The German-born Lieutenant Bootz glared at the officer. Bootz asked the observer what he was doing in the trenches. The Frenchman replied he was there to observe.

Bootz shouted, then you had better climb a tree and observe from there because we are here to fight, and that Irish flag is going over the top with us. On the night of the raid, the Germans bombarded the Third Battalion with mustard gas. Unfortunately, the soldiers (like the rest of the 42nd Division) had very little training in how to deal with a gas attack. In a supply blunder of dire consequences, the Division hadn't been issued gas masks until February 1918, three months after they had landed in France. Therefore, there was very little instruction on the use of gas masks. By the time soldiers reached the trenches, only thirty percent of the men had been through a gas chamber. Disaster struck Major Moynahan's Third Battalion. Between fourteen hundred and four thousand shells (most of them mustard gas) fell on the Third Battalion. Almost all the soldiers in "K" Company were blinded and transported to the hospital. There was nobody left to protect their abandoned weapons in the trenches.

After two months, the Regiment was sent to the Baccarat Sector. The Forty-second Division relieved three French divisions, which had been redeployed in the wake of Germany's latest offensive. Because of its numerous gas casualties, the Regiment was held in reserve. In Baccarat, the Regiment held the line and raided German trenches across no-man's land. In one of the daring raids, several prisoners were taken. In a moment of astonishing coincidence, Corporal Billy Munz was interrogating German prisoners in their native language when a captured officer spoke up. He asked Munz, where are you men from? "New York," Munz replied. The German officer said he had an aunt living there named Mrs. Bertha Bequest.

Munz's eyes widened. He said that's the name of my aunt, too. The German officer said I have another aunt in Hackensack named Mrs. Anna Munz. Billy Munz said, "She's my mother." You must be my cousin, Gustavo Wincklemann, of Bremen. The German said that he was. For the next hour Munz and Wincklemann happily discussed their family, then the prisoner was taken away.

Baccarat proved to be the quiet sector. Soldiers found small French cafes and restaurants. They supplemented their meals with omelets and French-fried potatoes, wine, and beer. Colonel Barker was recalled to Washington, and Colonel Frank McCoy took Command of the Regiment. Spring had come to the western front, and the 165th awaited orders. Joyce Kilmer had been promoted to sergeant and transferred into Elmer's Intelligence Section. The Intelligence Section's lookout post was a wooden platform built high in pine trees. They kept their eyes on the Germans through a long-range telescope.

Major Tim Moynahan, who was suffering from gas poisoning, was replaced by Captain Jim McKenna as Commander of the Third Battalion. Captain Alexander Anderson took Command of the Second Battalion. The

Regiment arrived in the Champagne region as part of the French Fifth Army. A new and deadlier phase of the war was about to begin. From mid-July through the first week of August, the Germans began an offensive. This time, the Allies counterattacked. Commonly known as the Second Battle of the Marne, it proved to be the turning point of the war. General Ludendorff's (the overall German Commander) daring gamble failed. The cost to both sides would be hundreds of thousands of casualties. The coming weeks would make the last six months feel like a picnic. The Regiment would reach the banks of a winding little river known as the Ourcq.

In mid-June, the Forty-second Division slipped quietly out of the Lorraine sector. The 165th Infantry departed Baccarat on June 18th. On the first night, the Regiment marched past replacement troops from the Seventy-Seventh Division from New York State. The 77th was composed of draftees from New York, and it was known as "New York's Own" (a moniker the Regiment resented). The Kelly brothers met each other, one from the 42nd Division and the other from the 77th. The brothers hugged each other and then parted. The Forty-second Division arrived at Camp de Chalons (part of the Marne salient). They were attached to the French Fifth Army, preparing for a push against the Germans on the fourth of July. The 165th moved to the

Suippes River, which ran through the village of St. Hillaire-Le-Grand. The Division's left flank was held by Major Alexander Anderson's Second Battalion. Donovan's First Battalion and McKenna's Third were kept in reserve.

Captain John T. Prout, Commander of Company "G," received an order from the French Commander in charge of the area to arm his most trusted non-commissioned officers with pistols and place them behind his troops. If anyone tried to run away, the non-commissioned officers were to shoot them on the spot. Prout tore up the order, flung it to the ground, and stomped on it. John T. Prout was born in Ireland. After serving with the Regiment in World War I, he joined the Irish Republican Army (IRA), serving as and intelligence officer in the Tipperary Brigade. Prout sided with the Pro-treaty forces in the Civil War, which began in Ireland in 1922. He reached the rank of Major General in the Irish Free State Army. In the movie "The Fighting 69th, Prout appears in the credits at the end of the movie as a Military Advisor. However, his rank is listed as Captain, the rank he held in the Regiment, not Major General, the rank he held in the Irish Army. Prout was not the only 69th soldier to reach a high rank in the Irish Army. Jeremiah (Ginger) O'Connell enlisted in the 69th in 1912. He returned to Ireland in 1914 to join the Irish Volunteers. He was involved in the War of Independence and the Civil War in Ireland. He held the rank of Major General in the Irish National Army. In recognition of the role of the Regiment in training Irish Republicans, an Irish Army publication referred to the 69th Regiment as the Irish Military College in New York.

Shortly after midnight, French artillery fired on the German lines. German artillery responded. The ground shook violently as each German shell landed. A hundred miles away in Paris, citizens felt and heard the shock of the bombardment. One of the shells smashed into Prout's Command Post, burying him, his First Sergeant Charles Grundy, and several others. The concussion blew off their helmets and covered them in white chalk. When they dug their way out, they looked more like ghosts than soldiers. At dawn, six German divisions moved forward behind a rolling barrage. The Germans had three other divisions held in reserve. The German plan was to push the Allies back and take the Suippes River by noon. By four the following morning, they expected to capture Chalons. As the German infantrymen advanced, airplanes fired their machine-guns into the American trenches, and German tanks attacked across no-mans-land. German long-range shells hit Chalons, collapsing buildings and ripping up cobbled streets. The Germans passed over the advance trenches and pressed on to meet the American units. To their surprise, the Allied line held. Anderson's Second Battalion stopped the enemy advance in his area. Prout looked on in front of "G" Company as the Germans attacked with bayonets. His First Platoon commander, Lieutenant Kenneth Ogle, ordered his men to fix their bayonets and charge the Germans. The charge drove the enemy back, and Prout's Company held its position.

Several Germans donned French helmets. A German platoon leader with a French helmet approached a machine gun crew, yelling not to shoot, as he and his men were French soldiers. When the Germans neared the Regiment's machine gunners, the German officer tossed a grenade into the American's midst. The explosion wounded the gunner, but his ammo bearer manned the machine gun, fired, and repelled the enemy. Four Germans with Red Cross armbands carried a stretcher up to the lines to infiltrate the Regiment's position. They failed.

Father Duffy stayed at the front, comforting his men during the worst of the shelling and the harrowing hand-to-hand combat. The Chaplain was constantly exposed to enemy fire as he tended to the wounded and carried them on stretchers to the nearest aid station. Major Anderson asked the Chaplain if he wanted some grenades. The Priest said no, every man to his trade. I'll stick to mine. Anderson handed Duffy the Third Battalion's Flag and asked the Priest to see that it didn't fall into enemy hands. Father Duffy said he would look out for the flag.

Although the Germans had withdrawn, they regrouped during the night. The next morning, they attacked again with artillery and airplanes. On the second day, there were sporadic infantry assaults. Each time, the enemy was repulsed. On the third day, Captain Elmer's intelligence team noted that the enemy was not returning fire. The enemy was withdrawing. Sixty men had been killed in the three-day battle. That was almost twenty-five percent of the total killed in the Division. Anderson's battalion suffered forty-seven dead. His "H" Company (caught out in no-man's land stringing wire) had been hit the hardest, with twenty-eight killed.

With the German army now in retreat, Foch believed the time was ripe for a bold counterattack. He set 18 July as the date to attack with the Americans fighting alongside the French. Foch believed the Germans would be routed in the Aisne-Marne sector. The problem was the Germans were not retreating. They were regrouping, setting up strong defenses along the Ourcq River (and other strategic points in the Aisne-Marne). General John Pershing had six combat divisions poised along the front from Chateau-Thierry to Belleau Wood (four were regular army, two were National Guard). On the day the Allies launched their counterattack, the Forty-second Division was sent to flush the Germans from the north bank of the Ourcq River.

The Ourcq River was a shallow tributary of the Marne. The Ourcq was fed by several smaller streams and was only eighteen feet across and about four feet deep. Two stone bridges crossed the Ourcq at Sergy and Seringes-et-Nesle. Large farms were located on both sides of the river. Their thick stone walls, huge barns, and walled courtyards offered ideal locations for machine gun positions. Each farm had been transformed into a lethal German stronghold. Among the strongest were Croix Rouge Farm on the south bank of the river and Meurcy Farm on the north. The capture of Meurcy Farm had been assigned to the Eighty-third Brigade. On the morning of 26 July, Donovan and McKenna (who still felt the lingering effects of the gas) were on a reconnaissance mission. They'd been ordered to see what lay ahead for their battalions. A gas shell exploded over Donovan's head. And he got a mouthful of gas. Donovan went to an aid station and was treated. He planned to spend the night there, but around midnight he was awakened. His battalion was to move to the south bank of the Ourcq. In the dark with intermittent rain falling, Donovan led his Battalion through dense woods. His soldiers hiked in columns a hundred yards between companies. When the battalion reached its assembly area, the tired men rested. Donovan wrapped himself in a blanket and slept for an hour. The enemy had pulled back in the night, heading for the heights across the Ourcq.

At midnight, the Forty-Second Division had its four infantry regiments in a straight line facing the northern heights of the Ourcq River. On the 69th's right flank were the Alabamians and, on the left, the Ohioans. No one knew for certain what lay ahead. The French commander believed the Germans would retreat at the first sign of an attack. He ordered the Americans to charge with bayonets only. A few hours before dawn on the morning of 28 July, the 69th assaulted an entrenched enemy in one of the first engagements of open warfare since 1914.

The Germans were still in control of the entire north side of the river. All three battalions of the 165th were engaged, poised to cross a river they contemptuously called the River O'Rourke. As "K" Company came down the hill to the river's edge, they were met by continuous German machine-gun fire. The company refused to stop and fought to the river's edge. Reaching the farm was going to test the courage of every soldier. Once "K" Company had made it over the Orucq, other companies in McKenna's battalion forded the stream. German machine gunners were everywhere, and their artillery had found its deadly range. At the regimental Command Post in Villers-sur-Fere, McCoy, at 11:20, sent the Brigade a message that the Third Battalion had reached the crest of the hill between Meurcy Farm and the village of Sergy. Since it had suffered heavy casualties, he ordered it withdrawn and Donovan's First Battalion to replace it.

In the morning of the 28th, Donovan's First Battalion moved across the Ourcq, to relieve Major McKenna's battered Third Battalion. The withdrawal of the Third had been orderly despite the harassing enemy machine-gun fire and artillery bombardment. In the relative safety of the woods west of Chateau de la Foret, what was left of the original one thousand Shamrock Battalion soldiers regrouped and marched back to Villers-sur-Fere. The Third Battalion only had six officers and four hundred and fourteen men.

Donovan's Battalion pressed the attack. Captain Henry Bootz (who received the Distinguished Service Cross at Luneville) was struck on one side of his chest by a bullet, which exited on the other. He was loaded on a litter and carried to an aid station. A German sniper fired at Donovan. Although the bullet missed Donovan, it killed his Adjutant, Second Lieutenant Oliver Ames. Donovan reached for Ames, and the sniper fired again, hitting Donovan in the hand. Ames' death deeply affected Donovan, but he had no time for grieving. Donovan needed a new adjutant. Sgt.

Joyce Kilmer volunteered, and Donovan agreed to take him on as Acting Adjutant.

He also needed him to serve as his Acting Sergeant Major. The poet left the Intelligence Section. There was no reason for Kilmer to serve with a front-line battalion. As a sergeant in the Intelligence Section, he was assigned to Regimental Headquarters, where he could have remained with complete honor in comparative safety. For Kilmer, leaving the Intelligence Section was bittersweet. He liked his intellectual companions there, and they, him. In one of his letters to his wife, he explained why they meant so much to him. He said that the dangers and hardships shared together develop friendships I never knew in civilian life. In another letter, he said that the soldiers of the 69th were risking their lives to bring peace to the people of France. The last poem he wrote he named it "The Peacemaker."

The attack lasted until the afternoon. The Regiment could not advance any farther due to heavy machine gun and artillery fire. The Brigade Commander ordered the regiment to dig in and wait until nightfall to continue the attack. The hillside was littered with the Regiment's dead and wounded. 145 soldiers of the Regiment were killed. Father Duffy was always in the midst of the heaviest fighting. He ministered to the wounded and dying soldiers. During the battle he had been seen weeping. Word came from the Brigade that the

Germans had retreated, and the advance would continue the next day, July 29th.

The line of battle was the First Battalion in front, with the Second Battalion in support and the Shamrock (Third) Battalion in reserve. Donovan's men were to clear out Meurcy Farm and advance north to Bois Colas and Bois Brule (small hillocks with little creeks that trickled down into the Ourcq River). The main objective was to secure Meurcy Farm and move on. But the Germans regrouped during the night. They reinforced their machine-gun squads. Their gun emplacements made it possible for then to control the valley.

Donovan's tactic was to send a few men at a time, darting forward and dropping to the ground. When they flanked a machinegun position, they would rush it. Donovan led an attack against a German emplacement. When he and his men arrived, they found a German platoon about to charge. The Americans killed all but two. In the assault, Donovan was struck on the head, left heel (which threw him off balance), and leg by shrapnel. The Second Battalion was brought up to protect Donovan's right flank.

The Regiment succeeded in taking Meurcy Farm after a hand-to-hand fight. Enemy machine gunners along the ridges north of Ourcq kept up a constant fire on the Regiment's lines. Donovan ordered Sergeant Richard

O'Neal to suppress the German machine guns in front of the Regiment. O'Neal was given command od "D" Company and promoted to Acting Captain. In the attack, O'Neill had outdistanced his platoon and charged the ridge alone with just a pistol and some grenades. The only protective bit of real estate was a camouflaged gravel pit. He dove in and found around him were twenty-five Germans manning machine guns. Yelling as loud as he could, O'Neill threw a grenade into their midst and fired his pistol, hitting three before the rest reacted.

A few Germans scrambled out the far end of the pit while the others charged him. He was shot seven times. Bullets pierced his side, his left shin, and his left arm. Still, he returned fire. The Germans surrendered. He called to his soldiers, saying he was with twenty German prisoners. He said he was pointing a pistol at them that probably didn't have any rounds left in it. As O'Neill marched the German prisoners down the ridge, a German machine gun opened fire. It killed several of their own men but also got O'Neill in his right leg. He couldn't walk or crawl, so he rolled down the hill. Even as he rolled, he was shot several times. He finally reached his own troops. O'Neill was wrapped in a blanket. He ordered the men carrying him to take him to Donovan. He had to tell the Major what the battalion faced when it fought its way to the top of the ridge. O'Neill made his report to Donovan and then passed out. He awoke several weeks later in a hospital. For his action, O'Neill earned the Medal of Honor.

At ten-fifty that morning, McCoy sent a message to Lenihan saying Donovan had repulsed the counterattack. German infantry got as far as the First Battalion's lines (attacking Brule). Three enemies were killed inside Regimental lines, and the rest driven off. Five minutes later, a message arrived from Donovan. Donovan had called for an artillery barrage, but he hadn't gotten it. Donovan said it was vital to shell Bois Brule where there were at least forty machine-gun emplacements.

That day, the Regiment suffered 12 killed, 90 wounded, and 130 missing. Donovan's Battalion lost thirty-seven men killed (nineteen from "A" Company and twelve from "D"). Although the Third Battalion had been held in reserve, it also suffered losses. Seventeen men lost their lives. "K" Company had eight killed. On July 5th, the battle was over. The casualty figures for the 165th for the entire battle were staggering. Fourteen officers and more than two hundred fifty men were killed, close to twelve hundred wounded, and another one hundred fifty missing. Total losses mounted to nearly sixteen hundred. Donovan was angry about the lack of artillery support during the battle.

Some historians report that Donovan complained to Colonel MacArthur. The Chief of Staff of the 42nd Division visited the Battery, which was supposed to support the First Battalion during the attack. MacArthur had harsh words for the Battery Commander, a Captain with the Missouri National Guard named Harry S. Truman. No one knows if Truman resented or even remembered the reprimand given by MacArthur. However, once President, Truman disbanded the unit Donovan organized and commanded during World War II, the Office of Strategic Services (OSS), and replaced it with the Central Intelligence Agency (CIA). Donovan was not offered a position in the CIA. Truman also relieved MacArthur during the Korean War. Some believe he never forgot the two men and his verbal reprimand.

MacArthur was assigned Commander of the Eighty-fourth Brigade, replacing Brig. Gen. Robert Brown. Hesitancy on the banks of the Ourcq likely cost Brown his post. McCoy received a promotion to Brigadier General and was transferred to the Army Transport Service. Donovan was promoted to Lieutenant Colonel. Father Duffy was promoted and awarded the Distinguished Service Cross. He was ordered by Colonel McCoy to go to the hospital in Vittel for rest.

On August 10th, Pershing took Command of the (All-American) First U.S. Army, which no longer answered to the

French. He ordered his Army to St. Mihiel, which the Germans had held for four years. The St. Mihiel salient was part of the Hindenburg Line between the Meuse and the Moselle rivers. The French tried to recapture it twice but failed each time. Strategically, it protected the huge railroad center at Metz, a fortress city twenty-five miles northeast. It interrupted the great rail line, which connected Paris to the vital iron mines and coalfields in the industrial Saar region. For several years, St. Mihiel had been a quiet sector.

Still, the St. Mihiel salient remained strongly fortified, with deep trenches and rock-solid artillery bunkers. At its southwestern point, the two-hundred-and-fifty square-mile salient, a triangle rather than a square, overlooked the Meuse River from high, wooded bluffs. Further back, as the salient widened out, it reached a flat section of land called the Woevre Plain. Covered with more woods, and streams and, lakes, and small villages in the rainy season, it mushed into a swampy morass. The rainy season usually started in mid-September. And when it got wet, the roads became impassable.

Attacking the St. Mihiel salient as the first offensive by the American Army. Pershing drew up plans for taking St. Mihiel, and on 24 July, he went over them with Foch and got his blessing. It was simple. The French would demonstrate in front of the salient while the Americans would attack its flanks. Pershing was ready. His army was ready. Troops were rolling in from all over France. Well over half a million enlisted men, five hundred officers, and a brigade full of tanks. They'd bust through the salient and then up to the Hindenburg Line. Foch had a change of plans. After the Allies stopped Germany's July offensive and counterattacked successfully, Foch believed an assault along the entire Hindenburg Line by Belgium, English, French, and American armies could end the war. There was no time to lose. The attack had to get under way before the end of September.

Foch envisioned a combined Franco-American force moving into the Meuse-Argonne valley, followed by the British First and Third Armies, the Belgians pushing eastward from the North Sea to Lys, and the British Fourth Army, supported by the French First Army, storming the Hindenburg Line between Cambrai and St. Quentin. A hold-up at St. Mihiel might keep Pershing's forces from joining the French in driving the Germans out of the Meuse-Argonne. Foch refused to take that risk. The Supreme Commander wanted a scaled-back attack on St. Mihiel, limiting it to just the eastern flank.

Afterward, Foch would peel off several of Pershing's divisions and move them west so they'd be ready to fight alongside the French in the Argonne. The remaining army would move into the Champagne sector to join Gen. Henri Gouraud's Fourth Army. If Pershing balked at his plan, Foch threatened to abandon the St. Mihiel operation. Pershing did not agree with Foch's plan. He told Foch the U.S. Army would fight wherever you may decide, it will not fight except as an independent American army. The U.S. Army must be employed as a whole, either east of the Argonne or west of the Argonne, and not four or five divisions here and six or seven there. Foch acquiesced.

Pershing's army wouldn't be divided, and the assault on St. Mihiel would go ahead, commencing 10 September (before the rains came and the battlefield was awash in mud). However, it would be the limited offensive that Foch wanted. Foch had set his dates for the grand assault, and the start was the 25th, with the Americans leading the way. Thus, when Pershing had finished with St. Mihiel, he was to move his army up the Meuse with great speed where, with the French Fourth Army in support, it would attack through the Argonne Forest.

The plans to take St. Mihiel were meticulous. The French force was set at nearly one-hundred thousand men while the Americans that Pershing was sending into battle was over two hundred thousand. On the eastern flank, one of the corps moving up for the assault was the Forty-second Division. The Division would attack in the center and deliver the main blow in the direction of the heights overlooking the Madine Creek, exerting its main effort east of Maizerais and Essey. The Ninetieth Aero Squadron had been placed at the Division's disposal along with the First Tank Brigade, Commanded by Lieutenant Colonel George Patton. The sector assigned to the Forty-second was in the center of the First Army. On the first day of the attack, the Division was to capture St. Benoit and go no further. As Pershing's First Army massed south of the St. Mihiel salient for its assault on the 12th of September, the Germans were reducing their forces. The Germans planned to let the Americans break through into the Woevre Plain, giving them a false sense of victory and then counterattack. The plan was scratched when they realized the Americans were coming at them from both sides of the salient. The German withdrawal was too slow. They rolled away the heavy guns two days before Pershing launched his attack. As "H Hour" approached on the morning of the 12th, it had been raining steadily for several days.

Donovan commanded the regiment in the field, and it worried him. For one thing, after the Ourcq, sixty-five percent of his enlisted men and close to seventy-five percent of its officers. The morning before the attack, intelligence reports brought into the Forty-second Division headquarters showed little enemy activity. Bad weather had obscured troop movement and kept enemy airplanes grounded. Smoke from a train was spotted, but because of poor visibility, there was no way to know if it was carrying troops. By afternoon, it had become evident that the Germans were moving back toward Metz. However, most of the German Tenth Division was still waiting for an attack. Pershing commenced his assault at one a.m. with a heavy bombardment. Four hours later, hundreds of thousands of soldiers, supported by tanks and French allies, rushed forward (the first time that an American army had gone on the attack since the Civil War). Behind the 165th Infantry, the 149th Field Artillery fired on enemy positions. Leading the First Battalion, Donovan told his men it would not be as bad as some of the cross-country runs I made you do. Duffy was with Donovan. He held his hands over the men and blessed them. The number of killed on the first day in the First Battalion was eleven. After the battle was over, the total was forty-seven. Division's Intelligence Report the next day stated only small parties of the enemy had been encountered and on the front of this Division. The enemy has evidently withdrawn to the Hindenburg Line. The Germans that stayed behind to fight surrendered in the thousands. Donovan was surprised at how the Germans quit fighting. Whole regiments surrendered at once. Pershing called the battle a striking victory. Foch called the victory a smashing success.

Elements of General Pershing's First Army were on the way to the Meuse-Argonne. As roads west became clogged with an army on the move. Almost half a million men, ninety thousand horses and mules, and four thousand artillery pieces were hurrying to keep its date of 26th September, when it would lead the Allied attack against the entire length of the Hindenburg Line. The Hindenburg Line (Siegfried Line) was a series of defensive strongholds, each one named after a hero of German folklore. The strongholds were comprised of a series of heavily fortified lines protected by coils of razor-sharp barbed wire, deep trenches, and honeycombed by thousands of concrete pillboxes manned by veteran machine-gun squads. Pershing planned a five-phase attack, with the Forty-Second Division taking part in the third phase. He felt that one attack after another would wear down the enemy and drive the Germans out of the Meuse-Argonne.

Pershing's army found itself stymied by the terrain and the enemy's overwhelming firepower. The Forty-Second Division got the call to join the battle. For nearly two weeks, the battle had gone badly. The easy romp through the St. Mihiel Salient had given the Americans a false sense of superiority. On October 12th, the 42nd Division relieved the First Division (Big Red One). The First Division had fought courageously, suffering nine thousand casualties in eleven days, but failed to crack through the enemy's defensive line. Because he was running the Regiment in the field, Donovan had turned over his battalion to Captain Mike Kelly. When the attack began, artillery blasted the ground three hundred yards in front of the division Regiment pushed forward from a sunken road. The start time had been set for seven-thirty, but the attack didn't begin until nearly nine. As Donovan feared, his men were struck by enfilading fire from Cote de Chatillon.

Mike Donaldson, the pugilist from Haverstraw who packed a pair of dynamite fists, was pinned down in a sunken road. His entire company had been stopped by intense machine-gun fire that poured down from the crest of a hill. As he regrouped his men, he saw in front of him several wounded soldiers. Donaldson left the protection of the sunken road and up the hill. The German guns roared, and bullets buzzed around him. He picked up one of the wounded and carried him back to the sunken road. He had to step over the other wounded soldiers scattered about the hillside. Donaldson braved enemy fire five more times, bringing back the wounded. For his action on the 14th, Donaldson was awarded the Medal of Honor.

Despite the early success, the fight wasn't going well. The Third Battalion lost half its strength. Only six officers survived. Donovan decided to stay with the Kelly's battalion.

He figured it might be able to sneak forward in the darkness. He talked the idea over with Mike Kelly and Henry Bootz (twice cited for valor, once at Luneville and again on the Ourcq River). Bootz reasoned that a single company might get through. Bootz led "B" Company, now filled with green replacements, toward the German defenses. Rockets exploded, and the sky lit. When Bootz returned after unsuccessfully trying to make it through, he said, I think we had better wait until morning. All we have done so far is wake up the Germans.

Donovan ordered the attack to stop for the night. The next morning, the Brigade sent a message saying the attack would continue at 7:15. The Regiment was ordered to move forward close to the artillery barrage line and, at 7:30 will, pass through the enemy's barbed wire and capture the village of Landres-et-St. Georges. Donovan was wounded ten minutes after the attack began. A bullet shattered his shinbone. As he struggled to sit up, the Germans counterattacked. Although the pain was unbearable, Donovan refused to be evacuated. He called in artillery support and ordered his Stokes mortars to fire on the enemy. The artillery fire proved weak and ineffective. The Germans kept coming. It was now up to the mortars to stop them. Unfortunately, from their position, the mortarmen could not tell where to fire their shells. Knowing the situation was desperate, Tom Fitzsimmons, a sergeant in one of the mortar platoons, ran up the slope for about one hundred yards under heavy machine gun fire. He found a spot at the crest of the hill, which gave him an excellent view of the approaching Germans. It also gave the enemy an excellent view of him. When Fitzsimmons figured the Germans were in range, he signaled for the mortars to open fire. The first shells struck the enemy, and Fitzsimmons called for rapid fire. The hits were on target, and the Germans faltered. For his actions, Fitzsimmons received the American Distinguished Service Cross.

Donovan decided to pull back, but Brigade Headquarters ordered the attack to be renewed. At ten-thirty, the Brigade Commander telephoned the attack order to Harry Mitchell at the

The Regimental Command Post. Relaying the order quickly to Donovan was difficult since the phone line between them had been cut. The only way to reach Donovan was by horseback. Mitchell dispatched two riders to tell Donovan to press the attack. He sent the same orders to Anderson and Kelly. By the time the orders reached Donovan, it was too late. Donovan had made up his mind to halt the attack. Mitchell relieved Donovan of his command and replaced him with Anderson. Even though his superiors felt he should have pressed the attack, Donovan received the

Medal of Honor for his actions during the battle. The First Battalion alone had lost seventy-four men killed while the total for the regiment reached one hundred-eleven. The total strength of the First Battalion was down to six officers and 186 men. The Second Battalion had only 480 men, and the Third (held in reserve had only 496 men. It took the First American Army a month to punch through the defenses of the Meuse Argonne and drive the Germans out of the steep ridges and narrow gorges. Once through, Pershing looked north to one last prize, a prize the French believed belonged to them and were not about to cede it to the Americans, the city of Sedan.

The Rainbow Division was on the march again. Now attached to Major General Joseph Dickman's First Corps, the Division was part of a massive push by Pershing's First Army toward the Meuse River south of Sedan. It was a different regiment that headed off once again to battle the enemy. Since the Meuse-Argonne engagement, replacements had poured in, with new officers, and new men. Many of the original soldiers were killed, wounded, or transferred. The 165th was still led by seasoned veterans, although Wild Bill Donovan was recuperating at a Paris hospital.

For the French, Sedan stood as a symbolic city. Capturing it meant more to the nation in the closing days of the war than any other event. Driving the Germans out was paramount, the French demanded. Pershing felt otherwise. He wanted his troops to capture Sedan. Pershing ordered I Corps to capture Sedan. As they marched to the Meuse, the 42nd Division was unaware that their rivals in the First Division were behind them, crossing into their territory. MacArthur went to investigate what was going on. He was afraid his troops would mistake them for Germans and open fire on the First Division. An officer in the First Division mistook MacArthur for a German and arrested him. He was held at gunpoint until he was recognized. He was released. The movement of the Big Red One into the 42nd Division's area created a dangerous situation for both divisions.

For political reasons, the French were given the right to enter Sedan first. The war was over, but it would be 6 months before the Regiment left Europe. The Regiment spent over 160 days in combat. The 165th had the most casualties in the Division. In killed died of wounds and disease, the number of deaths reached 844. Donovan's First Battalion had the most, with 299 killed in battle. His "A" Company suffered ninety-four dead. The Second Battalion had 213 men who lost their lives, while the Third Battalion had 255. The total figure for the Regiment was higher, but it is impossible to know because many, after returning to the United States, later died of complications from the gas they inhaled on the battlefield. Others committed suicide or turned to drinking.

On 7 March 1919, Wild Bill was promoted to Colonel and named Commander of the 165th Infantry, the Fighting Sixty-Ninth. On 21 April 1919, he led it home to New York City. During World War I, the Regiment participated in major operations: Champagne-Marne Defensive from July 15th to 17th, 1918, Champagne-Marne Offensive from July 25th to August 3rd, 1918, St. Mihiel Offensive from September 12th to 16th, 1918. Meuse-Argonne Offensive, October 12th to 31st, and Nov. 5th to 10th, 1918. The Regiment served in the Army of Occupation at Remagen, Germany, and returned to the U.S. in April 1919. The Regiment demobilized at Camp Upton, N.Y. Over 160 decorations from the U. S. or French were conferred upon personnel for conspicuous gallantry in action.

Chapter Six
Between the World Wars

In 1920, the 69th Infantry Regiment New York Guard was reorganized to conform to Federal Requirements, and the Companies were extended Federal Recognition. The New York Guard regiment was folded into the 165th Infantry Regiment, New York National Guard. Archbishop Hayes assigned Father Duffy as Pastor of Holy Cross parish on West 42nd Street. Father Duffy found that many Catholics worked the late shift in the hotels, restaurants, and newspaper plants in the Times Square area. Concerned that their late hours made it difficult for these workers to attend regular Sunday morning masses, he asked what time was convenient for them to attend services. The workers voted for the 2:15 a.m. (when many of them got off their shift). Father Duffy accommodated them by establishing a predawn liturgy.

The distinctive insignias were authorized by the War Department. Although the color of the field on distinctive unit insignia (DUI) for all Infantry Regiments was Infantry Blue, the DUI for the 165th (and 69th) is green. The Regiment is the only Infantry Regiment in the US. Army to have the color of the field other than Infantry Blue on its DUI. Green reflects the old facings of the 69th Infantry Regiment, the original organization. The rainbow is adapted from the shoulder sleeve insignia approved for the 42d Division during World War I. The wolfhound cap device was used by the Regiment since its organization. The distinctive unit insignia was originally approved for the 165th Infantry on 26 April 1924. It was amended to omit the motto from the design on 19 August 1924. On 17 March 1964, the insignia was redesignated for the 69th Infantry. It was redesignated on 9 Mar 1993 for the 69th Air Defense Artillery, and on 30 December 1996, the insignia was redesignated for the 69th Infantry.

In 1930, changes were proposed to the National Guard's relationship to the U.S. Army. In World War I, the National Guard was drafted into the Army and, at the conclusion of its active service, was discharged not only from Federal service but further State service as well. Under a proposed amendment to the National Defense Act, in. the event of a major emergency, the National Guard would be "called" or "ordered" into Federal service by the President without the necessity of being drafted. The National Guard would become a reserve of the U.S. Army. The proposed amendment would not affect the peace time status of National Guard troops in any way; they remain as, heretofore, under the sole jurisdiction, authority, and command of the Governors of the respective States. However, it becomes a reserve organization of the Army of the United States composed of those persons duly commissioned by the Governors of their respective States.

On June 26, 1932, Father Francis P. Duffy, the famed Chaplain of the Regiment, died after suffering from colitis and a liver infection. He served as Chaplain of the Regiment from July 6, 1916, and was promoted to Lieutenant Colonel on July 13, 1928. General Douglas MacArthur said he had recommended the priest for the colonelcy of the 165th Regiment. MacArthur was quoted as saying this is one of the few occasions in the history of the American Army when the suggestion was made that a minister of the gospel be converted into the commander of a fighting unit. On the day of Father Duffy's funeral, a thousand members of the 69th escorted his body from his parish church to St. Patrick's Cathedral. As Father Duffy's body was laid to rest at Raymond Cemetery in the Bronx that afternoon, a fleet of Army airplanes circled over the burial site. In 1933, a campaign to erect a memorial to the famous chaplain was begun. The following year, the sculptor Andrew O'Connor was offered the commission to design a suitable monument. About a year later, however, in July 1935, it was announced that Charles Keck would take over the commission of designing the statue following O'Connor's resignation from the project. The monument, which is located at the intersections of Broadway, Seventh Avenue, and West 47th Street at the north end of Times Square, features a nine-foot-high statue of Father Duffy standing in front of a twelve-foot Celtic cross. The figure is dressed in a military uniform and holds a breviary. The statue was unveiled by Agnes Bird, one of Father Duffy's nieces, and was blessed by Father Joseph McCaffrey, the chaplain of the 69th. On October 16, Duffy Square was opened again after being closed for almost three years for renovation.

On June 15th, 1933, the President approved the amendment, which changed the status of the National Guard to the extent of constituting it as a reserve component of the Army in peace as well as in war. The effect of the amendment is twofold in its provisions respecting National Guard forces. Namely, making them immediately available in the event of a national emergency through a "call" by the President without the necessity of "draft" under the provisions of a selective service law. Under the new amendment, all units of the National Guard that in the future may enter Federal service will retain their state identity and, at the conclusion of such service, return to their state status. Beyond this, the amendment makes no material change in the organization, policies, and functions of the National Guard of the respective States.

The 1937 AG Report noted concern about the possibility of mobilization of the National Guard and preparation necessary for the New York Guard for State service in the event the National Guard is called for Federal service. The report noted when the National Guard was federalized, it was necessary for the New York Guard to be organized for active duty during the absence of the National Guard. Furthermore, if it were necessary to organize the New York Guard of equipment, which would have to be supplied by the State, would present a serious problem. While uniforms could no doubt be supplied within a reasonable length of time, procurement of ordnance was another matter. Since the Federal government would have priority in obtaining rifles, pistols, and ammunition, it would likely these items would not be available to the New York Guard. The plan was to procure equipment and store it at the State Arsenal. It was estimated that approximately 6,000 rifles would be required and about 500 pistols. The report is also concerned with the number of officers in the State who have had prior service. Compared with data shown in the 1927 Report of The Adjutant General, when 67 percent of the officer personnel are shown to have had United States service, this indicates a loss of 25 percent of such officers over a period of ten years.

In 1938, the Sino-Japanese War moved into its second year. Adolf Hitler abolished the War Ministry, giving him direct control of the German military. German forces marched into Austria, and German annexation was declared. Soviet and Japanese forces were fighting in the Far East. Adolf Hitler and Neville Chamberlain met in Munich to partition Czechoslovakia. Chamberlain returns to Britain after the meeting and declares, "Peace for our time." The Japanese declared a New Order in East Asia. Americans wanted to stay neutral and stay out of any war. The mood in America was like it was before World War I. Once again America faced challenges regarding the size of the active army. The Country needed to prepare the National Guard for wartime service without making it obvious it was preparing for war.

The Regiment's arms and equipment consisted of items used in World War I. Soldiers still carried the M1903 Springfield rifle with bayonet. The Adjutant General's Report for 1938 expressed concerns regarding several issues. In 1939, the situation in Europe reflected an increased activity of U.S. military and naval forces. Authority was received to perform National Guard drills twice each week, with pay, which was the first time such authority had been extended in peacetime since 1847. Another requirement from the War Department was the fingerprinting of officers of the New York National Guard and the furnishing of a personal history of each officer.

On January 24, 1940, the annual reunion of veterans of the 69th New York paid a special tribute to Father Duffy. Besides the Regiment's current Commander, Colonel John Mangan, three of its former Commanding Officers were also present: Colonel William Donovan, Major General Frank McCoy, and Major General William Haskell. After praising Father Duffy as a brave and kindly priest who placed duty to God and man above all else, Governor Herbert Lehman of New York alluded to the new world war raging in Europe. It was, however, the remarks of General Douglas MacArthur, broadcast by radio from Manila, that the assembled veterans responded most enthusiastically. He said that no greater fighting regiment has ever existed than the One Hundred and Sixty-fifth Infantry of the Rainbow Division, formed from the old Sixty-ninth Regiment of New York. I cannot tell you how real and how sincere a pleasure I feel tonight in once more addressing the members of that famous unit. You need no eulogy from me or from any other man. You have written your own history and written it in red on your enemies' breast, but when I think of your patience under adversity, your courage under fire, and your modesty in victory, I am filled with an emotion of admiration I cannot express.

The annual reunion also featured a preview of "The Fighting 69th", the new motion picture about the famous regiment's World War I exploits. Actors Pat O'Brien, Jeffrey

Lind, and James Cagney were on hand for the evening's festivities. Pat O'Brien, who played the role of Father Duffy in the film, acknowledged the great honor it was to portray the beloved Chaplain. Jeffrey Lind reprised his film role as Joyce Kilmer that night by reading "Rouge Bouquet," a tribute by the famous soldier-poet to some of his fallen comrades. Cagney, meanwhile, expressed what he described as the cast's sense of responsibility to portray "the gallant Irish" justly. Major Donovan, whose role in the film was played by George Brent, also said a few words to the assembled veterans, many of whom had served under his command. He included a warning to representatives of the film industry to use the power of their medium to advance the cause of truth and not y to manipulate public opinion.

Europe was again about to be engulfed in a world war. Within six months, the Nazis controlled Denmark, Norway, the Netherlands, Belgium, and France, and in August Hitler began to prepare an invasion of Britain. In response to these developments, President Franklin Roosevelt began to turn the United States from "neutrality" to "non-belligerency," a shift that moved the country toward openly helping the Allies without going to war against the Axis Powers. Colonel Gardiner Conroy took command of the 165th Infantry in August 1940. Colonel Conroy would command the

Regiment until 1943, when he was killed in action on Makin Island.

On September 16, 1940, President Roosevelt signed the Selective Service Act requiring men between the ages of twenty-one and thirty-five to register for military training, the first step toward the first peacetime draft in American history. On August 27, 1940, the 76th Congress, in Public Resolution No. 96, conferred upon the President of the United States authority to order the National Guard into active military service of the United States for a period of twelve months unless sooner relieved. The Regiment was called to active duty with the 27th Division in October 1940. The Regiment, numbering about 1,700 men, was inducted into Federal service on October 15. About 70 percent of the men in the Regiment - which still bore the title "Fighting Irish" - were of Irish ancestry, down about 10 percent since 1917. One of the new recruits in the 165th was Private Christopher Kilmer, the twenty-three-year-old son of the famous poet Joyce Kilmer. Private Kilmer had been ten months old when his father was killed in 1918 while fighting with the 69th in France. On October 20, 1,200 men and officers of the Regiment attended a field mass in New York City's Central Park. The Mass was celebrated by the Regiments Chaplain, Father Thomas Egan. The Chaplain pointed out that the chalice used during the Mass had belonged to the Regiment since it was presented by Archbishop Hughes to Father Thomas Mooney, Chaplain of the 69th New York, during the early months of the Civil War. Three days later, on October 23, the 165th Infantry and about 10,000 onlookers participated in ceremonies at the statue of Father Duffy in midtown Manhattan. During the gathering, Mayor Fiorello LaGuardia expressed the city's best wishes for the regiment. That night, 500 men and twenty-five officers of the Second Battalion of the 165th Infantry left New York for Fort McClellan. Entry onto active duty was more rigorous than enlisting in the Regiment. Guardsman had to take comprehensive medical examinations and a battery of intelligence tests. Although many Guardsmen left the service in September and early October, more were discharged who were not physically capable or, did not meet mental standards, or had dependents. Of the approximately 90 soldiers in each company, only about 50 entered active service. Soldiers were assigned an 8-digit Serial Number. The first three digits were 2 0 2, indicating the National Guard, 2nd Corps Area (New York, New Jersey, and Delaware). Once arrived at Fort McClellan, the 165th Infantry began its military training in earnest. Within six weeks, more than 66 percent of its soldiers qualified as expert sharpshooters and marksmen with a rifle, and 87 percent of the men assigned to the machine guns achieved the expected competence.

The trip to Ft. McClellan, Alabama, in October took five days. The Regiment's training was different from what they had received at Camp Smith during the previous several summers. Although tent life was similar, instead of focusing on drills, their training stressed tactical training and marksmanship. The first two weeks were dedicated to the uniform issue, rifle marksmanship, and school of the soldier. The following eleven weeks focused on unit training. They began with squad training and progressed through company, battalion, and, finally, regimental operations. Throughout the 13-week period, only 26 hours were devoted to drill. Two hundred and forty-six hours had been devoted to tactical training and 111 hours to marksmanship. Training stopped in December for the holidays, and most soldiers boarded trains for a furlough in New York. The ranks of the Regiment began being filled by draftees, most being Irish Catholics from New York. The belief was that the Division would steer soldiers with Irish names to the 165th. ROTC officers also arrived to replace the officers who were too old or could not keep up with training. The regiment filled to wartime strength. In March the unit held a St. Patrick's Day Parade and celebrated as though they were back in New York. Soon, the Regiment and all other units in the 27th Division began to prepare for the season of maneuvers. Uniforms were still in short supply, and there was a mixture of khaki and olive drab uniforms at formations. There was also a shortage of mortars and machine guns, so stovepipes and wooden machine gun facsimiles were used instead during training exercises.

In the last week of May, the 27th Infantry Division left Ft. McClellan and began its field training period to prepare for the approaching Second Army Maneuvers. Training included numerous foot marches throughout Tennessee and the establishment of field camps with a stress on battalion-level training. The Regiment returned to Ft. McClellan for a short break and then traveled to the Alabama Maneuver Area for more training at the company, battalion, and regimental level. The soldiers participated in overnight marches and other rigorous training. At the end of August, the Regiment boarded trucks for the long road march to Arkansas, the staging area for General Ben Lear's Red Army.

During the 1941 maneuvers, every aspect of warfare was practiced. Soldiers wanted to return home at the end of their one year of service, and many talked about going AWOL if an extension of their term was authorized. "OHIO," which meant "Over the Hill in October," was scrawled on latrine walls, vehicles, and canvases. However, in August, Congress authorized the draft extension, and it was signed by President Roosevelt in September. Guardsman would spend another 18 months on active duty. In October, soldiers over 28 years old could ask for a discharge but those who got the opportunity to return home would be recalled in December after Pearl Harbor. Most did not return to the Regiment but would be assigned to units headed for Europe. The Second Army Maneuvers began in earnest on September 16th, and the Regiment fought battles in the pine forests northwest of Alexandria, Louisiana. Officers learned how to deploy and maneuver their units, and soldiers learned how to exist in a field environment, participating in endless marches on dirt roads. Umpires adjudicated combat between the Red and Blue armies, considering manpower, armament, and disposition of forces. The umpires used different colored flags to indicate whether a unit should retreat, but the only way soldiers could find out who was winning was to read the local newspapers.

Chapter Seven
World War II

At the completion of the Second Army Maneuvers, the Regiment returned to Ft. McClellan. The soldiers were facing another year and several months on active duty. In November, Thanksgiving dinners were served in the mess halls, and men prepared for their Christmas furloughs. The Japanese attack on Pearl Harbor on December 7th changed everything. President Roosevelt asked for a Declaration of War the following day. On December 16th, the Regiment traveled to Englewood, California. The rails were filled with military units, and it took a week to cross the country. In Englewood, the Regiment was assigned to guard vital installations, including aircraft plants. Sabotage was a major concern.

The War Department adopted a policy of releasing soldiers from active duty on their own application (e.g., enlisted men over twenty-eight years of age, married, soldiers whose absence from home caused family hardship, etc.). Officers were released on similar grounds or because they were over-age for the grade they held. The 69th Infantry Regiment, New York Guard (NYG), replaced the 165th Infantry Regiment when it was activated. The NYG

Regiment had 53 officers and 653 enlisted personnel assigned for a total strength of 706. The Regiment was headquartered in the armory on 26th Street. The NYG Regiment trained and prepared to operate as a regiment to become an efficient armed force within the borders of the State (e.g., to guard public utilities power plants, waterworks, vital highway bridges, railroad yards, and bridges, etc.) and to control crowds and prevent panics. The NYG Regiment also trained to observe and suppress active subversive elements. The Commander of the New York Guard believed the tactical teachings of the Regular Army in modern methods of combat between highly organized and trained forces, did not apply to State troops. A school for officers was conducted at Camp Smith from August 17 to 23, 1941. During the year, the 69th Regiment, NYG, lost 301 personnel. Most at the convenience of the State. Most companies had only 27 enlisted soldiers and one officer assigned.

The 165th was in Englewood, California living in tents. In February, soldiers trained using the M1 rifle for the first time. The unit prepared for overseas movement. Soldiers who did not pass the overseas physical were dropped from the rolls, and many untrained inductees joined the unit. On March 7th, the Regiment moved to Pier 22 in San Francisco and boarded the USAT President Grant. The berths in the holds were five high, with about 18 inches between berths. The next day, the ship sailed for Hawaii. The Regiment arrived in Kauai on March 16th and immediately began providing security and preparing beach defenses. Since most food had to be brought from the mainland, it was in short supply, and most of the food received arrived in cans. Curfew was 18:00 hours (6 PM), and soldiers who were not on guard duty were required to be in garrison. During the early months of 1942, the Regiment worked seven days a week digging foxholes and erecting concertina and double-apron barbed wire fences on the beaches. In late May, this high-intensity schedule lessened, and one-day passes were authorized. Things settled into a routine. Soldiers were assigned beach and airfield defense (where showers and clubs were available). In August, the Table of Organization and Equipment (TOE, the document which authorized personnel and equipment) for the infantry company changed to three rifle squads per platoon and three rifles and a weapons platoon for an infantry company. Squad leaders who were corporals were now sergeants. Weapons were essentially the same, but the weapons platoon was authorized the M1919A3 light machine guns and M2 60 mm mortar. Soldiers were issued the new M1 helmet and liner. The 165th Infantry was part of the first combat infantry division to be deployed overseas in World War II. It would be the longest wartime overseas service of any National Guard division in the American army. After spending six months in beach defense, the Regiment began training for offensive operations. In October, units of the 27th Division were recalled to Oahu to begin training for an invasion of the Gilbert Islands, the first American offensive in the Central Pacific.

New York Guard

The 69th Regiment, NYG, continued to improve after intensive training, including ten days of field training at Camp Smith, New York, during the summer. The State's National Guard had been completely inducted into the active service of the United States between the dates September 16, 1940, and March 10, 1941. The NYG Regiment now consisted of 66 officers and 577 enlisted soldiers for a total strength of 643, down over 50 from the previous year. Between December 1, 1941, to November 30, 1942, the 69th

Regiment, NYG, had lost 599 enlisted personnel. During field training at Camp Smith, the Regiment had 620 officers and enlisted soldiers attend, and 21 absent. During that training period, the Regiment had 360 infirmary cases and 9 hospital cases. The Regiment had 15 individuals complete the training at the Second Service Command Tactical School.

In May 1943, the 165th Infantry Regiment began intensive instruction in amphibious operations and spent weeks aboard amphibious transports practicing loading LCVs (Landing Craft Vehicles). The LCV formed into waves and assaulted the beaches of the Hawaiian Islands. The unit also trained on weapons and jungle obstacle courses. In June, Alpha Company received two silver rings for its guidon for participation in the Revolutionary War and the War of 1812. In August, the Regiment trained in high-risk, live-fire exercises in which soldiers assaulted objectives while live artillery, machine gun, and mortar were fired over the soldiers' heads. Some of the soldiers in the Regiment were killed by this "friendly fire. Squad leaders received the Thompson Machine Gun (Tommy Gun), which fired the standard 45 caliber round. Although the weapon was inaccurate at longer distances, it was hard to clean. However, it was the weapon of choice for close combat due to its rapid rate of fire and large caliber bullet. Soldiers practiced with the Mark 2 grenade (pineapple grenade), which consisted of 2 ounces of TNT surrounded by a serrated cast-iron shell. The grenade had a bursting radius of 35 yards, but the metal shards from the casing could travel as far as 100 yards.

On November 9th, the Regiment set sail aboard the Calvert for Makin Atoll in the Gilbert Islands. When the ship crossed the Equator, 164 soldiers who were "pollywogs (first time crossing the Equator) underwent the traditional naval rite and became "shellbacks" (person who has crossed the Equator in a ship) after paying the appropriate respect to the god of the sea, Neptune. Initiates dressed in wild costumes and festivities were held throughout the ship. Although most of the Regiment had been on active duty for more than two years, the combat which they would soon face was their first.

Before dawn on 20 November 1943, an American task force lay off the western shore of Makin Island (the northernmost atoll in the Gilbert Islands). Transports carrying men of the 165th Infantry Regiment were about to commence the assault on Makin. At Tarawa (about 105 miles to the south), an even larger force of U. S. Marines was poised to seize the airfield and destroy the Japanese there. From points as distant as the Hawaiian Islands and New Zealand (by several different routes), separate elements of an armada prepared to carry out our first aggressive mission in the Central Pacific. The attack upon Makin would be the first seizure of an atoll by an Army landing force. The invasion of the Gilbert Islands brought the war in the Central Pacific to a new phase. After almost two years of defense, the United States was taking the offensive. Japanese bases were to be recovered and used against the enemy in further strikes toward the heart of his empire.

Makin Island

The Japanese were driven from their bases in the Solomons and New Georgia. With the threat to the western coast of Canada and the United States removed, forces became available for simultaneous campaigns in Bougainville and the Gilberts. On 1 November, the hard battle for Bougainville was opened. At the same time, the expedition to the Gilberts was just beginning. The United States was opening what Admiral Chester W. Nimitz called "another road to Tokyo." The Gilberts straddle the equator some 2,000 miles southwest of Oahu. Most of them are low coral atolls, rising a few feet from the sea, supporting coconut palms, breadfruit trees, mangroves, and sandbrushes. The Japanese seized Makin on 10 December 1941 and converted it into a seaplane base. In September 1942, they occupied Tarawa and Apamama. At Tarawa, they built an airstrip and set up administrative headquarters for the naval forces in the Gilberts. On Apamama, an observation outpost was established. On Ocean and Nauru Islands, they also constructed air bases, and extracted phosphates important in their munitions industry. These Japanese bases and others in the Marshalls (to the northwest) were an interlocking system of defense.

The Gilberts and Marshalls were outer defenses of the empire of Japan. For the U.S., the enemy bases were a menace to the lines of communication from Hawaii to Australia. From the Gilberts and Marshalls, the Japanese struck Allied advanced staging positions on Canton Island and Funafuti (in the Ellice Islands). Also, Japanese observation planes could report the movements of Allied convoys and task forces and direct submarines and bombers to points of interception. Once the islands were in Allied hands, the route to the Southwest Pacific could be shortened sufficiently.

Makin atoll is an irregular formation of reefs and islands around a large lagoon, approximately triangular. The northern side is a reef 17 miles long, running east and west between islands. The western side (about 14 miles from tip to tip) consists of small islands, a reef broken by several channels, and the western end of Butaritari Island. The remainder of Butaritari and the island of Kuma (northeast of it) stretch for some 13 miles to the eastern corner of the atoll. The main passage into the lagoon runs through the reef at its southwest corner, passing just north of the northwestern tip of Butaritari. Other channels were suitable only for small boats. None of the other islands is as large or important as Butaritari, on which the Japanese had developed a seaplane base. Butaritari is shaped like a long, bending ribbon. Its western end resembles a fishtail with two main points projecting westward from the central shore, forming there a shallow curve. Eastward from the shore, the main body of the island narrows abruptly. It averages 500 yards from the ocean to the lagoon and, at some points, is much less. Butaritari and Kuma are connected by a reef, one side of which is high enough to permit crossing on foot at low tide. Butaritari is exposed to the open sea and heavy surf. From the northern shore, where the water is quieter, a wide reef covered with sticky mud extends into the lagoon. At the western end of the island, the smoother sections of the beach are very widely separated from each other and narrow, while jagged coral pinnacles make an approach to them an occasion for dexterous navigation. The Navy, whose task it would be to convey the assault troops to the beaches, believed landing boats could get ashore there at any time.

At 06:20, prearranged naval bombardment began. Striking first with the 14-inch guns of the four battleships and the 8-inch guns of three cruisers, this devastating attack was to rake the western shore from Kotabu Island to Ukiangong Point and to fall upon key points back from the beach. If need be, the range might be narrowed to 2,000 yards. A second bombardment was to be directed from 08:50 to 10:25 upon the area between the tank barriers and from the lagoon to the ocean shore. At approximately 06:00, when the task force reached the transport area, landing craft were lowered, and troops began descending cargo nets to the LCVs. When full, the LCVs proceeded to the rendezvous area and began circling. At approximately 08:18, the landing craft crossed the line of departure and headed toward the beach. When the first wave of boats was 800 yards from the Red Beaches (according to schedule, at 08:25), carrier-based fighters were to strafe the beaches and the area 100 yards inland and 500 yards north and south of the beaches' extremities. As the boats reached a point 100 yards from the shore, the fighters were to withdraw while bombers returned to hit every defense installation within 500 yards to 1,000 yards inland from the beaches. They were also to strike enemy positions on Ukiangong Point (e.g., mortars, pillboxes, and artillery). Unfortunately, things did not go as planned. Rocks and coral hindered the landing. LCVs became beached, and troops had to wade in chest-deep water. Maintaining footing was extremely difficult. Troops wading ashore came under small arms and machine gun fire. Once ashore, soldiers had to negotiate heavy vegetation, and they were under constant threat of sniper fire. Most of the snipers were on the ground, but many were in palm trees. Snipers cut foot holds into trees to make climbing easier. Soldiers soon learned to look for foothold cuts on trees to locate sniper nests.

Colonel J. Gardner Conroy was killed by a sniper on the first day. Before leaving the armory, Colonel Conroy took the crucifix, which hung from Joyce Kilmer's picture, and put it on. Kilmer was wearing the crucifix when he was killed in World War I. Donovan took the cross and wore it for the rest of the war. Donovan hung the crucifix on a picture of Kilmer he hung in his office at the armory. When Conroy was killed, his driver took the crucifix from Colonel Conroy's neck and kept it. He returned it to the armory after 9/11. The Commander, Colonel Geoffrey Slack, returned it to Kilmer's picture. When the Regiment left for deployment to Iraq in 2004, Colonel Slack took the crucifix from the picture and put it on. He wore it for the entire time the unit was deployed. For several years, Commanders always wore or carried the crucifix. After it was damaged, it was mounted in a frame and hung in the Commander's office. When the unit was activated and sent to the Horn of Africa, the Commander took the crucifix with him and always carried it (although he was Jewish).

After Colonel Conroy's death, Colonel Gerard W. Kelly took command of the Regiment. He would command the Regiment until 1944. On the first night on Makin, the Japanese tried to infiltrate the Regiment's lines. Japanese soldiers would call out "Hey, sarge" or "medic," and if a soldier engaged them with his rifle, it would give away his position. On the second night, soldiers were instructed to use hand grenades against Japanese probing. By the third day, Makin was secure. Day 4 and 5 the Regiment conducted mopping up operations and prepared for departure. Soldiers learned several lessons from Makin. If their ammunition got wet coming ashore, the cardboard boxes the rounds were in got soggy, and cardboard stuck to the rounds, making them useless (until the cardboard was removed from each individual round). They found out that they needed to keep their weapons clean since sand and rust would jam their weapons. Flamethrowers would not spark if their batteries got wet. By the second day, soldiers realized their canvas leggings were too long, and many cut them down. (The army would eventually shorten the leggings issued to soldiers). Soldiers also died, their white T-shirts brown with coffee. (Another innovation later adopted by the Army). Of the approximately 3,000 members of the Regiment who landed on Makin, 113 were casualties. Thirty-two men had been killed in action. The Regiment returned to Hawaii on December 2nd and was billeted in "hut city" at Schofield Barracks. Later, the Regiment moved to Bellows Field to rest and perform base security duty. Christmas Mass was held in the Regimental Chapel, and a Christmas dinner was served in the mess hall.

The 69th Regiment NYG discharged nine officers and placed six on the Reserve List. The regiment had 541 losses in 1943. Field Training was conducted at Camp Smith, and 625 members attended. The unit had 338 infirmary cases and 10 hospital cases. During the year, 42 officers and NCOs attended courses of instruction at the Second Tactical Command School. Pursuant to instructions issued by the War Department requiring the removal of Federal insignia from federally issued clothing and the wearing of distinctive insignia by the State Guard, procurement was affected of State shoulder patches to wear with the overcoat, coat, and shirt. Purchase was also affected of gilt buttons, with the

State Seal embossed to replace buttons on federally issued coats. Efforts were made to procure brass collar insignia, which were required for replacement purposes, but without avail. Substitute plastic collar insignia (22,000) was procured and distributed. During 1944, the basic weapon was changed from shotguns to rifles. Sub-machine guns 30 caliber and M1917AI machine guns were also issued to the NYG Regiment. The strength of the 69th Regiment, NYG, was 71 officers and 692 enlisted personnel, for a total of 763. Field Training at Camp Smith consisted of troop-leading procedures, tactics, and control measures in domestic disturbances, civil disorders, and riot duty, command post exercises for the staff, and instruction in chemical weapons. Demonstrations in the tactical training of the individual soldier (e.g., scouting, patrolling, riot control, weapons (including chemical warfare weapons), intelligence, military police, firing at moving targets, etc.). Leadership training of junior officers and of non-commissioned officers was stressed.

In Hawaii, training for the 165th began again in January (incorporating the lessons learned on Makin). Lessons focused on jungle warfare. In February, amphibious training was taught utilizing rubber boats and the newer Landing Craft Vehicle Personnel (LCVPs). The training stressed methods of eliminating Japanese fortified positions. A few replacements arrived in March, and the Regiment celebrated St. Patrick's Day in typical fashion with the Regimental Cocktail of Irish Whiskey and Champagne, games, and beer. After taking Makin, the United States continued its campaign across the Pacific using an "island-hoping" strategy. The next objective was Saipan in the Mariana Islands. Saipan is approximately about 1,400 miles south of Tokyo and from Aslito Airfield on the island, the U.S. could launch air strikes against the Philippines and the islands closer to the Japanese mainland.

On May 30th, the men of the Regiment held a memorial service for their fallen comrades. At 1300 hours the next day, they boarded the USS Harris. The Harris arrived near Saipan on June 16th. On the deck, soldiers watched the shelling of naval gunfire. Two Marine Divisions landed in Saipan on June 15th, and the 27th Infantry Division landed on June 17th. The first Army unit ashore was the 165th Infantry. The mission was to take Aslito Airfield and by nightfall. The 1st Battalion was in a fight for control of a ridge between the airfield and Cape Obian, and the 2nd Battalion was engaged with Japanese forces at the southwest corner of Aslito Airfield. On June 18th, the Marines' Fourth Division crossed the island to Magicienne Bay (on the east coast), and the 165th captured the airfield without opposition. The 165th then began clearing the southeastern end of the island at Nafutan

Point. On June 22nd, Army units, except the 2nd Battalion, were withdrawn from Nafutan Point. The repositioning of Army forces left the 2nd Battalion with the task of defeating the former defenders of Aslito Airfield. The effort did not go well, and on June 27th, the Japanese broke through the lines of the Second Battalion and reached the airfield before being repulsed.

The two Marine divisions began their advance up the lower slopes of Mount Tapotchau in the center of the island. On June 23rd, the 165th Regimental Combat Team prepared to attack an elevation that became known as Purple Heart Ridge. By June 27th, Purple Heart Ridge had been cleared but the 2nd Battalion had lost two commanders in two days. The enemy had entrenched positions in caves, and fighting was fierce. At Harikari Gulch, about 60 Japanese soldiers put grenades to their abdomens and committed suicide.

The largest Bansi attack of the war was conducted on July 7th. Saipan was declared secured on July 9th, but resistance continued for more than a year. The 27th Division left the island on October 4th. Thousands of Japanese soldiers and civilians committed suicide rather than surrender to the Americans.

The 165th Infantry never came off the line in Saipan except to move from one front to another. It served for twenty-five days of constant fighting. Each night, the

Japanese would probe the units' position. There were several night attacks and attempts at infiltration. The Regiment gained more ground and captured more important installations than any other comparable unit on the Island, Army or Marine. When the fighting was over, the Marines had redubbed the regiment, the "165th Marines," out of respect for the great fighting qualities shown in the struggle.

The 165th always referred to themselves as the "69th". They carried their green flags and referred to themselves as the "Fighting Irish." The 1st Battalion was Commanded by Jerry Kelley and later Jim Mahoney. The 2nd Battalion was Commanded by John McDonough (until he was wounded) and by Denis Claire, Jim Dooley, and Ben Ryan. The 3rd Battalion had several Commanders, Joseph Timothy Hart, Denny Claire, Martin Faery, and Herman Lutz (always fondly known as "Herman the German"). The Company Commanders included an O'Brien, two Ryans, a Kennedy, a Gallagher, a McManus, a Kiley, a Potter, and a Tuohy, among others. For some little time (under the command of General Haskell), all incoming 27th Division replacements were screened for the Irish names. Those soldiers were then sent to the 165th Infantry. However, under later generals, this practice was discontinued. Most of the esprit de corps was generated from within the Regiment by the soldiers who enlisted in the 165th when it was a National Guard Regiment.

As battles reduced, the number of these older members of the esprit went down. No effort was made by Division Headquarters to indoctrinate the men in the history and pride of the Regiment.

After the Battle for Saipan, Colonel Joseph Hart took command of the Regiment. In late September, the Regiment boarded the USAT Robin Doncaster enroute to Espiritu Santo in the New Hebrides. On October 7, 1944, the Regiment landed at Espiritu Santo and moved to one of the coconut plantations about 10 miles away from the naval base. In October and November, training was rigorous, intense, and professional. Soldiers requalified with their weapons and familiarized themselves with the heavier weapons (machine guns and mortars). Many went through another jungle training school.

Most of the New York Adjutant General's Report for 1945 is concerned with the activation of upstate units during civil emergencies (such as unexpected snowstorms). During Annual Training, the 69th Regiment New York Guard had 733 personnel present and 75 personnel absent. The Regiment's total strength was 808.

The oppressive heat of January through March 1945 caused many soldiers to suffer from heat-related illnesses (tropical skin diseases were rampant). When soldiers were not training, they were parading. Reviews, parades and awards ceremonies occurred monthly. In early March, there was a final ceremony where the 165th's three battalions received the

Combat Battalion Infantry Streamer (signifying that 65 percent of the battalions were recipients of the Combat Infantryman Badge). On March 19, in a driving rain, the Regiment boarded the USS Missoula for landing exercises at Turtle Bay. It then traveled onboard that ship to Okinawa. The next challenge for the Regiment was to participate in the Invasion of the Ryukyu Islands off Japan. On April 19th, the Regiment was on the right of the 27th Division line as it advanced toward Machinato Airfield. Prior to advancing on Machinato Airfield, however, the Regiment would have to overcome a system of Japanese defenses known as "Item Pocket." Item Pocket was three main ridges, two minor ones, and four gullies. The principal ridges came to be called Ryan's Ridge after the Commander of "F" Company, Charlie Ridge named after "C" Company, and Potter's Ridge after the Commander of "I" Company. Members of the Intelligence and Reconnaissance Platoon were issued a new weapon called a "Sniperscope." The Army had developed it for the sole purpose of thwarting Japanese infiltration. Using this weapon, a soldier could see in the dark to a range of about 70 yards. Objects appeared in the scope in various shades of green. About 30 percent of the total Japanese casualties inflicted through rifle fire during the first weeks of the Okinawa Operation were from the sniperscope and M2 carbine.

"A" and "G" Companies were to attack enemy positions along the crest of Charlie Ridge while the rest of the 1st and 2nd Battalions were to make their way across the bottomlands and rice paddies to Charlie and Potter's Ridges. By the end of the day, the crest of Charlie Ridge had been cleared, and the First Battalion had advanced as far south as Gusukuma. There, the Regiment received flanking fire from somewhere in the Pocket. Along the west side of the Charlie Ridge, the Second Battalion pushed forward to Potter's Ridge without opposition. But when "G" Company moved onto the ridge, it became engaged in a heavy firefight with the enemy dug in on the east nose of the ridge. Company "G" cleared enemy positions and took possession of a network of dugouts and tunnels. As "G" Company prepared to make contact with the First Battalion on its left, the Company (and the 1st Battalion) came under intense flanking fire from the Pocket. The enemy positions on the top of Ryan's Ridge opened fire with mortars. "F" Company pushed across open ground to Fox Ridge, where it waited for "G" Company to arrive. The next day, the Commander of the 2nd Battalion (Colonel Kelley) moved his battalion to the Division Reserve near Machinato Airfield (leaving Captain Ryan and

Company "F" to hold the right flank of the Division line west of Item Pocket). The enemy attacked "F" Company for three days, but "F" Company held their position. On April 25th, "F" Company was ordered to attack Item Pocket. The Company came under heavy fire, which continued all night. Captain Ryan was not able to assault the ridge until the following morning. In the morning, Ryan ordered his mortars, antitank guns, and machine guns to begin firing while two platoons attacked the ridge. Thirty-one men reached the top of the ridge. Suddenly, Japanese soldiers emerged from caves and tunnels while pillboxes opened fire on the Company's position. The men fought until their ammunition ran out. In the hand-to-hand fighting, the men used their rifles as clubs. "F" Company had established a foothold, but control of Ryan's Ridge was far from secure. Captain Ryan led the rest of his Company (twenty-one men) to the top of the ridge to reinforce his two platoons. Along with "K" Company, Company "F' continued operations on the ridge for several days. The men had not eaten in over two days. Finally, on April 26th, they received supplies and food. For their endurance under the most trying conditions, Company "F" and Captain Ryan received a Distinguished Unit Citation: "Company "F," 165th Infantry Regiment was cited for Conspicuous Valor and Outstanding Performance of a combat mission against the Japanese military forces in the Okinawan Phase of the Nansei Shoto Operation during the period 20-25 April 1945.

Although Company "F" had dislodged the enemy from the western side of Ryan's Ridge on April 27. The eastern side of the ridge was not cleared until nightfall of the following day. This was accomplished by Company "A," which had relieved Captain Ryan's men that morning. During that action, Private First-Class Alejandro Ruiz was awarded the Medal of Honor. The citation issued in June 1946 detailed Ruiz's heroism: "Sergeant Alejandro Renteria Ruiz (Army serial No. 38,442,412) (then Private First Class), Company "A," 165th Infantry Regiment, Army of the United States, on 28 April 1945, at Okinawa, when his unit was stopped by a skillfully camouflaged enemy pillbox, displayed conspicuous gallantry and intrepidity above and beyond the call of duty. His squad, suddenly brought under a hail of machine-gun fire and a vicious grenade attack, was pinned down. Jumping to his feet, Private Ruiz seized an automatic rifle and lunged through the flying grenades, rifles, and automatic fire for the top of the emplacement. An enemy soldier charged him, and his rifle jammed. Undaunted, he whirled on the assailant and clubbed him down. He then ran back through the bullets and grenades, seized more ammunition and another automatic rifle, and again made for the pillbox. Enemy fire was now concentrated on him, but he charged on, miraculously reaching the position, and, in plain view, climbed to the top. Leaping from one opening to another, he sent burst after burst into the pillbox, killing 12 of the enemy and destroying the position. Private Ruiz's heroic conduct, in the face of overwhelming odds, saved the lives of many comrades and eliminated an obstacle which would have long checked his unit's advance".

The Okinawa campaign was also the end of the "Fighting Irish" nickname for the Regiment. The esprit of the unit was instilled by the older, experienced, battle-hardened and Officers and NCOs. Although most of them had been overseas for four years and were eligible for rotation home, the majority wanted to stay with the Regiment and return home with it. This meant remaining with the Regiment for the future invasion of Japan. These leaders realized it would be a long, hard, and dangerous campaign. But the love of these men for their old 69th made them willing to forego their transfer back to the United States. This promised to furnish a core of seasoned men needed for future operations. The 27th Infantry Division had to be rebuilt to compensate for the tremendous battle losses it had suffered on Okinawa. Not only was the Division understrength due to battle losses, but because of the point system for rotation home, the Division had released all but 2,600 men. However, the new

Commanding Officer of the Division had other ideas. He assumed Command of the Division after the ugly "Smith versus Smith" affair on Saipan and he believed all the "old guard" must go. He put pressure on the older officers and men to leave. In July 1945, replaced Colonel Hart with a Regular Army Officer with a distinctly non-Irish name.

The next day, a division order was issued stating that press releases referring to the 165th as the "Fighting Irish" would no longer be issued. The effect of the order was instantaneous. As fast as they could, the remainder of the old guard took their rotation. On V-J Day there was not a single officer or man in the Regiment from the old outfit. The splendid esprit de corps, which had carried the 69th New York through Gettysburg, Antietam, St. Mihiel, and Saipan, was gone. All that remained was another colorless, inexperienced regiment of draftees.

The 165th Infantry Regiment deployed overseas in February 1942. It began combat operations on 21 November 1943. The Regiment suffered 113 battle casualties on Makin, 996 on Saipan, and 1,903 on Okinawa. The Regiment came home in December 1945 and furled its colors on 26 December 1945. There was only a handful of the men who were present in October 1940 to return with the Regimental Colors. The soldiers who were with the unit for activation were either dead, evacuated for wounds, or were sent home on furlough in May and June 1945 (because they had enough points). General Orders No. 16, Headquarters New York Guard, dated 29 November 1946, established the process of reorganization and re-establishment of the New York National Guard. The order called for the reorganization of the New York (State) Guard in preparation for its transition to the New York National Guard. When the necessary procedures were completed, and Federal and State requirements were met, the unit was Federally Recognized by the War Department. The 69th Infantry Regiment, New York Guard (less the band), was re-designated the 165th Infantry Regiment (less 3 rifle companies, the anti-tank company, and the cannon company), New York National Guard. The 165th was assigned to the 42nd Infantry Division. The 165th Infantry Regiment had 60 Officers, 4 Warrant Officers, and 1,424 Enlisted Soldiers for a total strength of 1,488. Colonel Martin H. Meaney took Command of the Regiment. He would command until 1949. The Regiment participated in a two-day exercise involving the theoretical use of the NYNG and NYG in the aid of civil authority.

The Korean War began on 25 June 1950. Lt. General W. B. Smith, Commander First Army, wrote to the Governors of New York, New Jersey, and Pennsylvania, pointing out the need for arrangements for the protection of interstate bridges, tunnels, and communications facilities. He suggested a conference to discuss the matter. On 20 September 1950, the Governors of New York and New Jersey signed an agreement for interstate cooperation and mutual aid in case of emergency. However, General Smith pointed out a problem with their agreement. Military principles require independent responsibility for protecting such structures, but the present laws do not permit the forces of one State to operate inside the borders of another.

The 165th Infantry Regiment celebrated its 150th centennial in New York on October 12, 2001. However, the Army Center of Military History (the proponent for Army Lineage) changed the lineage of the Regiment awarding the Regiment an earlier organization date. This change in lineage provided a more colorful early history and linked the Regiment much more closely to the Irish revolutionary movement in New York City. Before the lineage and was changed, the Army had not yet awarded the 69th Regiment the lineage and honors of the 1st Irish Regiment (9th Regiment) and the Fourth Irish Regiment (75th Regiment). The organizational date was changed to 1849 rather than 1851; the centennial was mistakenly celebrated in 1951 since the unit leadership did not realize there was a change in lineage. The 150th anniversary celebration should have been held on December 21, 1999.

In 1953, a ceremony was held which brought the 165th Infantry Regiment, the 167th (4th Alabama) Infantry Regiment, the Alabama National Guard, and the U. S. Navy's Aircraft Carrier, USS Antietam, together. The two National Guard Regiments had faced each other in the bloody Battle of Antietam during the Civil War. Each regiment placed its Civil War colors and battle standards aboard the USS Antietam. The Antietam was the only Naval vessel named after a Civil War battle. The program received national attention.

In 1954, the Regiment sent their Color Guard to Ireland to take part in the "A Tostal" Celebration, which was held in honor of General Thomas Francis Meagher. Ireland reestablished the practice of inviting representatives of the Regiment to participate in ceremonies for Meagher. Members of the Regiment have attended the "1848 Tricolour Celebration" in Waterford, Ireland, every year since its inception.

In 1960, the Regiment was reorganized as a parent regiment under the Combat Arms Regimental System to consist of the 1st Battle Group, an element of the 42nd Infantry Division.

1st Battle Group,165th Infantry (which is part of the lineage of the 69th Regiment) was inspected by the Secretary of the Army, Wilber M. Brucker, and Major General Charles

C. Nast, Commanding General, 42nd Infantry Division at Camp Drum during Annual Training. In 1963, during the presidency of John F. Kennedy, the designation "69th infantry" was restored. The 1st Battle Group, 165th Infantry, was reorganized and re-designated on 15 April 1963 as the 69th Infantry to consist of the 1st and 2nd Battalions, elements of the 42nd Infantry Division. The 1st Battalion was commanded by LTC John McCarthy, and the 2nd Battalion was commanded by LTC William Klauz. President Kenned presented one of the Regiment's Civil War Flags (Second Irish Colors) to Ireland. The presentation was held in the Irish Parliament, and it was the first time both houses of the Irish Parliament met in session.

In 1968, the Selected Reserve Force (SRF) program consisted of specially selected units, which were organized to full strength and equipment and trained and equipped for short-notice mobilization and deployment for Federal missions. The organization of these units into the new Selected Reserve Force II included both battalions of the 69th Infantry. On 6 March, Co "B" and Company "C" 107th Infantry, located in the Flushing Armory in Queens, NY) was transferred to the 2nd Bn 69th as Co "B and Company "C." The units remained in the Flushing Armory and were designated as Selected Reserve Force (SRF). On 30 March, Company "C" 2nd Bn, 69th Infantry, located in Manhattan, was disbanded. On 10 April, Company "B" 2nd Bn, 69th Infantry, located in Manhattan, was disbanded. There was a Snow Emergency in Jamaica, Queens, in February 1969.

The Flushing Armory was opened to house 348 individuals for a three-day period. On 28 August 1969, the Chief National Guard Bureau announced that the Secretary of the Army had directed the elimination of Selected Reserve Forces II (SRF) units, effective 30 September 1969. The 1st and 2nd Battalions were ordered into active Federal service on 24 March 1970 at home station in response to call up during the U.S. Postal Strike (Operation Graphic Hand). The units were released from active Federal service a week later and reverted to State control. Having been "ordered" instead of "called" to active duty by Presidential action, Federal law automatically reduced the obligated service of individuals from six to five years. The Viet Nam War was raging, and the President decided not to call the National Guard. During the year 1974, the Intelligence Section of the New York State Division of Military and Naval Affairs (DMNA) processed reports of one demonstration, 19 thefts, 8 bomb threats, 43 incidents of damage or forced entry, and 90 accidents affecting the DMNA facilities and personnel. During the year 1976, the Intelligence Section of the NYS Division of Military and Naval Affairs (DMNA) processed reports of 2 demonstrations at DMNA facilities, 16 thefts, 10 bomb threats, 20 incidents of damage or forced entry, and 96 accidents affecting the DMNA facilities and personnel. A major reorganization of the 42d Infantry Division took place on 1 April 1975. The reorganization resulted in deactivation of the 2nd Battalion, 69th Infantry. Lieutenant Colonel John O. Santelli, who commanded the 2nd Battalion from 1972, would be its last commander. The friendly rivalry between the 1st Bn, 69th Infantry, NYARNG, and the 101st Infantry, Massachusetts Army National Guard, date back to the Civil War. The Logan-Duffy Rifle Match has been an annual (although more on-again, off-again) event since 1936. The victor is awarded possession of the Logan-Duffy Silver Bowl with a matching tray. In 1976, the regiment had possession of the trophy. In 1979, the Battalion was mobilized by Governor Hugh L. Carey in response to a walkout of 7000 unionized prison guards involved in a contract dispute with the Department of Corrections. The call-up (Operation Gold Plum), the largest ever in State history, affected all the major forces of the State Militia and totaled 12000 members of the New York Army and Air National Guard, the New York Naval Militia, and the New York Guard.

In 1993, the Army re-established the Regimental System. Major General Martin E. Foery was appointed the first Honorary Colonel of the Regiment (HCOR) in accordance with Army Regulation / National Guard Regulation 600-82. Major General Joseph A. Healey was appointed Regimental Adjutant.

The Infantry Regiment was converted and re-designated on 1 September 1993 as the 69th Air Defense Artillery to consist of the 1st Battalion, an element of the 42nd Infantry Division. On June 4, 1994, Major General Martin Foery, Honorary Colonel of the Regiment, died. The Regimental Adjutant, Major General Joseph Healey, replaced him as the Honorary Colonel of the Regiment.

Major General Healy had been acting as the Honorary Colonel of the Regiment since the Regiment was established because of Major General Foery's poor health.

In 1996, The Regiment was converted and re-designated 1 October 1996 as the 69th Infantry to consist of the 1st Battalion, an element of the 42nd Infantry Division.

Chapter Eight
September 11, 2001

In 2000, LTC Jeffrey Slack took command of the Battalion. Slack had transferred into the Regiment as a Captain from the 71st Infantry in 1991. When he arrived, he believed the 69th was the worst unit In the National Guard. As far as he was concerned, it was the laughingstock of the Army. Slack believed the unit was in rough shape. But he felt it was far worse than he imagined. The 69th Infantry was an absolutely demoralizing pigpen of an operation. In Slack's estimation, 69th men were always unprofessional. Their equipment was always broken. And when they trained, they loaded their trucks with alcohol, Hibachi grills, and boom boxes instead of Army supplies. Slack believed the Fighting 69th embodied all the negative stereotypes held in the military about the National Guard. Captain Slack had been a Company Commander in the 71st Infantry, and he was sure that when the Army would eliminate one of the infantry battalions in New York, it would be the 69th, but he was wrong. It was his 71st Infantry, which was eliminated. Slack thought the decision was a travesty and was aghast when he learned he would be transferred to the loathsome 69th. There has always been competition between the 71st and the 69th, going back to before the Civil War. The 71st was formed to keep tabs on the 69th. Some of Colonel Slacks' assessments of the Regiment could have been due to the animosity between regiments, but overall, he was correct. The Regiment was in terrible shape.

Most of the men who served in the Fighting 69th throughout America's wars were poor, lean, and well-muscled from day-to-day life. They had hard edges etched into their faces that didn't necessarily reflect armed strife but rather an immigrant background and a tremendous struggle against prejudice, sickness, poverty, and conflicts with other races and ethnic groups. Most of the Irish Americans in the 69th in 2001 came from families that had long ago ascended to middle-class America. More than 80 percent lived in the suburbs and had completed or were enrolled in college. Lieutenant Mike Drew, the commander of Delta Company on Long Island, was typical of the Irish Americans in the 69th. In 2001, about 41 percent of the Regiment's officers claimed Irish American roots. The Irish were the first to immigrate en-masse to New York City and founded the 69th. But echelons of immigrants and dispossessed from other countries followed that path. In 2001, only about 13 percent of the soldiers were Irish American. After the 2001 St. Patrick's Day Parade, Lieutenant Colonel Geoff Slack cheered with the other Officers as the unit passed through the foyer of the Armory. He had just concluded his first march in command of the Fighting 69th, always the lead echelon in the massive St. Patrick's Day Parade.

Armory 9/11

Captain Chris Daniels commanded the Headquarters Company (HHC). Daniels had been a platoon leader in the 71st and a member of a Special Forces Reserve unit in Upstate New York. When his Special Forces unit shut down in 1998, an officer at the 69th urged Daniels to come aboard. Before taking command of HHC, Daniels led Charlie Company on Long Island. Though separated by only 50 miles, the two units were worlds apart. Charlie Company and the other Long Island units were largely white, middle class, and populated by experienced sergeants who were generally settled in their communities. The HHC and the other inner-city units were largely Hispanic and black, lower class, and populated by a transient group of teenagers and twenty-somethings trying to figure out what to do in life. The Long Islanders had joined the Guard for old-fashioned camaraderie, esprit-de-corps, and a place to drink cheap beer with their mates. When unit flags changed, they maintained their loyalties to their neighborhood armory. Whether they were infantry, signal, or air defense didn't make much of a difference. The inner-city units had lost their experienced leaders in the 1990s and struggled to recruit and retain quality soldiers. Most young men who sought Army service in New York were attracted to better-funded units that had the latest equipment and who traveled to Puerto Rico, Germany, and Iceland for training. Meanwhile, the 69th could only offer new recruits a rusted and aging fleet of vehicles and the chance to march in the St. Patrick's Day Parade. New York State put emphasis on recruiting but even with all the recruiting, Daniels found he was short more than 200 soldiers in his company alone by March 2001. The 69th Infantry Regiment was a sieve. For every recruit the unit brought on, it seemed two more walked out the door for any of a hundred reasons.

What would later be called Ground Zero was a scene from another world. Where the Twin Towers once soared, a couple hundred feet of skeletal remains projected from the ground like stakes. The remainder of the 110-story structure and its outlying buildings seemed to have pancaked into one pile. Flames shrouded vehicles and buildings at every turn. A group of firefighters stood around one of their own burning fire trucks, holding hands in prayer for the souls of their comrades who never made it out of the vehicle. By rushing to Ground Zero to conduct a reconnaissance with his Executive Officer, Slack had already exceeded the efforts of the entire National Guard in the wake of the 1993 terrorist bombing of the Trade Center. Following that first attack, Slack waited in vain for orders to move to the site. He thought the Guard should have at least assessed the situation and developed contingency plans. But without orders, the Fighting 69th did nothing in 1993. Slack was ashamed by their inaction and his own and was determined not to let that happen again. Within minutes of watching the second plane strike the towers, the battalion commander left his house 70 miles outside the city and sped to the Fighting 69th's motor pool at Farmingdale, Long Island. He traded in his green Ford Ranger pick-up for his camouflage Humvee, which would allow him to bypass all the police checkpoints and get into the city quickly.

Without orders from the Department of Military and Naval Affairs (DMNA), LTC Slack began to activate the unit. When a colonel from upstate New York called for an update, he got Daniels on the phone. "Right now, sir, it's mass chaos," Daniels said. "All the soldiers are coming in and we're getting prepared to deploy wherever the State needs us or to possibly go down to the World Trade Center just to help down there with the recovery efforts." "Stop right there," the colonel said. "You have no authorization to bring soldiers into the armory. Send everyone home right now. This is a local police matter." Daniels said, "Roger out, sir. He hung up the phone and continued to bring soldiers in for duty. While Slack and Daniels were doing what infantrymen were trained to do, move to the sound of the guns, the bureaucrats at the State headquarters were already prepping their memorandums. At 9:30 a.m. on September 11, 2001, a Colonel ordered the 69th to cease and desist any actions that might be construed as martial in nature. Daniels told Slack that he had been ordered to stand down. Slack told him to drive on. In Slack's opinion, many of the officers at the State Headquarters were careerists, people who didn't like sticking their necks out for fear a miss-step would cost them their next promotion. Later that day, one high-ranking civilian employee of the National Guard told Slack to send everyone home or be prepared to pay the salaries of all the soldiers he brought in because the State hadn't authorized it. Slack hung up on him.

"How dare you hang up on me!" the bureaucrat shouted at Slack when he called back. "Who do you think you are?"

Colonel Slack wondered the same thing about the civilians. He hung up on the bureaucrat again and instructed his staff not to take any more of his calls. Slack had called back from the World Trade Center and told Daniels he wanted to start getting platoon-sized elements down to the Trade Center as they reported in for duty. Slack and two other two battalion commanders devised a security plan in concert with the New York Police Department (NYPD) National Guard personnel (with its roughly 1200 soldiers) that would establish a cordon around Ground Zero. In general, actions inside the cordon would be under the control of the Fire Department, and actions outside the cordon would be controlled by the NYPD. More soldiers were needed during daylight operations, so the commanders decided to use one battalion as the night force and two battalions as the day force. The governor finally directed the National Guard to respond but without arms. Slack decided to issue Beretta 9mm pistols with one magazine to all his officers since they generally had more training with the rules of engagement. In addition, he stockpiled his rifles and ammunition near his command post at Battery Park, easily accessible in case the situation changed. When millions of television viewers turned on the news on September 12, 2001, they didn't see the 1st Battalion, 69th Infantry Regiment, New York National Guard. They saw the United States Army. As one group of soldiers moved into position at dawn, a civilian cheered from the sidewalk. He thought the men were paratroopers from the 82nd Airborne Division. "When did you guys get in?" he asked one of the troops. "Did you fly straight out of Fort Bragg?"

One of the first missions was to help the fire department search rooftops near Ground Zero for human remains and aircraft parts. Back at the 69th Armory, the outside walls of the building had become an endless sea of fliers, each featuring a photo of a smiling man, woman, or child. The words "missing," or "last seen," or "help" were typed out in large font below the pictures. The armory had become a shrine or, in the words of one soldier, a big graveyard of dead souls. Standing near the pictures in a line that stretched around the block were the thousands of people who hung the photos. Men and women, old and young, friends and family. They were panicked, desperate, scared. One man grabbed a Guardsman by the shoulders as he got off the bus. "Have you seen my baby?" he cried. "Have you seen my little girl?" While the 69th was working at Ground Zero, the City of New York's Office of Community Affairs had turned the armory into the Family Bereavement Center, the place people would come to register their missing children, spouses, parents, or friends. The drill floor, which had housed a trade show on Tuesday morning, was now carpeted, air-conditioned, filled with 2,000 chairs, dozens of desks and computers, and fold-out tables covered with fliers, forms, and booklets about how to deal with loss. Families sat alongside the desks. On the first day, they dropped off fliers. On subsequent trips, they provided DNA samples from combs or toothbrushes. More sheets of paper were taped to the walls, from the floor to the height of outstretched and shaking arms. Candles were lit on the sidewalks and people huddled in prayer groups or stared alone into nothing. One of the "missing" flyers for Lieutenant Baptiste, First Platoon Leader of Alpha Company. First Lieutenant Baptiste was a firefighter based out of Greenwich Village. He died in the south tower while trying to rescue civilians. Tommy Jurgens, another veteran who had finished his last drill with the Fighting 69th just weeks before, was also killed in the attack.

The world had changed. The purpose of an infantry battalion is to go to war, and the President had said that week that America was at war. Now, someone just had to give New York's old 69th Infantry Regiment a chance to fight again. In the week after the attacks, the 69th secured the perimeter of Ground Zero, assisted police and fire officials with recovery efforts, and escorted the residents of apartment buildings near the Trade Center in and out of their homes to recover pets, medications, and other key personal belongings. But when the U.S. launched air strikes against

Afghanistan, the 69th was ordered to push out the security perimeter. Instead of securing just Ground Zero, the 69th and other National Guard units assisted the police in securing Lower Manhattan. Platoons of soldiers left the Trade Center cordon and established positions at the entrances and exits of the bridges and tunnels leading into and out of Manhattan.

The planners and policymakers at the Pentagon designed the modern National Guard as a strategic reserve for the regular Army. The Guard was never meant to mobilize and deploy on short notice for a small regional conflict like Desert Storm or a peacekeeping mission like Bosnia. It was designed to be called up in the event of a major war. This institutionalized neglect was defined in the Pentagon's tiered readiness system. Every unit in the Army was assigned a force activity designator (FAD) that coincided with the unit's likelihood to fight. Units most likely to engage in combat received the best resources. After the Berlin Wall came down and the U.S.S.R broke up, the Army looked for a mission. The active force was structured for a major conflict, and if the U.S.S.R. was no longer a threat, the Country did not need all the soldiers who were on active duty. The Army started to downsize both the active and reserve forces. The National Guard received very little resources. The 69th completed its second rotation at Ground Zero on October 26. The Army was the smallest it had been since it was last called the Fighting 69th to Federal duty in 1940.

Moreover, the President had just launched a war in Afghanistan and was already planning an action in Iraq. The Army had no active forces to spare to secure the country's infrastructure, including West Point. That only left one viable option. The 69th was assigned security at West Point. Colonel Slack called the Bravo Company Commander and asked him if he would Command his company at the Academy, the officer said he'd rather not. He and many of the unit's soldiers, who had seen the devastation of New York, wanted to kill terrorists and guard against another attack, not babysit for cadets. And though Slack had told the men the mission was to defend the base, there were a handful among the Fighting 69th that thought the deployment to West Point was merely a ruse for public consumption. Many soldiers in the unit thought nothing could be worse than St. Patrick's Day with the Fighting 69th. Fifth Avenue in March was very cold and often snowing or hailing. Soldiers had to be at the Armory before 5 AM for formation.

However, March 17th at a guard shack at the U.S. Military Academy was worse. Soldiers spent their days standing like hall monitors among throngs of cadets. They searched squadrons of soccer mom minivans. They parked cars for the Blues Clues children's concert at the base theater. The goodwill shown to the Guardsmen when they first arrived was short-lived. By Christmas, the officers' wives yelled at the soldiers when they failed to salute the blue stickers on their windshields that proclaimed their status.

The unit had been gutted of NCO leadership in the 1990s but had rebounded enough that it could field an effective group of leaders for at least two companies in 2001 and 2002. the West Point mission gave the NCO Corps an opportunity to train their soldiers as infantrymen. The 69th was able to dedicate ten days out of every 30 at the Academy to training, all of it led by platoon sergeants. For the first time in years, the 69th started to develop its NCO Corp. Sergeants, who had no leadership experience and got valuable time in charge of men and a mission. The Officer Corps had similar experiences. Leadership was being learned and learned well. The Academy became a proving ground for all soldiers assigned there. As the months went by, each soldier demonstrated his level of competence, dedication, and reliability. With two of the companies on "Federal" duty at West Point, the rest of the Battalion was assigned "State" duty guarding the bridges and tunnels around the city, including the Brooklyn-Battery and Queens-Midtown Tunnels; the Brooklyn, Manhattan, and Williamsburg Bridges; and Grand Central and Pennsylvania rail stations. Slack shifted his Command Post from the Lexington Avenue Armory to Fort Hamilton in Bay Ridge, Brooklyn. The Bridge and Tunnel mission was slated to last three months. But LTC Slack was intent on keeping the battalion on duty until the troops who had deployed to West Point came home. Three months turned to six, then nine. Most of the men in the Battalion had begun full-time military duty on September 11, 2001, and served until October 2002 in the city or at the Academy with very few breaks.

The 69th was slated to mobilize for nine months in May 2004 as part of a Multinational Force and Observers (MFO) mission to the Sinai. The 42nd Infantry Division had directed all units to abandon collective training to focus on individual tasks. In The unit was in a poor state of readiness. There were soldiers in the unit who looked like they could have been grandfathers. There were soldiers who seemed to have no proficiency at even the most basic tasks. On one drill weekend, one of the officers found a soldier trying to load his bullets into his rifle magazine backward. Junior privates showed no respect for senior NCOs. They called them by their first names and didn't hesitate to tell them where to shove it. As for training, there was none. On Mar 17th, 2003 (Unit Day), it seemed nobody was focused on the parade. The march went off as usual, and everyone hurried home to watch what was going to happen in Iraq. The MFO mission was cancelled for the 69th would head to Bosnia in April 2004 instead. The Battalion needed another 163 more soldiers and leaders for the Bosnia mission, officially Stabilization Force (SFOR) 16.

In the 1970s, Captain John Green, a Company Commander in the 2nd Battalion, would tell his officers to "Remain flexible. It Will change." This was never truer than it was in 2003 and 2004. The mission to the Sinai had been changed to Bosnia. Now, the deployment to Kosovo instead. Kosovo was technically a peace-enforcement operation. Violence in the fractured state still flared from time to time. Former NATO Commander and then Presidential candidate Wesley Clark referred to Kosovo as the Wild West. In February 2004, at the National Guard Bureau (NGB) Sourcing Conference, the Army and NGB were in search of an infantry battalion to round out an enhanced National Guard brigade from Louisiana scheduled to deploy to Iraq. When the operations officer for the 42nd Infantry Division returned from the Sourcing Conference, he telephoned Slack and said: "Do you remember seeing the desert-pattern Rainbow patch?" Since January, the Division had been showing off the patch it would wear to Iraq. "Expect dramatic news when you get to Albany." Slack laughed off the remark. At a meeting in Albany on Friday, February 27th, 2004, rumors of a mission change picked up pace.

Major General Thomas Maguire, the Adjutant General of New York, made it official. "Guess what? You're not going to Kosovo; you're going to Iraq."

Chapter Nine
Operation Iraqi Freedom

Given the state of the Battalion's personnel and equipment, LTC Slack believed the unit would be lucky to get into Iraq at all. He thought the Battalion would be relegated to guarding an equipment depot in Kuwait, far from any action. Still, he realized that a deployment to a combat theater was far more complex than what he was planning for Kosovo. On March 17, 2004, Slack sat on the reviewing stand inside the armory for the annual St. Patrick's Day pass in review. The unit needed to deploy 760 soldiers (twice that of the requirement for Kosovo). The word was the 69th would mobilize in May 2004, train from May through September in the U.S., and then ship to the Iraq area of operations in October. Once in theater, the 69th would serve for one year. As Slack feared, the length of the tour meant all soldiers who served at West Point or on other Federal (Homeland Security) deployments now had to volunteer for service in Iraq because it would put them over 24 months of cumulative service. The rule affected more than 150 of Slack's remaining soldiers, and the Commander worried many of the men would bail out due to the amount of time already spent away from home. Headquarters Company (HHC), A, B, and companies were chosen to deploy, and C & D Companies were transferred into A. An entire company was transferred from the 101st Cavalry to make up the new D Company. Soldiers from the 101 Cavalry's D Company marched in St Patrick's Day Parade carrying their own Gideon. In the New York National Guard, it was normal for two battalions to be consolidated to make one. But in the case of the 69th Infantry, the State Headquarters in Albany had to break four other battalions to bring the unit up to wartime strength. When the 69th Infantry mustered on May 16, 2004, at Camp Smith in Peekskill for its first mobilization to a combat zone in more than 60 years, the Battalion included an entire company from the Staten Island-based 101st Cavalry Regiment, two New York City-based platoons from the 105th Infantry Regiment, and more than 100 soldiers from the 152nd Engineer and the 127th Armor Battalions out of Buffalo. Another group came as volunteers out of disparate units from as far away as California. Half of the Fighting 69th's men were strangers to the Battalion. In Alpha Company, now authorized 139 men, the number of outsiders topped 100 soldiers. On May 15, 2004, the unit was activated and proceeded to Camp Smith. An Advance Party, consisting of the Executive Officer, Adjutant, Logistics Officer, and representatives from the Companies and Staff Sections, proceeded to Fort Hood to prepare for the arrival of the Unit at their Mobilization

Station. On May 18, 2004, the unit flew from Newberg into the Army Airfield to Fort Hood, Texas.

When the 69th arrived at Fort Hood, it met the Tiger Brigade of Louisiana (which they fought during the Civil War). The Battalion's equipment was a disgrace, especially in comparison to the Louisiana Tigers, 256th Brigade Combat Team (which was a well-funded enhanced heavy brigade with Bradley Fighting vehicles and M1 Abrams tanks). One of the unit vehicles didn't have an engine, and another had to be towed off the train because its tires were flat. Slack was embarrassed and ashamed. He telephoned New York State Headquarters and accused the State of complicity. He was rude and confrontational to the officers who were supposedly supporting the mobilization. When the Commanding General of the Tiger Brigade, also called New York State Headquarters, a senior officer assured General Basilica, Commander of the Brigade, that they were doing everything they could for the 69th.

But the moment Basilica got off the phone, the senior New York officer was back on the line with Slack to put the rogue Commander back in his place. "You need to cease and desist," he ordered. The bureaucrat thought Slack was so far out of line in his accusations against New York that Slack should be relieved. Slack wasn't intimidated. He told the officer he didn't have the authority to give anyone in the 69th an order. "I'm no longer in the New York Army National Guard," Slack said. "I'm in the United States Army. I work for the Tiger Brigade. The only thing you are is a resource. New York State is a resource, and all I expect out of you is equipment and personnel, and that's all." Slack slammed down the phone. New York State offered to relieve LTC Slack immediately, but General Basilica thanked New York for its offer and said he intended to keep Lieutenant Colonel Slack on board. The 69th began to receive new equipment. When it came time to review training and equipment status reports and sensitive items inventories, the 69th normally came up woefully short. Slack made appropriate changes to Battalion Staff and attempted to make appropriate changes to the training schedules. But "checking the box" was the reality of the National Training Center at Fort Hood. Everything the soldiers did had to be recorded on a roster. Lieutenants and Sergeants stalked the training areas with clipboards. They had a list of some 100 tasks that needed to be done before anyone could be certified (e.g., driver's training. land navigation, weapons qualification, etc.,). But the unit would complete its training at Fort Hood in August 2004, whether all its soldiers had checked the boxes or not.

On October 5, 2004, the unit arrived at Camp Buehring in Kuwait, their home for the next three weeks. The men arrived by bus around Midnight and were told to hit the mess hall, a series of prefabricated trailers that had been pushed together to make a cafeteria. The Dining Facility (DFAC) was much better than anything the soldiers had ever experienced in the field. It was their first encounter with KBR Living. Kellogg Brown and Root was one of the larger defense contractors supporting the war effort (allowing the US to keep its numbers of soldiers on the ground low). They ran the mess halls, they set up the soldiers' tents, they maintained the air conditioning and they ran training areas. KBR did just about everything. But, the soldiers' primary interaction with the contractor was at mealtime. There was a main serving line, a grilled-to-order line, and no limit on the amount a soldier could eat. Steaks on Monday. Crab legs on Friday. Ice cream anytime.

After chow, the men were guided to a tent where their ID cards were officially "swiped in" to the theater. As of that day, the men's salary was no longer taxable, and they received extra pay for being in a combat zone. The purpose of the 69th's stop in Kuwait was called RSOI: reception, staging, and onward integration. Within a week of arriving in Kuwait, the men married up with their vehicles and connexes (short for container for export, a large box used by the military to ship equipment) and started preparing them for the drive north to Baghdad. The soldiers also used the time to sharpen their infantry skills. Most units spent their time shooting, rehearsing battle drills, and conducting physical training to speed the acclimation to the 120-degree temperatures. General Basilica was swapping infantry companies to balance the Tiger Brigade for its mission in Iraq.

Basilica had learned the 256th Brigade Combat Team would not be relegated to guarding an equipment depot in Kuwait or passing out chocolates in peaceful northern Iraq. The brigade and the 69th were going into the heart of Baghdad. By the summer of 2004, the city had erupted in a full-scale rebellion against the American occupation. To prepare for combat in urban areas, Basilica had to "task-organize" his units, had a similar complement of equipment, and was versatile enough to execute any mission in the AO (area of operations. A battalion of all tanks wouldn't have enough soldiers. A battalion of all dismounted infantry wouldn't have enough armor protection. Basilica's 1st Battalion was a tank unit armed with the M1A1 Abrams Tanks. His 2nd Battalion was a mechanized infantry unit armed with the Bradley Fighting Vehicle. His 3rd Battalion, which the General wasn't supposed to deploy with (but did anyway), was an understrength infantry battalion that would maneuver in Humvees (High Mobility Multipurpose Wheeled Vehicles).

The primary maneuver platform for the infantry in Iraq in 2004 was the M1114 up-armored Humvee. Ten days before the 69th was set to drive into combat, they still hadn't received a single 1114 (pronounced "eleven-fourteen" by the troops). All they had were six M1025 soft-skinned Humvees with an add-on-armor (AOA) kit. Compared to what the unit had, the 1025s with AOA were practically tanks. But the real benefit of the 1025s was that they came with a Blue Force Tracker (BFT). The BFT was a system new to the War on Terror. At its most basic function, the machine allowed the vehicle commander to see where he and other BFT-equipped vehicles were on a map. BFT operators could also send messages to each other.

Finally, the BFT provided a common operating picture for all forces in the theater. When the machines were turned on, commanders at all levels essentially knew who was where. On October 24, twenty 1114s with the 69th's name on them rolled into Camp Buehring. Although it was late in the evening, the men got up and ran to see their new trucks. The vehicle seats were still wrapped in plastic and the Hummers had that new car smell. The vehicles came complete with brand-new machine guns and radios as well.

In late October 2004, the unit deployed to Iraq via motor march. The unit spent four nights traveling to the Baghdad International Airport (BIAP) military base cluster (referred to as Camp Victory). The 69th reported to a small section of the Victory complex known as Camp Liberty on the northeast portion of the cluster, where a large billboard proclaimed, "Welcome Tiger Brigade!" The unit assigned an area of operation approximately 50 kilometers northwest of Baghdad around the town of Taji. Al Taji was crisscrossed by hundreds of reed-lined waterways, and Slack wondered how the Bradley Fighting Vehicles (Bradley's) could maneuver in such constricted terrain.

From 28 October to 6 November 2004, the Battalion was assigned the mission of seizing and holding a bridge over the Grand Canal. After approximately 5 days, it was decided there was no risk of enemy action at the bridge. Slack decided too much time was wasted traveling to Taji from Camp Victory and recommended deployment to Taji. The request was granted. The Fighting 69th (less one company which remained in Baghdad detailed to base security) traveled to Camp Cooke in Taji on November 8th to relieve the 2nd Battalion 7th Cavalry. Since the 7th had been sent to

support the attack on Fallujah, and the staff and soldiers had already left, the 69th did not receive a proper battle hand-off. Very little information was provided by the 7th. The 69th did not know that before the war, Taji was the home of the Iraqi artillery school, a Republican Guard tank division, an air base, several munitions factories, and a maintenance depot. Positioned strategically at the southern tip of the Sunni Triangle, Taji Base and its surrounding lands were the final line of defense before the heart of Saddam Hussein's tribal stronghold. If the Americans made it to Baghdad, the Iraqi Army planned to defend the heartland from the Taji area.

Ninety percent of the population were Sunnis, and Taji Base was the primary employer for everyone in the area, from senior Republican Guard Generals to the newspaper boys who depended on the base (and Saddam Hussein's regime) for their livelihood. If the 69th soldiers had been able to speak with the 7th soldiers who had worked in Taji, they would have learned that the people of the area were savagely anti-American. They had lost their livelihoods and their dignity when the U.S. came to town. And they now struggled to feed their families.

Some continued to farm. Some went to work in the black market that controlled the oil industry. Some took money from hardcore jihadist insurgents to continue low-level attacks against the Americans to degrade soldier morale and popular support for the war in the U.S. In the early days after the U.S. invasion, the disenfranchised Iraqis of Taji stored their Republic Guard uniforms in the back of their closets. They quickly consolidated whatever military hardware they could for on the black market to the jihadists. They dumped thousands of water-tight artillery shells into the canals; they buried untold numbers of rocket-propelled grenade (RPG) launchers and ammunition and looted the massive Airbase's ammunition bunker (a mile-long repository of bombs that ranged from 250 to 2000 pounds in size). Instead of dumping those in a canal, the Iraqis dug up roadbeds and buried the bombs in with a homemade fuse sticking out of the ground. These were no simple "roadside bombs," as they were used throughout Iraq. These were much more powerful and deadly. In some areas, the Iraqis placed them under a road and then paved the road over so they could continue regular civilian traffic until a U.S. patrol happened by. Among the handful of documents the 69th did get when they arrived at Camp Cooke was a picture of an M1 Abrams main battle tank that had been hit by one of these bombs. The hull of the tank was gored through the bottom, and the massive turret lay 40 meters from the site of the blast.

On November 6, 2004, the unit conducted "Presence Patrols" around Taji (consisting of convoying through areas and "showing the flag"). These are extremely dangerous operations since the unit was a target during patrols. The unit was set up in the Forward Operations Base (FOB) in Taji and continued to perform its mission. On November 29, 2004, Staff Sergeant Christian Engeldrum and Private First-Class Wilfredo Urbina were mortally wounded when their HUMVEE was struck by an improvised explosive device (IED). The Fighting 69th had just suffered its first killed in action since the battle of Okinawa. Sergeant Engeldrum had been out of the National Guard for a few years but re-enlisted when he heard several of his old comrades from the 27th Brigade were going to backfill the 69th for duty in Iraq. Things would get worse. On December 3, 2004, Staff Sergeant Henry Irizarry was killed when the HUMVEE in which he was riding was struck by a roadside explosive device. On January 5, 2005, the unit was redeployed to Camp Victory in Baghdad and was assigned the mission of patrolling and securing "Route Irish" from the airport to Baghdad. Route Irish runs from Baghdad's International Airport to the International Zone. In the early days of the war, the Americans labeled the road "Route Irish" after the Notre Dame football team.

But by February 2005, most people around the globe knew the freeway as "The Most Dangerous Road in the World." Route Irish was a four-lane highway with a 50-meter-wide median and 100-meter (garbage-strewn) grass shoulders. It was the main thoroughfare from the Baghdad International Airport to the center of the city and the Green Zone. Western diplomats, Iraqi officials, generals, journalists, contractors, and soldiers traversed the road all day and night, offering the insurgents lucrative targets. Contractors customarily sped down the road at high speeds, swerving in and out of traffic. American convoys cleared traffic with bursts from their machine guns and bumps from their grills. Iraqi civilians drove through the garbage on the shoulders and median to bypass congestion. It was every man for himself on Route Irish, a Wild West melee in the middle of the capital, and an embarrassment for top U.S. brass who struggled to answer the question: how do you expect to secure Iraq if you can't even secure a few miles of highway in the middle of Baghdad? Middle Eastern observers had long said, "As goes Baghdad goes Iraq."

In 2004 and 2005, Route Irish was added to the equation. "As goes the Airport Road goes Baghdad." The highway became a bell-weather for U.S. effectiveness in Iraq. General William Webster, whose 3rd Infantry Division replaced the 1st Cavalry in Baghdad after the elections, told his subordinate commanders that Route Irish was the only road in Iraq that President Bush knew by name. In the five months leading up to the January elections, insurgents sprayed bullets at highway drivers 63 times. They fired RPGs 70 times. They planted IEDs 42 times. Perhaps most disconcerting, they attacked military and civilian convoys with car bombs 25 times. Seventeen coalition soldiers and civilian contractors were killed. Seventy-five more were wounded. Task Force Wolfhound would replace the 1st Cavalry Division's 4th Battalion of the 5th Air Defense Artillery, which had suffered four killed on the highway in seven months. The 69th men had lost ten men in two-and-a-half months in Taji. A day after arrival on January 16, 2005, Specialist Alain Kamolvathin and Private First Class Francis Obaji were fatally injured when their HUMVEE rolled down an embankment into a river near Baghdad.

On March 2, 2005, SPC Wai P. Lwin and SPC Azhar Ali, patrolling with Sergeant Daniel Maiella, were headed east on Route Irish near the turn-off for the extension that ran to the Green Zone when insurgents hit them with an IED that was unusually effective for its small size. Explosively formed penetrators (EFPs) were in regular use in Israel and had recently begun showing up in attacks in eastern Baghdad. The weapons, which intelligence officers believed were coming from Iran, were typically about the size of a coffee can and featured a thick metal "lid" that coned into a dimple an inch deep in the center. When the EFPs were detonated, explosives re-shaped the metal into a compact projectile of molten steel that could penetrate the thickest armor the U.S. had. A Humvee was no match. The EFP that insurgents detonated against Lwin and Ali's truck sat just a couple of feet away from the vehicle in a pile of brush along a narrow center median. The penetrator entered the Humvee behind Lwin, who was driving. The molten steel killed him instantly. Ali was sitting in the gun turret facing rearward. The round exited Lwin then blew off Ali's hindquarters before sending shards of steel into Sergeant Maillela's chest cavity and head. Then, on March 15, 2005, Specialist Paul Heitzel (C/2/156th) was killed in Baghdad while conducting a mounted patrol on Route Irish when a vehicle-borne IED detonated. On May 24, 2005, SSG Peter Hahn was killed in action. On August 7, 2005, Sergeant Anthony N. Kalladeen and Private First-Class Hernando Rios were killed when their HUMVEE was struck by two improvised explosive devices, and they received small arms fire.

The next day, on January 6, 2005, several soldiers were killed in Taji, Iraq, when their Bradley Fighting Vehicle was struck by a massive bomb placed under the surface of a dirt road: Sergeant First Class Kurt Comeaux, Staff Sergeant Christopher Babin, Sergeant Bradley Bergeron, Sergeant Huey Fassbender III, and Sergeant Warren Murphy. Sergeant Kenneth G. Vonn Ronn, who was a Medic from Headquarters Company, 69th Infantry, was also killed.

In September 2005, the Unit returned to the U.S., turning the security of Route Irish over to the Iraqi Army.

The following soldiers were wounded while serving in Iraq:

SGT. Felix A. Vargas

PFC Richard A. Cornier

SPC Daniel Swift

SPC Todd Reed

SGT. Adrian Melendez

SGT Thomas Stevenson

SPC John Cushman

SPC Joseph Frisella

SPC Anthony Gilkes

SGT. Daniel Maiella

SPC Casey Carroll (C/2/156th)

SGT Jacque Bally (C/2/156th)

MAJ Michael Kazmierak (C/2/156th)

CPL Rusten May (C/2/156th)

SPC Damien Dickson (C/2/156th)

SGT Jose Dorsey (C/2/156th)

CPL Derrick Smith (C/2/156th)

SSG John Chalker (HHC 1/69)

SGT William H. Macy

1LT. Brian Rathburn (XO)

SSG. Sean Gilday

SGT. Sebastian Cila

SPC. Brian Lopez

SGT. Miguel Luna

SPC. Brian Lopez

SGT. Daniel Barr

SGT Donald Leinfelder (A Co 1/60)

SPC.Shannon Flahiv

SGT. Richard Strazalka

SSG. Vincent Brown

The Regimental Headquarters met when the unit was in Iraq to discuss what should be done to welcome the unit home. It was decided to renovate the historical displays throughout the armory. As the first part of the Armory Display Renovation Project, the Colors owned by the 69th Regiment were removed from the flag cases in the armory for preservation from June to December 2005 by a project team from the Fashion and Textile Studies, School of Graduate Studies at the Fashion Institute of Technology (Fit), New York, The purpose was to stabilize, protect, and properly store the Civil War flags located in two front hall cases in the Armory. Each flag had its own pole number and a State identifying number in the format of LX1996.xxx.

Almost all the flags were wrapped in dirty, brittle, yellowed acetate covering. The acetate was removed from each flag. An initial level of condition was determined, and the flags were either unrolled or not. If the flag was unrolled, it was photographed, aligned, laid on acid-free tissue paper, rolled in acid-free tissue paper, and then rolled again in a final covering of clear 4 ml mylar and tied with cotton twill tape. If the flag was not unrolled, it was photographed in its rolled state and then rolled in acid-free tissue paper and mylar as above. A record was made for each flag. Only archival materials were used in this re-housing project. For the 43 flags that were re-housed, there was considerable expense. Custom boxing made from double-walled acid-free corrugated board was created for the housing of the flags. Three flags were put into one box. Each of the flags were supported within each box to allow the boxes to fit on the shelving built for them; the lower end of each box was left open. At the top end of the box, the final end of the flag was supported on a notched bed of etha-foam. If there were plaques that were associated with the pole number, they were housed in the box also.

Chapter Ten
Post Iraqi Freedom

In 2005, LTC Charles Crosby took command of the Battalion. He had served as the Executive Officer in Iraq. Major General Joseph A. Healey, the Honorary Colonel of the Regiment, died on December 6, 2005, and LTC Robert Hutter (previously the Regimental Adjutant) was appointed the Honorary Colonel. Colonel Hutter remained the Honorary Colonel until 2013. The Regimental Staff, with assistance from the New York State Military Museum, continued to update and renovate the Armory Displays. In 2009, LTC John Andonie took command of the battalion. On January 28th, 2012, C Company was mobilized at Camp Smith, NY, and re-designated B Company 2-108 Infantry. Three days later, the company flew to Camp Shelby, Mississippi, for two months of individual and collective training, including mounted and dismounted live fire, cultural and threat training, and familiarization with specialized equipment. During this period, the Company was tasked to support two separate missions, with most of the Company preparing to deploy to Afghanistan and the rest training for a multi-faceted mission supporting the Third Army in Kuwait.

In April, the Afghanistan deployers attended a rotation at the National Training Center, Fort Irwin, California for nearly a month of demanding training in a realistic environment close to that of Afghanistan. Soon after the completion of this training on May 8th, those headed to Afghanistan were deployed. Their mission was to support the Afghan National Police in securing Highway One in western Afghanistan. Over the next five months, the company conducted over 200 dismounted, mounted, and aerial patrols along the highway, assisting and assessing police forces and collecting intelligence on insurgent and criminal networks in the area. In late September, the Company was ordered to redeploy earlier than expected and returned to Camp Shelby for demobilization and on to New York for a final homecoming.

In October 2012, during Hurricane (Superstorm) Sandy, members of the 69th were activated to assist Federal, State, and local authorities with the rescue and cleanup effort. Sandy was one of the largest storms to hit the East Coast. Three members of the unit, Sgt. Kenny Bharose, Sgt. 1st Class Israel Mahadeo, and Sgt. Michael Palopoli were awarded the New York State Medal of Valor, the State's highest military award.

Alpha Company was a part of the 13 December 2012 commemoration of the Battle of Fredericksburg, which was coordinated by the Town Council of the City of Fredericksburg, Virginia, and the National Park Service. The commemoration was attended by the public, Alpha Company, members of the Regimental Headquarters (RHQ), Veterans Corps, and dignitaries from the governments of the United States and the Republic of Ireland. The procession traced the Regiment's route from the location of the crossing of the Rappahannock River (which has a marker), through the streets of Fredericksburg, up the hill in front of Marye's Heights to the Sunken Road behind which Confederate Forces fired on attacking Union troops. During the entire time, the bells in all the town's churches tolled. Alpha Company marched behind the Battalion Color Guard and the Commander of the 69th. On top of Marye's Heights, the Color Guard from the 116th Infantry Regiment waited. The 116th Infantry Regiment of the Virginia National Guard was one of the Regiments which fought for the Confederacy during the Battle of Fredericksburg. Upon arrival at the top of Mayre's Heights, the 69th Color Guard faced the Color Guard of the 116th, and they saluted each other. Jim Finucane, Councilman from County Kerry, Ireland, who attended the event, said when the tenacity and courage of the 69th was seen by the world at Marye's Heights, it changed the perception of the Irish as "un-kept immigrants" to courageous soldiers. He believes it is a turning point for Irish

Heritage. John J. Hennessy, Chief Historian at Fredericksburg for the National Parks Service, said that after the charge up Marye's Heights, soldiers on both sides who fought in the battle would refer to their location on the battlefield in relation to where the Irish Brigade fought.

In March 2013. representatives from the 69th Regiment were invited to attend the 1848 Tricolour Celebration in Waterford, Ireland. Sergeant First Class Dennis Rick and Staff Sergeant Colin Stewart attended with Colonel (Retired) Jim Tierney, Honorary Colonel of the Regiment. The 1848 Tricolour Celebration (began in 2010) commemorates the first time the Irish National Flag was seen. Thomas Francis Meagher designed the Flag, which would become Ireland's National Color, and hung it out his window in Waterford City in March 1848. Before the Civil War, Meagher commanded one of the 69th lineage Regiments. He served with the 69th during the Battle of Bull Run and later formed and commanded the Irish Brigade. While in Ireland, the group visited the 69th Regiment Monument in Ballymote, County Sligo, which is dedicated to Colonel Michael Corcoran and the Regiment. The group stayed at the Granville Hotel in Waterford, where Thomas Francis Meagher was born. On March 17th, General Frank Grass, Chief of the National Guard Bureau, visited the 69th to attend the Unit Day festivities. March 17th is the 69th

Regiment's Unit Day, and each year, the Regiment leads the St. Patrick's Day Parade after attending a special Mass held for the unit at St. Patrick's Cathedral. In previous years, General Martin Dempsey, Chairman of the Joint Chiefs of Staff, visited the unit. In the Armory after the Parade, he sang for the soldiers "We are the Fighting 69th" (an old Civil War song) and had unit members sing the chorus.

The Battalion Headquarters established a forward Tactical Operations Center complete with satellite communications, which provided, in part, secure and non-secure network connections. The Mortar Platoon conducted various fire missions, expending over 500 rounds. The Mortars, Scouts, and Snipers coordinated to provide their own concurrent training scenarios. The result was the Mortars' training on occupation of a deliberate firing point while the Scouts conducted an area reconnaissance by establishing a patrol base and then observation posts from which they gathered and reported intelligence on the Mortar Platoon. While they were gathering intelligence, the Scouts were being stalked by the Snipers. All this training was supported by Medics who were attached to the maneuver elements. The Medical Platoon utilized its 40 assigned medics to treat over 140 patients while simultaneously supporting training efforts for the entire Battalion.

On October 15, 2013, the Command of the 1st Battalion 69th Infantry passed from LTC James C. Gonyo to the new Commander, LTC Vincent Heintz. Colonel Heintz's tenure as Commander would not be long. The unit was over-strength, and when higher headquarters decided to transfer soldiers on paper to another unit to bring up their strength figures, LTC Heintz vehemently argued against it, believing it would cause unit commanders to make inaccurate statements on the unit readiness reports. Furthermore, it would hurt the effected soldiers' promotion possibilities. LTC Heintz resigned his position as Commander a few months after taking command. On November 1st the Makin Day Dinner, which is held in the Mural Room in the Armory, marked the 70th anniversary of the successful invasion of the Central Pacific atoll by the 69th. As a memento of the anniversary, Makin Island Veterans, Major General Kenneth "Scooter" Barkley, and Sergeant Jack Munday were presented framed reproductions of a landing beach photo taken on Makin.

In 2013, LTC (Retired) Bob Hutter turned the Honorary Colonel of the Regiment position over to Colonel (Retired) Jim Tierney. Colonel Tierney had served as the Regimental Historian for the previous 10 years. LTC (Retired) Walter Montagno remained as the Regimental Adjutant. Bert Cunningham, who had served as the Executive Officer of

Charlie Company, 2nd Bn in the 1970s, was appointed Regimental Historian. Command Sergeant Major (Retired) Brett was appointed Regimental Sergeant Major. In 2014 Lieutenant Colonel Sean Flynn assumed command of the 1st Battalion, 69th Infantry in January 2014. Prior to taking command of the Fighting 69th, LTC Flynn served as the Chief of Operations for New York's Joint Force Headquarters in Latham, NY. LTC Flynn joined the New York Army National Guard in 2000 after six years of active and reserve commissioned service in the U.S. Air Force. He spent his first seven years in the Army with the 69th Infantry, including five years as a Rifle Company Commander. He Commanded a Company during Operation Iraqi Freedom and served on active duty when he returned to the U.S. Military Academy at West Point.

In 2007 and 2008, LTC Flynn served as the Chief of Operations for the 42nd Infantry Division in Troy, NY. In 2009, LTC Flynn was named the Executive Officer and Chief of Staff of the 2nd Battalion, 108th Infantry, in Utica, NY. He deployed with the 108th to Afghanistan in 2012. Prior to joining the National Guard, LTC Flynn served as a Public Affairs Officer for the U.S. Air Force from 1994 until 1997. He worked in New York as a financial communications and public relations consultant from 1997 to 2000. LTC Flynn earned his commission through the Air

Force Reserve Officer Training Corps at the University of Maryland at College Park and holds a BA in Journalism. LTC Flynn's family has a long history serving in the 69th Regiment. His family members served with Colonel Corcoran and General Meagher during the Civil War and one of his family served with the Regiment in World War I and II.

The Corona Virus Epidemic hit New York early in 2020. In response to the epidemic, the Governor of New York State and the Mayor of New York City canceled the St. Patrick's Day Parade. They also closed St. Patrick's Cathedral to the public. During a Commander's Meeting in the Armory a few days prior to St. Patrick's Day, the Battalion Commander, LTC Joseph Whaley, discussed options with his staff and company commanders. Although his active-duty staff recommended that the unit not march, LTC Whaley decided to uphold the tradition of marching on St. Patrick's Day. The Regiment had been leading the Parade since 1851. On March 17, 2020, members of the Regiment voluntarily marched with a police escort from the Armory to St. Patrick's Cathedral. Members of the New York St. Patrick's Day Parade Committee followed, carrying the Parade's Banner. Upon arrival at St. Patrick's Cathedral, Monsignor Ritchie, Rector of St. Patrick's Cathedral, blessed the assembly in front of the Cathedral. The Parade Committee, with their banner and representatives from the Regiment, then walked the parade route up Fifth Avenue to 86th Street. LTC Whaley had saved one of the Regiment's and the City of New York's oldest traditions. The day after the Parade (March 18, 2020), the unit was activated to assist in fighting the Corona Virus Pandemic. They were deployed to testing sites, hospitals, Javits Center and other areas in the City and State to assist with testing of over 400,000 individuals. Unit members helped distribute 350,000 gallons of hand sanitizer and provided security and access control at two city hospitals.

In September 2022, the unit received orders to deploy to the Horn of Africa to relieve the 116th Task Force (Task Force Red Dragon), which had been serving there for a year. Task Force Red Dragon was composed of Virginia and Kentucky National Guard Soldiers, primarily from the 116th Infantry Regiment. The 116rg Infantry Regiment last met the 69th Infantry Regiment at Marye's Heights. The mission of Operation Horn of Africa is to provide security to the East African region.

The Battalion would serve on active duty in Djibouti, Somalia, and Kenya as part of the Combined Joint Task Force-Horn of Africa (CJTF_HOA) and Task Force Wolfhound. Major General Shawley, Commander of CJTF-HOA, described the region as a geo-strategically place molded by competing forces of prosperity and poverty, peace and conflict, plenty and famine, good governance, and corruption. The region is challenged with instability caused by violent extremist organizations and the U.S.' competitors, which continue to weaken the world order. Task Force Wolfhound and the Regiment provided security forces throughout the region to maintain a presence in Djibouti, Somalia, and Kenya. The defensive mission included 24/7 perimeter security of military installation. Unit members manned guard towers and vehicle entry control to points to safeguard U.S. forces and civilian contractors.

They also provided land-based security for U.S. Navy ports of call, which enabled refueling operations for U.S. ships. During the deployment, Task Force Wolfhound augmented medical personnel and established indirect fire capabilities to improve their defensive posture. Unit members were also the ground component of the East Africa Response Force, tasked with a broad range of military operations, including crisis response and security augmentation. The Unit conducted multiple staff exercises, rehearsals, security patrols, joint exercises, live fire exercises, and battle drills during the time they were deployed. Task Force Wolfhound built relationships with its foreign partners, French, Kenyan, Japanese, Italian, Spanish and Djiboutian armed forces. They also worked closely with U.S. Marines.

On March 17, 2024, in the Armory after the Parade, the Adjutant General, Major General Shields, announced that funding for the renovation of the Armory had been approved. The $125,000,000 project would completely renovate the Armory and take approximately four years. Everything in the Armory would have to be either stored or thrown out. All historical property had to be inventoried, boxed inappropriate material, and transported to a storage facility somewhere in the State. Drill locations for the Companies had to be found, and Company property had to be transported to the new location. The plan would be to house the Companies in several armories throughout the downstate area. The project was enormous in scope. Numerous questions had to be answered.

Knicks playing in armory. January 21, 1956

The members of the regiment had secured the historic artifacts in the armory. Would the artifacts ever be returned, or would they be stored in some facility upstate? What should be done with the current furniture? What should be done with the basketball court on the drill floor (the court was put in New York Knicks and was their original home court)? What would be the effect on retention when soldiers are told they must travel to a new location for drills? Which space would be allocated to who? Which display cases would be kept, and which would be thrown out? What furniture, lighting, and various other things that had been in the building for over 100 years would be discarded?

The plan was to empty the armory by October and close it by November. During the months of June, July, and August, everything was packed and transported. The Armory was opened in 1906, and it had the look and feel of a historic place. Everyone wondered what it would look and feel like when the modernization and renovation was completed. Would it be just another colorless modern building without the ghosts which haunted the old place.

On January 25, 2025, Pete Hegseth, a veteran of the regiment was confirmed as the U.S. Secretary of Defense.

Chapter Eleven
Traditions of the Regiment

Regimental Cocktail

The Regimental Cocktail, made of one-part Irish whiskey and two/three parts champagne, is prepared for toasting at all regimental affairs. At Fredericksburg, General Thomas Francis Meagher, who liked to drink whiskey mixed with Vichy water, sent a soldier to get the effervescent mineral water. Unable to find the water, the soldier returned with champagne. General Meagher mixed the two, and the Regimental Cocktail was born.

Makin Day Dinner

Held the first Friday in November, the Makin Day Dinner celebrates the invasion of Makin Island during World War II when the 69th Regiment (165th Regimental Combat Team) spearheaded the beach landing on this central Pacific atoll on November 23, 1943. Originally called the Beefsteak Dinner, the name was changed to honor the veterans of Makin Island. The Makin Day Dinner is organized by the members of the Veteran Corps 69th Regiment.

St. Patrick's Day Parade, Unit Day - March 17th

Around 1850, the recently formed 69th Regiment became the official military escort, and the Ancient Order of

Hibernians became the official sponsor of the parade. Ever since the 69th has been the first unit to march in the parade both in wartime and peacetime. The 69th celebrates March 17 as Unit Day and proudly marches to honor its great history.

Blackthorn Stick

Blackthorn Sticks 1951

Officers and NCOs of the 69th Regiment traditionally carry swagger sticks made of blackthorn wood during the St. Patrick's Day Parade and on other ceremonial occasions. Ancient Celts revered the blackthorn tree, and in Irish folklore, the blackthorn tree has supernatural associations.

Garryowen

"Garryowen" has been the unofficial Regimental March since prior to the Civil War. The tune was written in the 1770s and became popular among Irish regiments of the British Army through the 19th century. It naturally spread to America and became the signature march of the 69th Regiment. The 7th U.S. Cavalry subsequently adopted the tune under General George Custer.

"Fighting 69th"

Because the regiment fought so bravely and ferociously during the Civil War, Confederate General Robert E. Lee nicknamed it the "Fighting Sixty-Ninth" at the Battle of Fredericksburg in 1862. Proudly used since that time, the name became the title of a major movie about the 69th's exploits during World War I, starring James Cagney and Pat O'Brien.

Regimental Motto "Gentle When Stroked, Fierce When Provoked"

Irish wolfhounds were companions to the Kings of Ireland and are prominently featured on the regimental coat of arms. Despite its large size, the Irish wolfhound has a generally calm disposition but can become ferocious when aggravated. The Irish wolfhound is the Regiment's traditional mascot.

The Logan – Duffy Trophy Rifle Match

This rifle match began in 1936 when the commanders of the 101st Infantry, Massachusetts Army National Guard, and the 69th Infantry New York Army National Guard organized a friendly marksmanship match. The regiments, each with an Irish history and a friendship dating to the Civil War, annually compete for the ornamental trophy which is retained each year by the organization winning the rifle match.

Length of Color-Staff

When General John J. "Blackjack" Pershing, commander of the American Expeditionary Force, officially reviewed the 42nd (Rainbow) Division in 1919, he hesitated before one of the regimental color guards, noting that the color staff was one foot longer than regulations permitted. Upon examination, the reason for the discrepancy was clear--the unit's inordinate amount of engraved silver battle rings had to be accommodated on the staff. "What regiment is this?" asked the general. "The 165th Infantry, Sir," responded the soldier. "What regiment was it?" continued the chief. "The 69th New York, Sir," came the proud reply. "The 69th New York, I understand now." Thus, did General John J. "Blackjack" Pershing acknowledge the reputation of "The Fighting 69th." Having originally gained its fame during the Civil War, the regiment gathered nine more battle honors during World War I.

Calvary Cemetery

Calvary Cemetery in Queens contains the remains of many unit casualties of the Civil War, Spanish-American War, and World War I, and one day each May, members of the Veterans Corps, 69th Regiment gather at two special memorials dedicated to the Regiment to conduct formal Memorial Day ceremonies.

Rouge Bouquet

On March 7, 1918, a shell from a German artillery barrage landed on the roof of a dugout in the Rouge Bouquet Sector, burying 1st Lieutenant John Norman and a group of men of E Company under mud, dirt, and beams. After hours of intense rescue efforts, under continued enemy artillery fire, efforts to reach the soldiers were halted. Twenty-one were killed because of the explosion, including Lt. Norman and fifteen others who remained entombed in the collapsed dugout. Father Duffy conducted Last Rights and the men placed a marker at the dugout. Joyce Kilmer wrote the poem "Rouge Bouquet" to memorialize the men who died, and Father Duffy read it aloud for the first time on St. Patrick's Day 1918. From that time to this Joyce Kilmer's poem "Rouge Bouquet" is read at funeral services for veterans and members of the 69th Regiment.

Boxwood on St. Patrick's Day

At the Battle of Fredericksburg, the soldiers of the Irish Brigade wore sprigs of Boxwood in their hats because their Green Flags had been returned to New York. In commemoration of that Battle where many of the Regiment lost their lives, the soldiers and veterans of the 69th wore sprigs of boxwood during the St. Patrick's Day Parade.

9 781917 553018